Web Aesthetics

STUDIES IN NETWORK CULTURES
Geert Lovink, *Series Editor*

This series of books investigates concepts and practices special to network cultures. Exploring the spectrum of new media and society, we see network cultures as a strategic term to enlist in diagnosing political and aesthetic developments in user-driven communications. Network cultures can be understood as social-technical formations under construction. They rapidly assemble, and can just as quickly disappear, creating a sense of spontaneity, transience and even uncertainty. Yet they are here to stay. However self-evident it is, collaboration is a foundation of network cultures. Working with others frequently brings about tensions that have no recourse to modern protocols of conflict resolution. Networks are not parliaments. How to conduct research within such a shifting environment is a key interest to this series.

Studies in Network Cultures *is an initiative of the Institute of Network Cultures (INC). The INC was founded in 2004 by its director Geert Lovink and is situated at the Amsterdam Polytechnic (Hogeschool van Amsterdam), as a research programme inside the School for Interactive Media. Since its inception, the INC has organized international conferences about the history of webdesign, netporn, the critique of ICT for development, new network theory, creative industries rhetoric, online video, search and Wikipedia research. For more information please visit: http: //networkcultures.org/publications/studies-in-network-cultures/*

The series Studies in Network Cultures *is published by the Institute of Network Cultures in collaboration with NAi Publishers, Rotterdam.*

Series Coordinator: Sabine Niederer, Institute of Network Cultures
For more information please visit www.networkcultures.org/naiseries

Previously published in this series:

Ned Rossiter, Organized Networks: Media Theory, Creative Labour, New Institutions *(Rotterdam: NAi Publishers and Amsterdam: Institute of Network Cultures, 2006)*

Eric Kluitenberg, Delusive Spaces: Essays on Culture, Media and Technology *(Rotterdam: NAi Publishers and Amsterdam: Institute of Network Cultures, 2008)*

Matteo Pasquinelli, Animal Spirits: A Bestiary of the Commons *(Rotterdam: NAi Publishers and Amsterdam: Institute of Network Cultures, 2008)*

Web Aesthetics

*How Digital Media Affect
Culture and Society*

Vito Campanelli

NAi Publishers
Institute of Network Cultures

Series editor: Geert Lovink, Institute of Network Cultures, Hogeschool van Amsterdam (HvA)
Series coordinator: Sabine Niederer, Institute of Network Cultures, Hogeschool van Amsterdam
Coordinator of this publication: Rachel Somers Miles
Translation from Italian: Francesco Bardo, edited by Nicole Heber
Copy editor: D'Laine Camp
Design: Studio Tint, Huug Schipper, The Hague
Cover design: Studio Léon&Loes, Rotterdam
Type setting and printing: Die Keure, Bruges, Belgium
Binding: Catherine Binding
Paper: Munken Lynx 100 gr
Project coordination: Barbera van Kooij, NAi Publishers, Rotterdam
Publisher: NAi Publishers, Rotterdam

NAi Publishers is an internationally orientated publisher specialized in developing, producing
and distributing books on architecture, visual arts and related disciplines.
www.naipublishers.nl info@naipublishers.nl

Available in North, South and Central America through D.A.P./Distributed Art Publishers Inc,
155 Sixth Avenue 2nd Floor, New York, NY 10013-1507, Tel 212 6271999, Fax 212 6279484.

Available in the United Kingdom and Ireland through Art Data, 12 Bell Industrial Estate,
50 Cunnington Street, London W4 5HB, Tel 208 7471061, Fax 208 7422319.

Printed and bound in Belgium

ISBN 978-90-5662-770-6

Contents

This useless and wordy epistle itself already exists in one of the thirty volumes of the five shelves in one of the uncountable hexagons – and so does its refutation.

Jorge Luis Borges, *Ficciones* (1944)

Acknowledgments

The idea for this work was born in May 2008 during a weekend in Procida, a small island in the Gulf of Naples. As Geert Lovink and I sat beside a calm sea, and I explained my research on the aesthetic forms of the Web to him, he proposed that I give this work the completed form of a book. He has prompted me to see things from a different point of view, and encouraged me to confront the views of others. My first and most heartfelt thanks therefore belong to Geert.

I am grateful to all the people with whom I have exchanged ideas, impressions and feelings over the last few years, and to those who encouraged me to contribute to the debate on digital media. I thank Sabine Niederer and Rachel Somers Miles of the Institute of Network Cultures for their incredible efficiency, and their unfailing support and sympathy. At NAi Publishers in Rotterdam I thank Barbera van Kooij and D'Laine Camp for the exceptional care with which they treated this work. A vital contribution was offered by Nicole Heber with her brilliant editing work, I thank her sincerely. I feel a deep sense of gratitude for Francesco Bordo's enthusiasm and seriousness as he helped me translate this text from the initial Italian version, succeeding in the *mission impossible* of transferring to English, the rhythm of my writing.

I owe a special thanks to Iain Chambers for having supported this editorial project, and to the Department of American, Cultural and Linguistic Studies of the University of Naples *l'Orientale*, which has provided me with a peaceful and stimulating research environment. I won't ever find words to express my thanks to my students for their contagious enthusiasm. I am grateful to all my colleagues (precarious or not), and to all the young researchers and PhD students with whom I have shared enjoyable discussions over the years, but especially to Serena Guarracino, Mariangela Orabona, Katherine Russo and Maria Domenica Arcuri. This book would never have assumed its present shape without the continuous and valuable exchange of ideas with Cosimo Campanelli, whom I wish to thank for his patient endurance of my frequent abuse of the philosophical discipline to which he has devoted a lifetime. I am indebted to Tiziana Terranova for her invaluable criticism, which confronted me with a different way of thinking about aesthetic phenomena, and to Francesco De Sio Lazzari for his crucial advice regarding the organization of the Index. I thank Cecile Landman for offering me a refuge and the opportunity for long and passionate conversation during each of my *sorties* to Amsterdam. I thank Alessandro Ludovico for the opportunity to collaborate with *Neural* magazine, which also allowed me to stay updated on the most interesting innovations in the field of new media art.

Thanks also to my 'unfortunate' hometown, to whose proverbial porosity and ability to contain within itself so many forms of polarity I should, perhaps, attribute my aversion to anything that appears univocal and definitive. My warmest thanks go to Mimmo and Silvana, whose voices – among a thousand and more – will continue to sound dearest to me, and to Giusy and Nicola, without whom it would not be possible to maintain the triangle of my identity. This book was written at Largo Baracche, in the popular heart of the Spanish Naples: an ancient place, noisy, full of contradictions; a place in which ethnic groups and social classes, 'strange trades' and workers who wake up in the early morning, night shootings and music that accompanies housework, are mixed; a place – since now – also of writings.

***

I dedicate this book to Katia who describes orbits around which the turning is sweet to me.
This is in thanks for having transformed our life together into an adventure in which I am happy to wake up every single day, and for having supported me with such determination that, in the end, even my fickle nature was infected.

Vito Campanelli
June 2010

Introduction

Web Aesthetics deals with two major topics: the aestheticization of society and the global diffusion of Web-related forms. Those who expect a text regarding the Web and digital worlds might be surprised by the room left for the analysis of phenomena that take place outside these two major contexts. The premise with which I have begun, however, is that new media take part in an underlying tendency in contemporary society: the progressive aestheticization of reality and its main cultural expressions. When the Web is located inside this sociocultural process, it becomes a powerful, globally acting agent for aestheticization. Hence, I envision a continuous flow between the Web and society, and I formulate this in a way that requires the reader constantly to re-position themselves accordingly.

My thesis takes the form of a *pars destruens* because I believe that aesthetics offers the most effective tool to reveal the violence of contemporary communication. By observing the essential phenomena of contemporary communication, *Web Aesthetics* aims to build the foundation for an organic theory of digital media aesthetics. I want to construct an active aesthetics, a tool for persons or for multitudes to turn themselves from victims of the media agon into active aesthetic subjects, capable of formulating aesthetic strategies able to unmask the strategies used by powerful elites. A counter offensive requires an awareness of the enemy, and I see *Web Aesthetics* as the ground zero of aesthetic research into digital networks. Because I wish to understand the relationship between human beings and the Web, and between the creative act and human and machinic subjectivity, I do not delve into the policies and economic interests giving shape to the Internet. I view aesthetic experience on the Web as a giving over of oneself to an aesthetic flow; a flow that is fuelled by the logic underlying digital technology and that increasingly encompasses contemporary existence. Because my priority has been to comprehend the terms of the relationship between human beings, machinic blocks and aesthetic perceptions, I have postponed discussion of significant issues, such as the extraordinary stratification of content into massive databases, and the difficulty of interacting with such complex phenomena separately from that opaque tool, the search engine.

Web Aesthetics opens with a chapter on dialogue. This is because I believe that the constraints upon dialogue within both online and offline contexts constitute the principal blockage to the rising of a collective consciousness of Web dynamics and its spreading aesthetic forms. The invitation to dialogue prepares the ground for the consciousness of the aesthetics of new media. A further challenge for new media culture is to depart from its Anglo-centric orientation in favour of a molecularization of cultural and linguistic backgrounds. One must push unrelentingly to reveal the intrinsic limits of what falsely represents itself as an international debate.

In Chapter Two, I demonstrate the typically European tendency to link the new to its historical foundations. I offer a brief history of the concept of aesthetic experience, and in particular to the Italian aesthetologist Ernesto Francalanci's conception of diffuse aesthetics. At the close of this chapter, I explain the theory of memes and connect this theory to Albert-László Barabási's generative model of the 'scale-free network', and to the art historian Aby Warburg's concept of the engram. Of course, those who are already familiar with these issues can feel free to press skip, just as in a Flash intro, and move ahead.

I have already mentioned that the concept of flow is crucial to my interpretation of aesthetic experience on the Web. I need only add that Chapter Three deals with two antinomies that characterize that experience: between form and content, and between optical and haptic perception.

The experience of travelling across digital networks using modern tools of archiving and reproduction of media objects is characterized by a state of latency or of waiting, and by the desire to collate massive archives of cultural data. In Chapter Four, I locate these phenomena in relation to aesthetic feelings. The focus then shifts to the material exchanged on P2P networks, and to what are the values involved in these disturbed aesthetic experiences, and the consequences they have for the taste and the style of the present age. I focus on several contemporary obsessions such as personal digital camcorders and cameras, trying to establish the result of this confrontation between human and machinic will. Finally, I analyse the repetitiveness of 'amatorial productions', emphasizing the feature that characterizes society as a whole: the new aesthetic category of 'cool'.

Many of these reflections come together in the fifth and final chapter, but I do not attempt to synthesize them. Rather, they blend together in a way analogous to that which by its very nature blends together heterogeneous and opposing elements: the remix. We have arrived at a stage of *total remixability*, a stage at which everything can be mixed with everything else. This, I contend, establishes a chain of imitative or repetitive behaviours. When the logic of the remix encounters the amateurization of media production, the result might be summarized in the formula *Remix It Yourself. Web Aesthetics* closes with a few reflections on the relationship between human and machinic subjectivity and the rise of a *technological hyper-subject* in the contemporary age. Although the constraints of time and space prevent me from delving too far into this issue, I intend to return to this vital field of research in the future.

***

This book represents a first attempt to give shape to reflections that have emerged in the last few years, which I have spent researching the forms of aesthetic expression encountered when inhabiting digital networks. The initial aim of this work was to apply features of aesthetic thought to my observation of the Web. However, the research field has widened to encompass activities connected to the use of digital tools such as cameras, MP3 players, and increasingly complex mobile devices, and has gradually become more fully oriented towards contemporary everyday life.

This is a text that does not want to be finite, both because it represents only the very first step towards a wider reflection about the aesthetics of digital media that I aim to realize in the future, and because the concept of finitude is itself nonsensical in the digital environment in which these reflections have been born. In the digital sea that is the Web, everything is fluid – and so it flows, leaving behind every attempt towards the absolute. As I share Deleuze and Guattari's horror of 'making the point', rather than just making points, I have tried to trace several trajectories between thoughts and realities belonging to different fields and to different times. The aim of this work is to intro-

——

duce several proposals into an open space of ideas, and to let them find their own life. My hope is that these ideas will collide with, overturn, contaminate, confuse and converse with one another, and with present or future ideas.

It was my belief that very few authors had attempted to give life to a new media theory that began from – or that at least took into consideration – aesthetic categories, even if only to question them. The principal studies on the topic that I have accessed seemed to reflect on the aesthetic implications of new media without making any reference to classical, modern or even postmodern aesthetic theories. It was as if new media had come from nowhere, rather than belonging to a continuum of human thought; as if it was possible to discuss this specific topic without a general frame of reference. Furthermore, a rather common supposition of the major works has been that aesthetics *affects* computing. Thus, the majority of research has been dedicated to understanding this process. I wanted the opposite starting point for *Web Aesthetics*: my research would be mainly focused on the specificity of aesthetic experience in relation to the Web, and to digital networks more widely. In other words, I have addressed my efforts towards understanding the processes through which interaction with digital technologies clears the path for new forms of aesthetic perception, which reverberate throughout society and other contemporary cultural expressions.

I was, however, risking a mistake that, according to the Italian aesthetologist Mario Costa, plagues a significant number of contemporary aesthetic theories: wanting to apply reflections and criteria formulated in previous technological periods to the present period, which Costa terms 'neo-technological'. Therefore, I returned my focus to the main object of my research, which was the aesthetic form of the Web, and those forms being made possible by the spreading of digital media. In this way, I was slowly persuaded that the true starting point must be the description of what I was observing, and I knew that what I must do was to try to set the grounds for a phenomenological observation of new media aesthetics. Adopting a phenomenological point of view is a way of being in society, and it also means accepting the future without necessarily attempting to trace trajectories of cause and effect. It means giving up on an ideological point of view, and accepting the ontological perspective instead. The postmodernist attitude of recent times in particular seems to necessarily foreclose any debate concerning being, and hence ontology. Once I began this project, I became aware of Husserl's crucial formulation of phenomenology, in which he places among *epoché* a series of *different* options; suspending judgment of things in order to allow those phenomena that reach consciousness to be viewed as they are, free of preconceptions. This is, perhaps, the only possible approach to the exploration of contemporary aesthetic forms, and in particular those forms belonging to the Web and digital meta-worlds. Proof of this is to be found in one of the most highly praised conceptualizations of digital culture: Deleuze and Guattari's rhizomatic interpretation, in which 'lines of flight' are to be found within rather than outside the rhizome. From this perspective, ethical judgment becomes a burden for those who want to understand the phenomenological reality of the Web.

In this work, I aim to map out the first stage of a more complex project. I outline an organic theory of Web aesthetics, a theory that is adequate to the new, emerging modes of perception in network society, and to the shifting and hybridizing senses and meanings definitive of that society. I am aware of the imprecision entailed by the word 'Web', and of the fact that it is not the only network, although it is one of the most important. In the sense that I use the word here, the Web comprises phenomena related to digital media, including those that are not necessarily represented by the Internet. On the one hand, this choice of terminology has been made due to the need for a word that captures the diversity of the observed phenomena. On the other hand (and this explains the arbitrariness of this option) it is true that the Web is nothing but the most popular expression of the so-called digital revolution. The Web has become the place where the infinite potentials of the present encounter a recombinant simulacrum. It is on the Web that its inhabitants hope to find the wire that reconnects them to the web of narratives that encircle their everyday lives. From this point of view, talking about the Web means looking beyond its 'physical' state (the pages that open once an alphanumeric sequence preceded by 'www' is keyed in) in order to embrace the whole media complex. It should come as no surprise, then, to find in the following pages an analysis of offline phenomena, for the Web is always in the background, acting as the main reference point for each and every reflection.

17

Nevertheless, some might ask: why 'Web' and not 'Internet'? I find this question deeply intriguing, because the two words are frequently treated as interchangeable. Still, it can be argued that referring to the Internet leads us to focus on the *medium*, and on understanding the Net as a network of computers. Referring to the Web leads us to focus on the Net as an entity that is also anthropological: a network of individuals that relate to each other, or who have the illusion of doing so. This is not a mere terminological matter, however, it is a decision resulting from the will to distance this work from all those that mainly concern communication, even when they are labelled as works addressing digital aesthetics. Discussing media is always tricky, yet I believe it is worth highlighting the aesthetic perspective, even when analysing the specificity of a medium.

Although there are a number of political implications to the issues discussed in this book, I chose not to go into these matters in too much depth. There are many works on these issues that deal with it far more incisively that I could ever hope to: works by Tiziana Terranova, Ned Rossiter, Michel Bauwens, Brett Neilson and Brian Holmes, to name just a few. However, this decision was made mainly because of Danilo Kiš's warning that one must always make a distinction between *Homo politicus* and *Homo poeticus*, and I believe I belong to the second category. I am aware of the fact that this decision might lead to the criticism that *Web Aesthetics* is a work that is inadequately situated. I believe, however, that for those who have the will and the patience to go beyond a superficial reading, my position will become clear in and through the ways my points are developed and linked to one another.

One last remark is required to define the topic of this work. I am rather sceptical when it comes to the matter of 'the next thing'. I have, therefore, focused upon recounting what has happened in the last few years and on what is happening today – which, as I write, has already become yesterday. After all, the point of aesthetics is to reflect on its own time. Rather than the evolutionary trajectories of the future, I am intrigued by the challenge of making connections between what has just happened and the historical bases of these events, while remaining fully aware of the fragmentation of the postmodern age, and of the impossibility of creating a grand unifying story.

Chapter 1

Dialogue Inside and Outside the Web

Closed Monads

The art of moderation concerns virtual diplomacy of the highest
rank. List aesthetics is about the creation of a text-only social
sculpture. It is meta-visual process art.
Geert Lovink, *Dark Fiber* (2002)

The first topic I want to analyse from the point of view of aesthetics is
the dialogue that takes place both within and around the Web.[1] The
concept of an 'aesthetics of dialogue' is not well-known, for, as an independent sector of philosophy, the main concern of aesthetics is believed
to be the 'judgment of taste'.

Polyphonies and Patchworks

In literary studies, we find frequent reference to the Russian philosopher and literary theorist Mikhail Bakhtin's concept of *vnenachodimost*:
that interpretation according to which, when a work of art is excellent,
it gives rise to a condition in which one is able to live simultaneously
in the place of oneself and in what is other than the self. In other words,
the Self and the Other come into contact. It is primarily in the 'polyphonic' Dostoevsky that Bakhtin glimpses the capacity to give aesthetic
form to the multiplicity of possible worlds that are composed precisely
within the polyphony of the literary text. Hence, to Bakhtin, difference
is the essential condition of dialogue: it is difference that shows that
identity is never complete, autonomous or definitive; that shows the
necessity of shifting from oneself. According to Bakhtin, the artist is
the person who does not take part in life only from the inside, but who
also loves it from the outside. Artistic activity stimulates an action out
of life and out of sense.[2] Furthermore, as philosopher and literary theorist Tzvetan Todorov observes, Bakhtin remains sceptical of Hegelian
dialectics, and works on a 'dialogics of culture' rather than a 'dialectics
of nature'.[3] He is aware that: 'Life is dialogical by its very nature. To live
means to engage in dialogue.'[4]

The Italian sociologist and philosopher Maurizio Lazzarato develops
a theory that begins with Bakhtinian dialogism and extends to the Web
via television. The purpose of such a theory is to involve those social
and expressive dynamics that would be omitted from a 'short geneal-

ogy', thus considering the sphere of new technologies and the Internet in isolation from the rest.[5] To Lazzarato, the Internet releases the centrifugal forces that had been captured and homogenized by the analogue networks of television, and opens the field to new potential worlds. Whereas television immediately arises as a monopoly, the cooperation of brains that grounds the spreading telematic networks makes them appear from the very earliest stages as a 'patchwork' of, for instance, communication protocols, hardware and software devices, copyright and copyleft. Thus digital networks do not follow the television model of a 'collective whole', but are set to work as 'distributed wholes' that encourage the development of 'multilingualism':[6]

> The individual, with his/her own computer, is an open monad, that communicates with other monads, all included in a non-hierarchical and acentrical network. The *net* is a net of nets; its heterogeneous nature is reluctant to unification, to homologation, to the melting of the differences into a 'collective whole'. . . . The monad is included in a flow of signs, sounds, images, information, that can either split (invention) or reproduce (repetition). Surfing the *net* means constantly experiencing conjunctions and disjunctions of flows. By entering a network a relationship of either unilateral or mutual appropriation, sympathetic or opposite cooperation, with other monads is built. . . . The subjectivization of the monad is in the refrain. Numeric flows wrap around the monads and from their meeting a refrain comes out, an act of subjectivization, that moves towards the meeting of other refrains in the network (polyphonic composition).[7]

To Lazzarato, the attempts to push digital networks towards a hierarchical centralization by means of monopolies (for instance that of the 'new economy') have failed because monads work according to a cooperative principle: they are cooperators and not clients. Acting inside the Internet becomes a 'feeling together', a building of common perception and an organization of common intelligence. In Lazzarato's work, this observation enables a definition of the new expression machines in the Bakhtinian terms of multi-perception and multi-intelligence.[8] The struggle between monolingualism and plurilingualism becomes, for Lazzarato, the struggle between the 'authority word' (that which to

Bakhtin is of religion, politics, moral, adults, professors and fathers)[9] and the 'persuasive word', which is the word of peers and contemporaries, and which enables the creation of infinite possible worlds. Lazzarato's interpretation is particularly successful at describing the origins of the Internet, which is characterized by what he terms a 'cooperation of brains'. However, although they appear to encourage a higher degree of interaction between users, I believe that the latest developments of the digital networks and the new philosophy that takes life on the Web – or in what is usually labelled as Web 2.0 – requires further reflection. Rather than forms of dialogue, the Web is often characterized by an autistic mode of expression, in which self-referentiality is the rule.

Homogeneous Clouds

Nowadays, the envisioned dialogue within Web 2.0 seems to have been just an illusion. As Dutch media theorist Geert Lovink observes, the blogosphere that by its very nature should have constituted a polyphonic space looks very much like a closed environment. Bearing in mind that a blog user is not on the same level as its author, the user cannot be considered an antagonist; rather, they are merely a guest. To Lovink, bloggers cannot be considered to fuel a public debate. Blogs give life to communities of like-minded people, while debates stagnate within clouds of homogeneous blogs. In such a condition, the exclusion of dissent is not even necessary, since nobody actually posts on an opposing blog. This is, for Lovink, the limitation of these media: even when the chance to reply is not cancelled, it is considered senseless to comment on a blog with content that one disagrees with.[10] Paraphrasing Lazzarato, we might say that the individual in concert with his or her own computer is in the process of returning to the status of closed monad.

Of this issue, Bakhtin might state that every statement (or every post) bears a link that connects it to all the actors that have appeared and that will appear on the word scene (the blogosphere). Yet for the purposes of this work, it may be more useful to analyse opinions expressed by French philosopher Pierre Lévy that seem to deny Lovink's theory of the Web's self-referentiality. According to Levy, the hypertext logic that rules the Web – for example, the links that lead to contrasting political views – encourages the creation of a virtual *agorà*, in which citizens become familiar with the opinions of their opponents. By participating in a daily dialogue with others, citizens build a context that leaves behind common political activity and its own self-reference in favour of a 'conversing political reason' and finally constitutes an 'electronic cyberdemocracy'.[11] The cyberdemocracy is defined by the art of a dialogue that does not aim to change the positions of the interlocutors, but which helps everyone to include an awareness of the other's point of view within their own perspective. A new, collective world takes shape, richer because the individuals it is made of are closer to each other, thanks to the mutual acquaintances forged through virtual communities, emails and above all hyperlinks.[12] Digital technologies help to mingle linguistic bodies, so that 'the other becomes closer to us through the tie of dialogue'.[13] They impose an ethics of dialogue, according to which sense does not come from the material universe composed of technological or economic relations, but from the connections between human spirits, each of which represents an original source of sense and is both autonomous and responsible, though conditioned by its own cultural and social background.[14]

In the introduction to the Italian translation of Lévy's work, philosopher Giuseppe Bianco makes the point that the chance to partake in dialogue and to access information does not mean that one is free to decide. In Lévy's discussion, Bianco observes, the 'invisible hand' of the market is replaced by a 'beneficial virtual hand' that would regulate the 'naturally' democratic development of technology, 'messianically walking mankind by the hand towards the Omega point of collective intelligence'.[15] Just a few years after the publication of Lévy's work, it is obvious that the development of digital technologies, and of the Web in particular, aims towards an 'only ostensible pluralism, actually domesticated to the interests of the big info-economical monopolies'[16] (Google's fate *docet*). There are problems, too, with Lévy's claim that the Web leads to a turn away from self-referentiality. A closer look at the main trends of the spaces that are supposedly aimed at the exchange of opinions (which have proliferated in the last few years thanks to the 'social' perspective pervading Web 2.0) leads me to conclusions directly opposed to Lévy's. As mentioned above, for Lovink debate takes place inside clouds of homogeneous blogs that remain closed in on themselves, and deny any contact with different or contrasting opinions.

If it is true that the software platforms upon which social networks are based allow everyone to articulate their opinions in a public forum, it is also indisputable that those 'meetings of spirits' that Lévy discusses take place with decreasing frequency. In fact, we increasingly observe the opposite scenario: in which everybody writes but almost nobody reads what others have written; everybody expresses their own opinions but almost nobody recalls the opposing opinions expressed by others; everybody is busy increasing the number of their 'friends' (virtual entities that share the same *Weltanschauungen*) but nobody considers confronting or arguing with one's ostensible 'enemies'. As Zygmunt Bauman claims: 'The Other is reduced by the internaut (the Internet user) to what really counts: to the status of the instrument of one's own self-endorsement.'[17]

In order to clarify these issues, it might be worth making a comparison with forms of dialogue that took place prior to Web 2.0, and in particular with mailing lists. The main feature that differentiates a mailing list from a blog is that any participant in a discussion that uses a mailing list must read what others have written. In fact, the debate develops through a series of posts, each one of which ends up constituting the logical premise of the discussion to follow. In mailing lists as well as in online forums, quoting what another user has written and developing a personal idea from that is a widespread practice. If one wants to understand the contrasting positions in the debate, one needs to walk backwards, following the *fil rouge* that links the different messages. In a mailing list, the different positions – whether in agreement or disagreement – are always related to one another, and it is only by considering the whole that these positions embody that 'collective' sense to which Lévy refers. As these digital environments are also typified by clashes that are often of a personal nature, a moderator is needed, as Lovink reminds us in the epigraph opening this chapter. Thus, we could say that the dialogic aesthetics instituted by mailing lists is about collectively building dialectic spaces, in which different opinions openly clash and overlap, without disregarding the two main premises of these forms of discussion: peer users (excepting the moderator, who is widely accepted to have a privileged position in order to facilitate the dialogue); and the partiality of single posts that only have a meaning if related to the whole they aim at building. Finally, bearing Bakhtin's theory in mind, it is possible to state that in mailing lists, the Self and the Other come into relation. In the blogosphere, and in social networks in general, we seem to have moved far away from any such dialectic. Rather, it seems that individuals and groups speak on their own terms, resulting in an enormous number of opinions travelling on parallel tracks, destined never to meet.

Another significant and distinctive feature of mailing lists is their private aspect, as opposed to the public nature of blogs and social networking platforms. It is important to note, however, that the messages that are sent to a list are sent to all the members of the list, which is often a significant number. The list is not an intimate conversation, nor is it like an email sent to a single addressee. However, the messages received from a mailing list are received in the same space in which all the other emails are read; a space that is often experienced as private and is password protected. Furthermore, the messages received from a list are often saved in a specific folder, so as to always have a history of the discussions that have enlivened *one's own* little community on hand. As banal as it is, even this last example is proof of the feeling of intimacy that characterizes the act of taking part in a mailing list. On the other hand, a discussion that takes place on a blog or on Twitter is public because it is visible to anyone, and this public mode clearly influences the dialogue. There is no manifestation of the Self in which its public and private versions match. In the case of mailing lists, however, a dialectic tension prevails in the dialogue involving two or more subjects, whereas in those opinions that are supposedly addressed to a potentially infinite audience such as Web users, it is the rhetorical features of language that dominate. We might state that the more intimate the dialogue is perceived to be, the more the subjects involved are open to the Other. In the more public forums, the risk is that we end up in a mode of self-celebration and become increasingly closed to those opinions that are seen as a threat to the Self.

There appears to be an ineradicable difference between an ideal of what the dialogue within the Web could be, and what it really is. The dialogic potential of digital networks do justify theories such as Lévy's, which view the Web as a sort of promised land in which the salvific power of dialogue can finally be revealed. Yet, the same potential enables the marketing campaigns of those parties that reap increasingly higher profits from the Web, thanks to the content generated by millions of enthusiastic users. Thus, the Web could be described as a vast amusement park, in which everyone experiences the excitement of the potential for an unlimited and unbounded dialogue to take place. In actuality, because the dialogue lacks any political, social, cultural or ethical premise, it never gets off the ground. Instead, groups of individuals wallow in their shallow puddles of self-reference while, behind the counter, the 'usual suspects' count up their cash. As Bauman states: 'The powerful flow of information is not a confluent of the river of democracy, but an insatiable intake intercepting its contents and channelling them away into magnificently huge, yet stale and stagnant artificial lakes.'[18] To sum up, it is possible to state that the debates that currently take place within the Web seem to be characterized by three principal features: autism, self-referentiality and monolingualism.

Autism and Self-Referentiality

Autism is a strong term to use, and I want to make clear that I do not use it carelessly. For both personal and ethical reasons, I have a great deal of respect for anyone who has experienced the pain caused by this condition. However, I believe it is reasonable to view the attitudes of many bloggers as a sort of 'media autism', characterized by repetitive actions, the loss of contact with external reality, and finally becoming locked up in a personal, autocentric life.[19] Here, I have in mind those bloggers that spend their time reviewing consumer goods, movies and video games, rather than those who relate their personal emotions or experiences. In these types of expression, there appears to be no will to engage with other opinions, or to open up a discussion, as signalled by the statement that 'the comments to this entry are closed'. In these cases, it is clearly pointless to speak of a 'dialogue', unless we consider it in highly idealized terms. We could, for example, speak of the cohabitation of ideas in the common space of the Web, and hence of a *potential* for dialectic among them. Yet, I believe we inhabit a stage of self-referentiality, which takes place when individuals gather, either in big or small groups, in an environment that fosters a dialogue that takes place exclusively within a single community. Only rarely do these groups open up to the outside, and only towards very similar realities. In these cases, the dialogue is reduced to sharing values within a culture or a subculture, an activity that serves a dual function: strengthening the internal cohesion of the community; and emphasizing the differences between one's own community and those other communities that are ostensibly populated by enemies, strangers, and those who are different.

Monolingualism

The third factor is the most complex, as it is possible to speak of the Web's monolingualism both literally and metaphorically. I will begin with the literal meaning of the term, by pointing out that the *institutional* dialogue within the Web takes place in English, regardless of the number of, say, Spanish or Mandarin-speaking users, which statistics show is far higher than the number of users from English-speaking countries.[20] In the last few years especially, the emergence of several forms of monolingualism has become visible in those networks of websites in which users talk exclusively in, for example, Hindi, Iranian, Portuguese, Japanese or Korean. In the international debates that take place on the Web, the use of English as a 'career language' leads to significant consequences that few seem to have noticed. The first, and worst, consequence is the total exclusion of all those who do not speak English at all. This comprises a huge number of Web citizens, whose exclusion massively depletes the global quality, the complexity and the multicultural nature of the debates. The high cost of translation, as well as of training and hiring specialists such as cultural mediators, are the main reasons for discouragement.

What is surprising, however, is the complete vacuity of those who do not realize how partial the debates they are involved in are. Until a way is found to include those who are now excluded by linguistic barriers, these debates can never be considered truly international, by which I mean representing the whole of those who use the Web. Another significant consequence is the inferior status conferred upon all those who cannot fully develop their thought in the English language, though they are able to read and write in that language. Struggling with the hardship of translating the complexity of their own cultural background into another linguistic system, these people find themselves in a situation I would term a kind of 'involvement with handicap', and which Marc Augé has evocatively termed a 'mutilated relationship' of 'linguistic infirmity'.[21] In other words, one is involved in the debate, but one's own potential to contribute cannot be fully realized. These people end up being ridiculed, treated with detachment or considered as inconveniences. As has been stated by Emmanuel Levinas and later by Jacques Derrida, 'language is hospitality'. However, that very hospitality is based on a paradox: the guest simultaneously offers the promise of escaping from loneliness, and represents a threat to one's own sovereignty. When the door is opened to the guest who is both friend and foe, the Other is being both accepted and challenged. As one's own hegemony is forced upon them and one's own code imposed, the guest becomes a hostage.[22] On the Net, the tendency to impose one's own code is very dangerous, as it can create new monolingual ghettos. As has happened in Spanish-speaking communities among many others, dialogue takes place solely in the mother-tongue, in order for the interlocutors to avoid feeling like uninvited guests in international discussions.

The debate on the Web can also be described as monolingual due to the ritualization and constant repetition of certain expressive modes. In this context, it is worth mentioning that, since the ancient Greek period, the purpose of dialogue – as a symbolic battle for the truth – is to realize a 'world' built according to particular formal rules. Thus, the ritualization of forms is not a result of mutual respect, but of the fact that both interlocutors are 'armed'. Compared to this conception of dialogue, the monolingualism I want to talk about arises from the flattening of dialogue into expressive clichés that are endlessly repeated, thus typifying the diffuse aesthetics of the present time. If the idea of building the form of dialogue together is abandoned in favour of the deployment of ritual and hence predetermined expressive forms, the dialogue itself is degraded. As the components of dialogue drift further from the original and true thoughts that are the natural referents of debate, the act of choosing an expressive model comes to precede the formulation of the thought itself. The result is that it becomes impossible for the dialogue to move beyond the mere exchange of symbols lacking any substantial content. In Jean Baudrillard's words, we end up with a situation in which signs 'are exchanged against each other rather than against the real'.[23] Finally, one ends up not saying anything at all. In other words, if dialogue becomes aestheticized, the contents are reduced to their formal qualities, and any semantic, moral or ethical properties are left aside.

In order to demonstrate my point, a simple game might be useful and perhaps provocative. I have identified some of the most frequent formulas used in the mailing lists I subscribe to and in the forums I observe, as follows:

I very much/wholeheartedly/wholly agree with that conclusion.
That's really interesting and I really wish/want/think...
Indeed an interesting topic.
The point is to think in terms of...
This is the key question...
There is only one way to address such questions...

Clearly, these phrases are commonly used in English, and so it is not surprising to find them widely used in online discussions. Nevertheless, each of the above phrases occurs so frequently that one must ask: How is it possible that so many different people, from so many different geographical areas, are unable to find a better way to express their enthusiasm for a particular topic than by stating, for example, 'indeed an interesting topic'? Scrolling the messages of any mailing list, what strikes me is the tendency to use a profoundly limited variety of adjectives, verbs and adverbs, for example: interesting, real, effective, wholly, mostly, embodied, addressed, distributed, based, to suggest, to struggle, to strengthen, to point. Rather than supposing that the English vocabulary is impoverished – a claim that is very difficult to credit – this lack of variety is in fact an expression of the conformism that rules online discussions. Rather than freely and effectively expressing their thoughts, many users seem concerned only to conform as closely as possible to the 'aesthetic canons' that rule specific discussion forums. Thus dialogue becomes increasingly ritualized, and composed solely of mantra and cliché. Increasingly, this formulaic repetition becomes the price to pay for anyone who wishes to be immediately and universally comprehensible. Once again, we see that process of spectacularization that has turned the advertising model into the main reference point for any form of communication. More specifically, we see the tendency for those who are uncertain of their ability to formulate their thoughts in English to simply copy and paste in those sentences that seem capable of expressing their own point of view.

Another feature that typifies these discussion environments is an 'aesthetics of dissent'. Here are some expressions of ritualized dissent that I have observed:

> I agree with much of what you say, but I would only add that...
> Although I do agree with most of your arguments, what I think is lacking...
> I have to agree with the assertion that... although I do think...
> xxxx, with respect, I heartily/wholly/wholeheartedly disagree with your arguments.
> While I wholly agree with xxxx's comments about..., I would like to point out that...
> I do agree that..., but to put it in perspective...
> The discussion on... has been very interesting, but seems to be...
> I'm not sure I agree with the statement that...
> I sincerely doubt that...

In these examples, the adoption of a ritualized form pre-existing the formulation of one's own thought denies the actuality of the opposing argument. Rather than a meeting of different opinions, what takes shape is a kind of role play in which the actors faithfully follow their scripts. In light of these expressions, one wonders if we should refer to the staging of fictions or of entertainments rather than dialogues. Whatever the case, the key point is that such expressions of apparent dissent are actually aesthetic attitudes aimed at taking part in a system – a system that could not be what it is without incorporating into itself the presence of forms of dissent. These expressions function to safeguard the health of the system, but they require ritualization and institutionalization in order to be integrated, finally, within the system itself.

The only escape from these ritualized, shallow and pointless exchanges, it seems, are personal insults, vilification and politically incorrect statements. To insult is an irrational act; thus the insult is capable of fracturing the structure of diffuse aesthetics and of disturbing falsely dialogic routines. Those who insult reinstate the individual at the core of the relations, thus transgressing the ossifying rules of the debate. They marginalize themselves, but reinsert elements of unpredictability into the exchange. The insult sounds an alarm to the whole community: to the moderators, who will have to use all their diplomatic skills to repair the relations (or who will simply act as censors *tout court*), and to the other members of the group, who will be required to exhibit their disdain for such lapses in taste. The opportunity to rail against the rebel who has disturbed the placid flow of the discussion allows the community to consolidate its internal ties, and to reassert the good old 'rules of the house'. However, although insults are capable of breaking the rules, not even they can elude the tendency to ritualize. Eventually, they lose their subversive drive and end up repeating well-known epithets, usually ending in 'uck'. How, then, do we allow the Web to develop forms of genuine dialogue and to avoid the tendency towards monolingualism?

Dialogic Conditions

The conditions for dialogue constitute a highly complex issue, because it is not only utopian but completely misguided to consider the Web as an entity that is independent from the dominant cultural and social trends of society. However, it is still possible to identify some premises for dialogue that are valid in relation to any medium. Dialogue requires the willingness on the part of the interlocutors to re-discuss and re-evaluate their own positions, ideas and values, time and time again. This mutual re-positioning is what allows the interlocutors to give life to the form – to construct the formal rules – of their dialogue. This form can never be pre-given, for it needs to be built by the interlocutors through the discussion. Another essential requirement for dialogue to take place is to be aware of the presence of the Other. This seems obvious, but it is actually the foundation of the relationship of responsibility that must characterize any form of dialogue. Dialogue requires a choice for the Other from both the interlocutors – in Jean-Paul Sartre's words, it requires *taking care of the other*. This seems to me a crucial point, because it recalls an ethical vision of dialogue; it implies the mutual responsibility of the interlocutors to each other, and the awareness that the failure of the dialogue will affect both of them equally. If this premise is accepted, one must conclude that taking part in a dialogue always involves an ethical choice. The issue is to establish the kind of ethics.

In this light, the work of Italian philosopher Guido Calogero is instructive. Calogero has theorized a secular ethics that leads to tolerance and to the cohabitation of men and women in a 'common house', in which 'none has to feel like a stranger, as an inhabitant without rights, even if his beliefs are not shared by anyone else'.[24] The concept of laicism, which Calogero relates to dialogue, is the best guarantee against the temptation of 'pretending to be a repository of the truth more than anybody else can pretend to be',[25] but also against the temptation to slip into dogmatism. Thus, Calogero encourages us to develop a double ability: to live together with differences, and to doubt the truth of which we are certain. In Calogero's perspective, the 'truth' can only come into light through dialogue: through exchange and discussion with the Other; through the common building of a shared ethics; and through what might be considered a *minimal common platform*. In other words, the aim is to construct a shared ethics that does not entail some final agreement (which can easily become a flattening of difference) but rather offers the chance for the interlocutors to continue their discussion without sacrificing their personal values.[26]

Travelling in Surface
At this point, I would like to consider how the ritual forms of communication might be interpreted from a different perspective; one seemingly opposed to the ethical vision of dialogue that I have discussed thus far. As opposed to the language that *humbly* adapts itself to the requirements of dialogue, rituals are extremely resistant to change. This is the starting point for Italian aesthetologist Mario Perniola in *Contro la comunicazione*,[27] in which Perniola, drawing on George A. Lindbeck,[28] considers the ritual, as a self-referential and autotelic practice, as a potential aesthetic strategy that contrasts with the movements that characterize the mass media. For Perniola, the mass media moves in a way similar to a continuously turning wheel. To the spins of communication, *habitus*, forms, and rituals might be opposed, entities that:

> ... stay in their exteriority as something stable and shared even when their meaning has disappeared or has become unconscious or has never existed at all. The chance for a social connection is based on these dimensions that show a non organic physicality and then are not subject to the twisting and turning of the spin.[29]

In Perniola's work, the concept of 'intrasystemic consistency' is crucial, as 'every single culture is made up of a vocabulary of discursive and non-discursive elements as well as the specific logic or grammar they are based upon and develop'.[30] If this is true, then it is not difficult to understand why rituals are capable of resisting the 'muddy flowing of communication' better than cognitive and expressive dimensions are able to, as these offer only 'low resistance to the communication spin'.[31] Perniola's reflections offer us the opportunity to integrate the concept of dialogue with that of diffuse aesthetics, in order to emphasize that, in light of the present dominance of digital media, identities are able to form from contact with bodies that communicate exclusively in an electronic mode. Thoughts move only in extension, intermingling with other thoughts that are structured within networks, and which finally remain on the surface. For Ernesto Francalanci, this very inability of thought to enter into depth is the reason for its present crisis.[32]

The shift from modernity to postmodernity has been characterized by the arrival at non-places and an endless present. The price to pay for this new, completely fake, global dimension has been the loss of the space and time for reflection. Without such space and time, moving beyond the aesthetically harmonized surface of things has become impossible. The contemporary subject is wrapped up in webs that give rise to a shallow uniformity, and has lost the ability to make critical or moral incisions into the webs in which they are enfolded. In this condition, dialogue is reduced to an exchange of thoughts in which contents have been replaced by formal or spectacular elements. We are far from Plato's speleological 'lunges', as well as from Fontana's pictures, which still possessed the capacity to impact upon the surface of a reality that was only experienced superficially. In the contemporary age, it is easy to travel in any direction, as long as we travel on the surface. We are prevented from accessing the depths, and we lose the capacity to cut through or even to scratch the surface of things. Present times are *deeply* anti-dialogical.

Spam and Viruses:
The Evil to be Eradicated

Le rhizome est l'image du chiendent qui pousse dans toutes les
directions, avec des nœuds et de multiples contacts souterrains.
Gilles Deleuze and Félix Guattari, *Rhizome* (1976)

A dialogic effort should also include those phenomena capable of diso-
rienting or harassing users of the Web. I am referring to practices such
as spamming, or the uncontrollable sending of viruses, Trojan Horses,
back doors, and any other phenomena that alter the relationships between human beings and computers.

The Problem of Legitimation
This issue is usually discussed in a defensive key, by those who wish
to protect their own privacy, their PCs, and their businesses. I wish to
approach these phenomena differently, by focusing on their peculiar
nature. It seems to me that we need to understand these practices
within the line of flight of the rhizome – that line which, once followed,
brings multiplicity to the entity, mutating its own nature. Placing the
activity of spammers and the modern 'digital anointer' on the line of
flight means applying the principles according to which Gilles Deleuze
and Felix Guattari define the rhizome:

> There is a rupture in the rhizome whenever segmentary lines ex-
> plode into a line of flight, but the line of flight is part of the rhizome.
> These lines always tie back to one another. That is why one can never
> posit a dualism or a dichotomy, even in rudimentary form of the
> good and the bad.[1]

The practices I have described above are a crucial part of the Net or, in
Deleuze and Guattari's terminology, the rhizome.[2] In the end, those who
discuss spam and viruses in terms of the degeneration of the system[3]
confer a negativity upon these phenomena that denies their very existence. They are the 'couchgrass' to be eradicated, and yet, as Deleuze
and Guattari write: 'Yes, couchgrass is also a rhizome. Good and bad are

only the products of an active and temporary selection, which must be renewed.'[4] Therefore, we can establish a first principle that I will term *legitimation*. No one can deny that spam and viruses, as well as those who profit from these practices, are in actual fact citizens of the global hypertext. Once they are legitimized, the point will be to identify the political significance of these phenomena, by following the line of flight that they express. This direction has been taken in a few publications. The first, by Spammer-X (aka Jeffrey Posluns), begins with the hypothesis that the activity of spamming can be understood as a 'spam cartel', and can be connected to specific economic interests. Posluns' conclusion is that as long as spamming remains remunerative, users will have no other choice than to accept its existence, just as they accept the constant intrusions of telemarketers. One feature of this work is its exhibition of the wit and technical skill of spammers. The key point, however, is to understand the philosophy shared by spammers, which is encapsulated in the statements: 'I can do it, and you can't stop me, so it's all right. Besides, I get paid to do it.'[5] In his review of this work, Alessandro Ludovico writes:

> The simple but straightforward terms used by Spammer-X to express his thought, unveil tricks, strategies and numbers that open the doors of a world that is actually only imagined by the average user. By looking at the net with the tools of a spammer, it takes the shape of a fascinating toy, that, as easy as it seems to be managed, it can so easily become uncontrollable, letting itself be tamed only until the next technical or legal upgrade. The (noticeable) ethical compromises, as well as the money involved and the technical skills needed to survive in a system that involves a surprising solidarity among single beings, reminds one of an eternal chess game between spammers and the front that tries to block them.[6]

Ludovico's reference to solidarity is not accidental. In fact, this is a topic that is discussed in a second work on the issue, Danny Goodman's *Spam Wars*.[7] Rather than providing a 'magical' remedy capable of freeing the mailbox, Goodman's work clearly shows that the measures for restricting spam (anti-spam filters, blacklists, etcetera) end up blocking messages that have nothing to do with the danger that one is trying to avoid. From these two texts, we can discern a significant point: while the mass of users annoyed by spam appears a broken and fragmented multitude, the spammers' cartel is a supportive community, composed of subjects with extraordinary skills, working towards a common *telos*. There is always the temptation to reduce spam and viruses to economic phenomena, existing only for profit. Yet, from this point of view, we can conceive of an economy that takes advantage of the desire of users, as Ludovico brilliantly states:

> Spam acts as an updated survey of the most basic desire and taboos incarnations (having sex with unknown people, owning status symbol objects, owning more money, being more healthy). It deals with some of the most common contemporary men's social weakness, and the mirage of obtaining them quickly and without a big effort.[8]

World Visions

However, there is a perspective that encourages us to view these practices in terms of culture, rather than solely in terms of economics.[9] If spam is part of contemporary reality, the same is true of computer viruses: they are elements of the daily digital that enter the collective imaginary, and sometimes become an artistic 'ready-made'. For example, projects such as the famous *Biennale.py* (2001) by EpidemiC and 0100101110101101.ORG,[10] and the provocative website *spamshirt.com* (from which it is possible to purchase a personalized T-shirt with one's own favourite spam subject), clearly show that spam and viruses have become pop objects, just as Andy Warhol's *Campbell Soup* (1962) turned that product into an icon of 1960s' consumerist society. Historically, the artist's task is to perceive social and cultural transformations before they begin to affect the wider population. So, if an analysis of these works of pop art is undertaken, it seems that these practices are not mere 'couchgrass' to be eradicated, but rather that they are *Weltanschauungen*, entire worldviews, or more specifically Net views, and hence systems of values that are endlessly multiplied. After all, what is the postmodern condition if not the end of history as a central and unifying point of view, and the subsequent liberation of the many cultures and worldviews that typify the present time?[11]

A further step towards understanding these phenomena might be the adoption of a mystico-religious mode of interpretation, particularly if we accept the arguments of those who view the Internet as a cult object. This is the hypothesis put forward by the French philosophers Pierre Lévy and Philippe Breton, although echoes of this view can be found in writers belonging to different cultures as well as throughout a great deal of cyberpunk literature. Furthermore, recent anthropological studies have demonstrated a tendency for an infatuation with the Internet to develop among users, and hence for the Internet to gain the aura of a new religion. I use the adjective 'new', though I am aware that the present cult derives to some extent from another, much wider, cult: that of information, which arose in the 1940s and is most closely associated with the work of the American mathematician Norbert Wiener.[12] At this time, cyberneticians popularized a worldview that made information the central component of the real. According to cyberneticians, the world is composed of two elements: on the one hand, forms, ideas, messages and information; on the other hand, disorder, chaos and entropy. Though an atheist, Wiener links disorder and entropy to the Devil, just as Internet users characterize any obstruction to technological progress as the worst of evils.[13] Discussing this issue, Breton employs the expression *ontologie radicale du message*, by which he means that nothing exists if it cannot be conceived in the form of a message, or as information.[14] This is a mystic of communication: since the aim of the message is its own circulation, anything furthering this movement is positive, while anything that prevents its movement can only be disorder, entropy or evil. From a metaphysical perspective, the real becomes conflated with the constant exchange of information, and ends by being reduced to the information that constitutes it. Thus, the real is confined to the relational (the constant exchange of messages), and the relational, in turn, is confined to the informational.[15] Although Wiener's paradigm has influenced several schools of thought, it was only the inception of a global network of connections that provided the *humus* for the full realization of the cybernetic worldview. To its supporters, the Net represents the promise of a new Jerusalem, a new conscience, and a new spirit. It has also, however, become the promise of a better world and even of better men and women, if we take conscience in its wider sense of a *collective* (or *connective*, to mention De Kerckhove) *conscience*. As Breton reminds us, it is in the Net that the 'noosphere' – as conceived in the 1950s by the Jesuit priest Teilhard de Chardin as a meeting point of col-

37

lective ideas – is finally realized.[16] The cult of the Internet is mainly that of a transparent society in which the movement of information is no longer mediated, and in which the distance between the producer and the user of the information, the two entities that results from the modernist split, finally meet in the same noosphere.

Apart from reconfiguring the terms of the producer/user dialectic, we can reconsider those practices that some would like to define as outside the Net. For example, the essential attitude of what is commonly known as 'computer piracy' is nothing but a statement of this transparency. Anyone who takes possession of computer data is refusing the authority of the law, is contesting any kind of regulation of the circulation of information, and is refuting any distinction between public and private. Whatever limits the free movement of information – the private sphere, intellectual property, or the law more generally – is continuously violated by Web users. Political representation, along with information that is 'packeted' according to the needs of mass communication, is both refused and sabotaged because they are obstacles between the 'freed' human being and a real that has been rendered completely transparent. From this point of view, it is clear that spam and viruses, however obnoxious, must be considered full citizens of digital networks. The aim is to establish a more critical, dialectical approach, one that is capable of bringing to light the worldviews that these practices express.

New Media Culture

Yes, I only have one language, yet it is not mine.
Jacques Derrida, *Le Monolinguisme de l'autre* (1996)

The debate surrounding the cultural implications of the Web, and new media more generally, is dogged by monolingualism and self-referentiality. Even in new media, familiar problems are in evidence: practical problems such as the high costs of translation and the difficulty of training cultural mediators, and ideological problems such as the blind faith in English as an international language. Outside the Web, however, monolingualism and self-referentiality become grotesque. The difficulty that new media scholars have finding a specific place within Media Studies, for example, or the shallow approach of the mainstream media towards a culture that is still wrongly referred to as 'underground' or 'niche', have resulted in the ghettoization of new media theory. All this only deepens the fracture between the cultural approach of new media theory and society.

Limits and Prospects

For those who wish to make a 'professional' contribution to the development of new media theory, the alternatives are well defined, and can be seen as constituting three main options: firstly, trying to forge a career within an academic institution, a task which is often difficult and unsatisfactory; secondly, contributing to the ideological productions and marketing campaigns of those companies that wish to profit from new media; thirdly, living a *bohémien* life as a free thinker, in which case one will be forced to live by one's wits alone. In regard to the first option, it is worth mentioning that the situation varies between countries, and that the universities located in the more technologically developed countries do not find it difficult to introduce courses and departments focused on theoretical research into new media, often by integrating it into Media Studies departments, although it sometimes functions independently. In contrast, in those countries in which the academic world is still tied to the traditions of classical studies, any opening to the new is continually obstructed, so that building an academic career as a theorist of new media becomes an almost utopian aim. In general, there is significant interest in the study of new subjects focusing on digital media in English-speaking countries. This, however, only reinforces the monolingualism of the study of new media: an Italian, a Greek or an Iranian who wants to engage with these topics has no choice but to move to a more academically developed country. Eventually, the most probable outcome for such a scholar is to publish their work in a language other than their own, almost always in English. What is more, it is very rare to read an English translation of a book written in another language, and simultaneous translations are almost never provided in international lectures.

In regard to those who choose to use their knowledge in their work for commercial industry, I do not believe that their arguments can ever really be considered objective, because the first priority will always be to protect the interests and the ideology of the company. However, I would like to focus on a second, less dogmatic aspect of the work of these authors: the tendency to be constantly oriented towards the future, to the *next thing*. This attitude is surely detrimental to the development of a critical view of reality.

The third option, the *bohémien* life, is the most frequently chosen. However, this is not actually a choice; as Lovink observes, it is really the only option left. The number of those who experience firsthand the hardship of intellectual uncertainty is increasing. It is also worth mentioning the difference between those who seek to work in countries in which forms of welfare still exist and those who live in countries without a welfare system. What is surprising is that it is very often the 'free thinkers' who make the most interesting contributions to new media theory. As they do not belong to any specific institution, these authors can develop their thoughts in a freer, and less self-referential, way. Furthermore, the lives of these people are not subject to strict rules or schedules, so that they can follow the rhythms of their own artistic urges, rather than following a precise research plan and suffering the concomitant 'scientific compromises'. Often, the work of these authors is more flexible than that arising from academic or institutional contexts, in which work often stagnates and becomes detached from reality. This is particularly clear in the field of aesthetics, in which the understanding according to which, as Fredric Jameson puts it, 'everything is cultural' makes it crucial to abandon academic strictures for a methodo-

logical flexibility that allows us to comprehend the complexity of contemporary phenomena. However, if the 'free thinker' has a weakness,
it is a tendency to fall into radical anti-academicism, and to refuse any
cultural establishment whatsoever.[1]

One of the challenges of new media culture, then, is to bring into
contact those realities that are otherwise destined to travel on parallel
paths. The development of theories of new technologies should take
place both from within academia and from outside, and even from within commercial industries themselves. The debate should flow without
regard to the status of the participants, and should be based above all on
the willingness of the interlocutors to always question themselves and
to be ready to take sudden and unpredictable directions in their work.
Only in this way can we avoid the force of self-referentiality, which
reduces all new media theory to a few predefined lines of inquiry.

One clear example of self-referentiality is to be found in the bib-
liographies of books about digital media theory. In such works, the
references are so similar that one feels as if one is reading photocopies.
Certainly, one of the major reasons for the similarity of the bibliogra-
phies of different authors is the brief history of new media as a subject.
Yet, although there can be relatively few texts relating to a specific
theme, there is still a reluctance to create a genuine exchange with different fields, and to seek out authors from outside the main channels of
research, with genuinely innovative points of view. If one were to list
the speakers taking part in the majority of conferences, lectures, meetings and festivals related to digital culture, the prevalence of guests
from visible cultural contexts (usually Northern Europe and California)
would be obvious. There are 'openings to multiculturality', yet the *conditio sine qua non* is a prevalence of scholars connected to international
(read: English-speaking) cultural institutions.

It does not seem to occur to anyone that the most interesting work
might be done in languages other than English, nor that it might be
done by people who are unattached to a specific cultural institution.
In ten or 20 years' time, perhaps this will become evident, and all the
material that is currently lost to new media studies will be recovered
through translations, critical reviews, or any other format capable of
including these works within new media culture. What new media culture needs is intellectuals who, thanks to a global and interconnected

view of the relevant fields of knowledge, are capable of understanding the relativity and partiality of current intellectual speculation on new media, and who are authoritative enough to denounce the limits and the narrowness of the present perspectives. We need thinkers who are able to make connections with schools of thought, whether they are well-established or progressive, other than the ones the debate is currently suffocating in.

New Media Art

The debate on new media art is emblematic of self-referentiality and monolingualism. Certainly, there is no agreed-upon definition of new media art as yet. Even so, it is tragic how little openness there is to different opinions in this field. Anyone who has experienced self-celebratory arts festivals such as Transmediale or Ars Electronica will understand my point. One theorist who is able to fully grasp this reality is Lovink, who characterizes the situation as follows:

> The collective discursive poverty within new media arts explains the virtual absence of lively debates about the art works in general. There is little institutional criticism. With mainstream media uninterested, the new media arts scene is fearful of potentially devastating internal debates . . . a fuzzy tribal culture of consensus rules, based on good-will and mutual trust.[2]

According to Lovink, new media art needs to be viewed from the perspective of completely different fields, such as design, commercial art, or dance music. A genuinely critical perspective will only be built if we are willing to depart from the present suffocating scene. The barriers of the ghetto will only be transcended by those who are willing to make a 'quantum leap',[3] or to denounce the mistakes perpetrated by those who presently populate the scene.

Lovink's criticism is clear. I would, however, like to add a point in relation to that which Lovink terms a 'tribal culture of consensus'. After spending several days at a major European festival of digital art and culture, I had the impression of a community in which good manners and friendship were the rule. Smiles, handshakes and back-patting dominated within this laidback atmosphere, in which the participants

42

were safe from unwanted or threatening currents. This brings to mind Baudrillard's reference to a certain 'accomplice paranoia' (*paranoïa complice*) in the world of contemporary art. In other words, this is a scene that constantly eludes the possibility of critical judgment, and leaves space only for 'a friendly, necessarily convivial, sharing of nothingness' (*un partage à l'amiable, ément convival, de la nullité*).[4] In such a context, open dissent is seen as utterly inappropriate. Nothing is allowed to disturb the quiet harmony of a community that in fact comes together for comfort rather than to confront.

The result is an aestheticization of forms of dissent, which are expressed very stylishly through the litany of phrases such as: 'I would only add that ...', 'but I also think that ...' or 'to put this in perspective ...'. This is an ethereal, insubstantial form of dissent, which expresses only the frailty of the community, and its desire to remain protected from any disturbance. Proof of this is the determined unity that characterizes the tribe's reaction to any potential critique or provocation. In the Artist's Statement[5] that Parker Ito has published on his personal website, the dogmatic nature of the premises of new media art are treated with refreshing irony. Here, the Californian artist has his weird characters reading out a list of 'new aesthetic principles', their robotic voices stating that: 'C++ has replaced the brush', that 'the hand is dead', and that 'Cyberspace is the contemporary muse'. This litany of mechanically repeated statements brilliantly satirizes the reality of new media art, and its lack of critical theoretical approaches and perspectives.

The Utopia of a Consensual World

At this stage, one might wonder if there are reasons for new media art to be so enclosed within its ghetto, apart from the community's need to protect its own weak premises. In order to answer this question, I would like to draw on a concept introduced by Philippe Breton. In order to describe one of the main obsessions of the cybernetic school of thought, which I have mentioned briefly above, Breton conceives of a *utopie de la communication*: the will to create a peaceable and dispute-free society, one that is based on rules that are agreed to by all the members of the society. In particular, Breton believes that this is the aim of neurolinguistic programming, in which communicating means, *in primis*, defining a clear target and then identifying the other's target. Following the stage of identification, communication becomes a positive action, in which subjects aim to harmonize their targets.

For Breton, this is a utopian aim, which functions to deny and to demonize conflict. In other words, this is a binary view that only recognizes 'good' (harmony of the elements) and 'evil' (conflict), so that no room is left for 'negotiation of the conflict'. An effective community does not deny the presence of differences and disagreements[6] but recognizes both the need for such conflicts and the need for an effort to resolve them. The debate around new media art is characterized by an obsession with positivity that precludes the possibility of criticism. The critical attitude is viewed as a hurdle to communication and to the development of new media culture, with the result that critics are demonized, confined within the evil universe of entropic disorder, and excluded from festivals, meetings, lectures and publications.

To Open Oneself to Difference

In conclusion, my invitation is to open ourselves to difference, to denials and to critique, wherever they are and whatever their form, for it is only by recognizing and negotiating conflict that it becomes possible to increase the quality of thought in regard to digital media. In particular, it is important to stop strutting about one's own *international language*, and to begin looking for more suitable ways to comprehend what is being discussed in languages other than English. It is my hope that more people will be offered the opportunity to express their thoughts in the way that is best for them, that the specificity of different cultural backgrounds will be realized and encouraged, and that tools will be created that will facilitate the involvement of a greater variety of thinkers in the debate around new media. For example, in place of the umpteenth massive and massively expensive installation in a publically financed festival, we might instead finance the simultaneous translation of discussions and lectures. The silly habit of parallel sessions could be avoided, and a smaller number of speakers would be able to give their speech in a language of their own choosing.[7]

I am also suggesting that we move beyond the perspective of multiculturalism. Too often, this manifests itself as a hypocritical tolerance of the Other, the different, the stranger.[8] In actuality, 'multiculturalism' has ended up destroying differences, and crushing them under a single code – the experience of the European Union might ring a bell. What new media culture, and Western society in general, really needs is to move beyond the mere acceptance of the Other and to learn, as Iain Chambers writes, to 'dwell in *hybridity as home*'. That is to say, we need to learn to '[occupy] a further space in which both the familiar and the foreign are conjoined and mutually interrogated'.[9]

Chapter II

Aesthetic Diffusion

A Short History of the Concept of Aesthetic Experience

Art is the imposing of a pattern on experience, and our aesthetic
enjoyment is recognition of the pattern.
Alfred North Whitehead, *Dialogues* (1954)

Before delving into the analysis of aesthetic experience in digital
networks, I will offer a short summary of critical positions regarding
aesthetic experience. There has never been an accepted definition of
aesthetic experience, and there is still some confusion over how aesthetic experience differs from the experience of beauty. The Polish philosopher Władysław Tatarkiewicz, whose *A History of Six Ideas*[1] will be
the main reference point for this short *excursus*, points out that each of
the three great aesthetic concepts – beauty, art and aesthetic experience
– has a slightly different meaning. Concepts such as the sublime, tragic,
comic or pictorial are included in the concept of aesthetic experience,
for example, but not within the concept of beauty.

In the Footsteps of Tatarkiewicz

According to Tatarkiewicz, the expression 'aesthetic experience'
developed much later than its corresponding concept. The Greeks, for
example, used the expression αἴσθησις to describe sensory impression
and the expression νόησις to describe thought; a distinction that is mir-
rored in the Latin terms *sensatio* and *intellectus*. Although these terms
were used in debates on beauty and on art, the term 'aesthetics' was not
used until the second half of the eighteenth century by the German
philosopher Alexander Baumgarten. Baumgarten, writes Tatarkiewicz:

> ... identified *cognitio sensitiva*, sensitive cognition, with the cognition
> of beauty and gave to the study of the cognition of beauty the Greco-
> Latin name *cognitio aesthetica*, or *aesthetica* for short. It was thus, from
> modern Latin, that the noun 'aesthetics' and the adjective 'aesthetic'
> entered the modern languages.[2]

As Tatarkiewicz notes, the late development of the term for aesthetic experience is further proof that the history of concepts often differs from the history of terms. Although Aristotle did not use the term aesthetic experience, he defines six features of the experience of beauty in the *Etica Eudemia*, his works on ethics: intense pleasure; suspension of the will; various degrees of intensity; that it is an experience characteristic of man; that it originates in the sense; and that its origin is from the sensations themselves and not from associations. Plato, who claimed that true beauty did not reside in things but in ideas, believed the faculty of intellect essential to the aesthetic sense. Plato's views are apparent in Plotinus, who stated that the beauty of the world can only be seen by those who possess beauty within themselves.

As there were no significant developments during the Middle Ages, it is not until the Renaissance, and in particular in the work of humanist philosopher Marsilio Ficino, that we find the concept of a particular faculty of the intellect and an appropriate attitude of the subject. At this time, the humanist polymath Leon Battista Alberti introduced the concept of 'soul slowness',[3] and recommended 'passive submission' to beauty, so that the passive attitude overtook the idea of the intellect as the active component of experience.[4] Although the traditions of Ancient history are alive in fifteenth-century Florence, it was not until the late baroque age and Gian Vincenzo Gravina's *Poetic Reason* (1708) that we find the assertion that the experience of beauty uniquely involves the mind's seizure by irrational feelings. Thus, Gravina uses the expression 'delirium'[5] and speaks of 'people (who) dream with their eyes open'.[6]

During the Enlightenment, there is a surge in interest in aesthetic experience. In Britain, for example, Locke's psychologism and his 'sober intellectualism' is confronted with Shaftesbury's emphasis upon feelings and values and 'poetical anti-intellectualism'.[7] The contribution made by Enlightenment thinkers is the attempt to explain aesthetic experience regardless of the hypothesis of a specific 'sense of beauty'. Yet, in spite of the coherence of this method, there was conflict between the positions: to Shaftesbury, beauty is an absolutely objective feature of things; to Hutcherson aesthetic experience is a subjective reaction of the senses to objective stimuli; to Hume 'beauty exists only in the perceiving mind'; and to Burke beauty is 'some quality in bodies, acting mechanically upon the human mind by the intervention of the senses'.[8]

Simultaneously, German scholars were formulating very different theories of aesthetic experience. For example, Baumgarten, who is mentioned above, believed aesthetic experience to be a wholly sensible and ultimately irrational form of knowledge. However, in the history of aesthetic theory, the most important synthesis is to be found in Immanuel Kant's *Critique of Judgment* (1790). In this work, Kant denies the cognitive (and hence logical) nature of aesthetic judgment, and asserts that 'its basis can only be subjective'. For Kant, aesthetic experience is uniquely 'disinterested': it exists as an image independent of the object's real existence; it is 'non-conceptual', concerning only the 'form of the object'; it is a 'pleasure for the whole mind' (it is a pleasure related to that which has an appropriate form in human intellect and that is therefore objectively liked, even if it is a subjective need). Finally, aesthetic judgment is not subject to a general rule, for every single object is to be considered separately. Thus, judgments of aesthetic pleasure can only be subjective, although it is probable that something enjoyed by a single person will be enjoyed by others. For this reason, it is possible to speak of universal aesthetic judgments, even if this universality cannot be defined by means of proper rules.

For Tatarkiewicz, Kant's theory is paradoxical, because it 'applies the measure of cognition whereas the aesthetic experience is of an entirely different nature than cognition'.[9] More importantly, its complexity gives rise to a search for simpler formulations, such as German philosopher Arthur Schopenhauer's theory of aesthetic contemplation. As expounded in his major work, *The World as Will and Idea* (1818), Schopenhauer's theory recovers Pythagoras' intuition of the attitude of the 'beholder'. According to this view, aesthetic experience consists solely in contemplation, and in the lived experience of a spectator wholly absorbed in what he sees in front of him. In order to partake in this experience, one must detach oneself from all practicalities as well as from abstract thought, in order for one's consciousness to be filled with the images that one is confronting. Thus, Schopenauer conceives of a state of mind in which the subject becomes a mirror of the object, and consciousness (in which the difference between the observer and the observed object disappears) is filled with the representation of the world in the form of the image.[10]

In the eighteenth and nineteenth centuries, we find the adoption of the hedonistic theory, according to which aesthetic experience is nothing but a feeling of pleasure (or, in the case of ugliness, of pain). This theory is rooted in the dawn of aesthetic reflection (in Hippias), echoes through the Aristotelian and Platonic traditions, as well as the Middle Ages and the Renaissance. In the modern age, the theory is propagated thanks to Descartes, who equates beauty with pleasure in his letter to Mersenne, dated 18 March 1630. A radical view of his formulation may be ascribed to George Santayana, according to whom beauty is simply 'a pleasure regarded as the quality of a thing'.[11] Simultaneously with hedonistic theories, a diverse set of theories developed that Tatarkiewicz terms 'cognitive', as they are based on the assumption that aesthetic experience is a type of knowledge. It is worth recalling, for example, Benedetto Croce's conviction that aesthetic experience involves an illumination of mind, an 'intuition', or a 'spiritual synthesis' (*The Essence of Aesthetic*, 1913). An additional cognitive theory is 'illusionism', which was expounded by Konrad Lange, Eduard von Hartmann and Moritz Geiger, among others, and which places aesthetic experience outside reality, in a world of illusions, appearance and imagination. A third cognitive theory, adapted by Darwin and Spencer from Kant and Schiller, conceives of aesthetic experience as a 'game', although this theory might be considered a theory of art more than a theory of aesthetics. Meanwhile, the theory of the 'active nature of aesthetic experiences' (*Einfühlung*), arises in Germany from the work of Vischer, Lotze and Lipps. This theory contends that aesthetic experience takes place when the subject actively confers features upon the object that it does not inherently possess. This is conceived of as a phenomenon of 'psychic resonance', in which a subject recognizes themselves in the object.[12] For Tatarkiewicz, however, the theory is 'exaggerated', for it 'universalizes a phenomenon that occurs occasionally, and which takes the prerequisites of the aesthetic attitude for its essence'.[13]

During this period, the contemplation theory that will later be recast by Schopenhauer also emerges in opposition to the cognitive theory. This theory, recall, affirms the passive character of aesthetic experience: the focus on external objects rather than on the subject, and the submission to beauty. However, the emphasis on passivity does not exclude intellectual activity; rather it emphasizes a gradual 'taking possession of' in place of a still, detached mode of observation. A theory complementary to 'contemplation theory' is 'isolation theory', according to which 'the isolation of the object and detachment of the subject' is the fundamental condition of aesthetic experience. Art historian Richard Hamann's more radical formulation of the theory, however, states that it is necessary to isolate oneself not only from practicalities but also from the environment surrounding the object. A final contribution to contemplation theory is made by *Gestalt* psychology. According to this school of psychology, 'the whole is primary to the part'; in perception, a subject necessarily conjoins external stimuli in order to form a whole, coherent system. Rudolf Arnheim extended *Gestalt* theory to painting, and the Polish scholar Zórawski to architecture.[14]

In accordance with the attitude of early nineteenth-century scholars, the theories examined thus far take a predominantly intellectual approach. Around the late nineteenth century, however, the idea that aesthetic experience is purely emotional emerges. In the early twentieth century, theories are put forward that emphasize the involvement of feeling and emotion in aesthetic experience, and particularly in relation to poetry. Although both Paul Valéry and Ernest de Selincourt support these theories, the most radical proponent is French literary scholar Henrie Brémond, according to whom poetry is a euphoric, 'indefinable *enchantment*', uniquely capable of establishing a 'contact with a mysterious reality' and able to 'convey the depths of our soul'.[15] According to Tatarkiewicz, the emotional and anti-intellectual conception of aesthetic experience that develops in relation to poetry may be extended to all of the arts, especially if euphoria is considered a form of aesthetic experience. It is, for example, precisely this idea that Nietzsche employs in his dualistic conception of aesthetic experience which is partially 'Apollonian' and partially 'Dyonisiac' (*Geburt der Tragödie*, 1871).[16]

It is in the twentieth century, Tatarkiewicz writes, that scholars begin to seek a theory that will mediate between these positions. Tatarkiewicz admires the work of Polish philosopher Roman Ingarden, according to whom aesthetic experience is manifold and develops in distinct stages. Ingarden states that the preliminary emotion is pity, and it is pity that causes one to direct one's consciousness towards the object that has stimulated the emotion. Thus, the second stage involves a narrowing of the field of consciousness, in order to focus on the quality of the object. In the third stage, one focuses wholly on that quality, and it is at this point that the aesthetic experience can either come to an end, or live on.

If the latter is the case, the subject will find themselves facing an object that they have, in a sense, created, and have established a relationship with. Thus, aesthetic experience involves 'the pure excitement on the part of the subject, the forming of the object by the subject, and the perceptive experiencing of the object'. We might say that Ingarden's theory represents a brilliant summary of many of the theories displayed: the experience is emotional and dynamic in nature, and it turns, in the final stage, into contemplation.[17]

However, Tatarkiewicz himself supports a pluralistic theory (*Skupienie i marzenie*, 1934), which differs from Ingarden's. Whereas for Ingarden aesthetic experience exists as dream before it becomes a form of concentration, for Tatarkiewicz both dream (as *rêverie*, a sort of daydream) and concentration are possible at once. Or, there might be only dream or only concentration: 'Only by means of alternatives can one describe the concept of the aesthetic experience, so very general is it and indeterminate.'[18]

Art as Experience

In the work of American philosopher and psychologist John Dewey, the concept of aesthetic experience widens considerably, to encompass any act or object with the potential to intensify, enrich, broaden, or refine experience:

> ... that limitation of fineness of art to paintings, statues, poems, songs and symphonies is conventional, or even verbal. Any activity that is productive of objects whose perception is an immediate good, and whose operation is a continual source of enjoyable perception of other events exhibits fineness of art. There are acts of all kinds that directly refresh and enlarge the spirit and that are instrumental to the productions of new objects and dispositions which are in turn productive of further refinements and replenishments.[19]

In *Art as Experience*, Dewey reiterates his objection to those theories which bracket aesthetic experience facts from the continuum of experience. The aim of a new theory of aesthetics is to 'restore continuity' between works of art and everyday events, or those actions that are 'universally recognized to constitute experience'.[20] Thus, Dewey does not

53

share the concerns of the Frankfurt School in relation to popular culture, and he is critical of cultural elitism in general. For Dewey, aesthetic
experience is possible in many kinds of experience, including work,
games, dance, reading, and thought. Aestheticity, Dewey asserts,

> . . . is a quality that permeates an experience; it is not, save by figure
> of speech, the experience itself. Esthetic experience is always more
> than aesthetic. In it a body of matters and meanings, not in them-
> selves esthetic, become aesthetic as they enter into an ordered rhyth-
> mic movement toward consummation.

Furthermore, Dewey writes that:

> The material of aesthetic experience in being human – human in
> connection with the nature of which is a part – is social. Aesthetic
> experience is a manifestation, a record and celebration of the life of
> a civilization, a means of promoting its development, and is also the
> ultimate judgment upon the quality of a civilization. For while it is
> produced and is enjoyed by individuals, those individuals are what
> they are in the content of their experience because of the cultures in
> which they participate.[21]

Thus, Dewey places nature, society, culture, art and experience on a
continuum with each other. Furthermore, rather than presenting as
a hindrance to artistic creation, Dewey considers the technological
development of society to offer new opportunities for artistic creation
and aesthetic experience. Dewey offers a conception of aesthetics that is
foundational to the present work, the aim of which is to extend the categories of aesthetics beyond the field of art to the Web, as the medium
that seems most crucial to contemporary culture.[22]

The Technological Sublime

Among several theories that have recently been put forward, Italian
philosopher Mario Costa's conception of the 'technological sublime'[23] is
particularly valuable.[24] Costa marks a postmodern condition of sublimity, characterized by a final turn away from the *aesthetic dimension of art*
and towards a new dimension that, though it is still aesthetic, is funda-

mentally distinct from art. 'It simply has to be accepted that the one of art is too much narrow a dimension,' Costa writes, 'and inappropriate in the times of computers and networks, genetic manipulation and unification of species.'[25] For Costa, the notion of the sublime no longer applies to works of art, because 'the feeling of sublime rises ... from real things or occurrences ... that represent a virtual threat for the subject, since they show themselves as threatening or anyway exceeding'.[26] As in Edmund Burke's and Schopenhauer's theories, one 'feels pleasure' in the sense that one is living the threat while being 'safe' from the reality of the pain that threat might bring. As in Kant's theory, it is in recognizing one's pre-eminence as a thinking being over a threatening natural world that one experiences the sublime. Finally, as in Sade and Bataille, it is in experiencing the submission of subjectivity in the face of a threatening excess that we encounter the sublime.[27] A further premise is that the sublime 'is *inexpressible* in its essence', so that 'nothing that has taken the form of the symbolic can be really considered sublime'.[28] Costa points out that the concept of the sublime metamorphosed dramatically during the last decades of the eighteenth century and the early decades of the nineteenth, from the 'natural sublime'[29] to the 'new excess' of the metropolis and the machine. These modern mechanical and electric objects and environments bring with them a new form of excess, a new mode of dissolution of the Self, and a 'new kind of inebriation' that, continued into the electronic and synthetic postmodern age, gave rise to a 'new vertigo of technological sublime'.[30] Technology, carrying the 'supreme danger of radical expropriation on human', has given birth to the 'technological terrifying':

> *Sublimity* is no longer connected to an object or an event that is natural, it rather arises from an *event* or an *activity* that is technological; this means that new technologies finally make a *domestication of the sublime* possible and that for the first time in the history of aesthetic experience *sublimity* can be the object of a controlled production and a socialized and repeatable use.[31]

If it is true that in pre-technological ages no work of art can re-create that feeling of sublimity that only arises from the experience of the shapeless and the inexpressible, this situation alters profoundly with increased technological development. In the technological age, in fact, 'the *sublime* ceases to belong only to nature and starts to really belong also to "art"'.[32] According to Costa, this takes place in two major ways. First of all, through technique, the 'aesthetics of communication', which can capture Kant's natural sublime and render it as an 'opportunity of socialized and controlled fruition'. Secondly, in 'synthesis technologies', technology is robbed of its capacity to terrify, mainly because technique 'reveals its essence in the form of the aesthetic showing itself as *technological sublimity*'.[33]

What is it, then, that typifies contemporary aesthetic experience? To Costa, the 'technological sublime' will replace the traditional concepts that define what is artistic, with the following results:

- a *decline of the subject and the artistic personality*: subjectivity is no longer the subject matter of art. Rather, the aesthetic must be conceived in the terms of a 'neo-technological epic', in terms of 'an aestheticization of technological objective signifiers completely lacking meaning';[34]
- *the aseity*[35] *of the product is fully realized*: technological productions are not essentially linguistic, so that emphasis is placed on the signifier and the aesthetic work becomes either a remaining will to 'put into shape' the signifiers or, even more often, an activation of them;[36]
- *personal style is eradicated*: the weakening of the subject entails the end of the age of style. Attention shifts from the 'style of the author' to the specificity or the 'style of the product' which may reflect either an individual or collective intention;[37]
- *the concept of 'epistemological fantasy' replaces that of 'intuition'*: contemporary productions have increasingly become cognitive and intellectual projects; 'aesthetic-epistemological investigation(s)', as Costa labels it,[38] so that it is possible to explore and use the dimensions and structures of the actual techno-anthropological universe;
- a *'hyper-subject' takes shape*: the weakening of the individual subject entails the birth of a 'hyper-subject' that resides in a body made of networks;

- *an aesthetic-sensorial experience:* this replaces contemplative and immaterial forms of experience, which heightens and widens the perception of the actual techno-cosmos.

This last point is a particularly crucial stage in the creation of the 'technological sublime'. According to Costa, new technologies lead feeling and sensation to turn from mere containers of aesthetic experience, and to become the objects themselves of research. The consequence is that the contemporary 'artist producers' or 'aesthetic researchers' evince interest only in sensorial experience, and it is 'only in this that the aesthetic experience of the user takes place and has a conclusion'.[39] Costa does not neglect the transformation in the field of aesthetic production that took place in the avant-garde works of Gabo, Moholy-Nagy or Duchamp in the early twentieth century. In recent years, however, the machines of artistic experiments, but also those that we encounter every day, involve the whole body, so that experience makes sense only as asensorial experience:

> The sensorial experience, the will to create an experience of senses, muddling them up, placing them into a new situation, stimulating them, extending them, twisting them ... the object of the operation both from the point of view of the product and the kind of fruition it requires is sensoriality and nothing else, which for aesthetics is almost blasphemy.[40]

Well aware of the pointlessness of lingering among archaic and reassuring aesthetic categories, *Web Aesthetics* takes up Costa's challenge, and aims to contribute to the development of a theory of the aesthetics of communication that owes much to the concept of the 'technological sublime'.

Diffuse Aesthetics

> Beneath the sky of the aesthetic everything is light, pleasant and fleeting.
>
> Søren Kierkegaard, *Enten-Eller* (1843)

In my opinion, there are two concepts that are essential to the specificity of the aesthetic experience in digital networks and on the Web: that of 'diffuse aesthetics', and that of memes. Diffuse aesthetics is a typical feature of a world, like the present one, that has turned into a global shop. In it, objects, people and experiences conform to a diffuse aesthetic dimension. As everything becomes aesthetic, the debasement of value that typifies modernity proceeds apace, as does the ubiquity of the spectacle that typifies the postmodern age.

A notable observer of this phenomenon is art historian and aesthetic philosopher Ernesto Francalanci. Francalanci locates features of diffuse aesthetics[1] in the early nineteenth century: in, for example, Wölfflin's studies on shapelessness, and in Riegl's *Kunstwollen* (the will to form). Nevertheless, the crucial shift is evident in the work of Walter Benjamin who, in his famous essay on the mechanical reproduction of the work of art,[2] links fascistic and imperialistic forms of governments to the reproductive techniques of media, thus giving rise to the first stage of the aestheticization of both politics and the masses.[3]

Indeed, Mussolini saw the Italian population as a mass to be moulded, and himself as a craftsman able to turn that formless material into a perfect work: *the new Italians*. In this regard, Todorov notes that for *Il Duce* it was not enough to be the craftsman of the Italian people – Mussolini needed to present himself as the perfect product, as both artist and work of art.[4] When, close to defeat, Mussolini admits to failing to produce *the new Italians*, he is then able to blame the 'material' for not being robust enough. As he confessed to Galeazzo Ciano a few months before his death:[5] 'Even Michelangelo needed marble for his statues. If he did not have but clay, he would not have been much more than a ceramist.'[6] In the case of Nazism, Todorov observes, there is an equally close relationship between political action and artistic activity, as Hitler also considers himself the artist who will bring in to being the new German population as a total work of art – although Hitler does not identify himself with the work of art itself, as does Mussolini. As Todorov recognizes, totalitarian dictators are attracted to art because it 'is not content with conveying a message, but does transform those who receive it without them knowing'.[7] Thus, for Hitler it is not enough to aestheticize his political activity through processions, gatherings, architecture and film. He must merge politics with aesthetics in order to give birth to a new population, both spiritually and physically: 'The artist has made himself demiurge.'[8]

In regard to the Nazi's adoption of classical Greek imagery, Francalanci observes that: 'The aesthetics of absolute power, crossing and modelling every space, every time, as well as every entity and subject, turns into an omnipresent force ... a true "virus" that will increasingly and unstoppably feed on the society.'[9]

Nowadays, the spectacularization of politics is taken for granted, most obviously in Italy. Even that individual considered a genuine novelty in the international political environment, and towards whom many address their hopes for change, could not resist the temptation to become an icon by encouraging the 'Obamamania' that has rapidly spread throughout the West. Although I have identified the origins of the aestheticization of society in the early nineteenth century, I want to make it clear that this is a process that becomes complete only in contemporary times; its epicentre is the West, and in the acceptance and standardization of Western values – the cultural *imperium* so well depicted by Michael Hardt and Antonio Negri.[10]

At this point, I will elaborate on several of Francalanci's concepts that I believe are vital to the argument I wish to make: the 'virtualization of reality'; the 'spectacularization of society'; the 'metamorphization of things'; the 'spillage of the aesthetic from the artistic sphere'; and the 'domestic as aesthetic'.

The Virtualization of Reality

When Francalanci refers to virtual reality, he is making reference to a phenomenon that exceeds the experience of a multidimensional graphic space. He is invoking the massive totality of data and digital programmes linked to each other by means of global computer networks. He is speaking of a parallel reality that overlaps and replaces physical reality. In Baudrillard's words:

[Images] are no longer the mirror of reality, they are living in the heart of reality – aliens, no more reflecting, but haunting reality – and have transformed it into hyperreality, where, from screen to screen, the only destiny of the image is the image itself. The image cannot imagine the real any longer, because it has become the real. It can no longer transcend reality, transfigure it, nor dream it, because it has become its own reality.[11]

According to Baudrillard, if there are no longer any secrets, it is no longer possible to create illusions. Life happens in an unrelenting visibility and – mostly thanks to digital media – in a perfect (numeric) transcription. In a virtual reality, both reality and its image have disappeared.[12] For Francalanci, something absolutely new happens: 'For the first time, this system becomes a prosthesis that interfaces the subject and the object *within the image itself*.'[13] That is, the distance between the representation and the observer is erased: the subject is forced never to close their eyes, hence never to imagine. *Conditio sine qua non*, to preserve the submersion in the boundless reign of images is in fact to keep one's eyes always open; to look is to take part in a journey in which one is simultaneously user and pilot. We are ceaselessly thrown into a realm of imagination – a realm that for centuries was only accessed through fantasy, dream and art. In order to adapt to the massive technological developments of recent decades, aesthetics must confront the virtual dimension. Every age and culture has tasked art with building a *different* world. What we need to realize is that this task is today accomplished by technology. Aimed at complete interactivity between human and machine, this technology must, as Francalanci observes, abandon the complexity of the philosophical language of art for formal strategies that do not require semantic encoding. Lacking any depth, images become universally comprehensible. Indeed, the concept of 'image' itself is in crisis, as it no longer retains any physical, pre-existing referent. Rather, it constitutes an 'autonomous information of self'.[14]

In present times, Francalanci asserts, the relationship between human beings and objects, or between the material and the digital, is increasingly maintained by 'unnatural mediators', or interfaces, a view that differs from Manovich's, in which the human-computer interface is on a continuum with other cultural interfaces – for example, we acquire from print and from cinema the metaphors of the rectangular page and the frame.[15] Recalling Fredric Jameson and Baudrillard, Francalanci terms the complete harmony which is the aim of the interface a progressive aestheticization of the relationship between human beings and objects.[16] Thus, in the virtual dimension under consideration in this work, it is above all vital to resist the temptation to use ethical and moral categories.

Society and Global Spectacle

Grounding the concept of the 'spectacularization of society' is the platonic ideal of the image as simulacrum or, in the words of Jameson, as 'the identical copy for which no original has ever existed'.[17] Furthermore, Francalanci's conceptualization explicitly recalls theorists Guy Debord's and Daniel Boorstin's separate definitions of contemporary culture as a 'society of the spectacle'. At the dawn of the television age, Debord understood that spectacle would soon become society's most significant product. La société du spectacle (1967)[18] identifies a bipolarity between the 'concentrated spectacle' of communism and the 'diffuse spectacle' of capitalism. In Commentaires sur la société du spectacle (1988),[19] however, Debord asserts that this bipolarity has been dissolved in an 'integrated spectacle'. Spectacle is definitive of a world dominated by media, in which appearance and value are equated, and history has been abandoned for an eternal present. The society of the 'integrated spectacle' is finally one that celebrates the conversion of truth to falsity, and of the real into the simulacrum. In the present context, the following remarks by Debord appear particularly prescient:

> Images can tolerate anything and everything; because within the same image all things can be juxtaposed without contradiction.... Since no one may contradict it, it has the right to contradict itself, to correct its own past.... In the same way, the computer's binary language is an irresistible inducement to the continual and unreserved acceptance of what has been programmed according to the wishes of someone else and passes for the timeless source of a superior, impartial and total logic.[20]

Boorstin refers to the 'pseudo-event': those non-random events that are organized or produced with the aim of being reported, and continually reproduced, by the media. Whereas propaganda is opinion masquerading as fact, the pseudo-event is neither true nor false, rather it is a factual, existent, but entirely synthetic event.[21]

In present times, the process of news production renders it virtually impossible to distinguish between real and fake news. This, at least, is the thesis of Walter Molino's and Stefano Porro's *Disinformation Technology*.[22] In this brief but provocative essay, the two authors analyse several urban myths, such as that of 'bonsai kittens', a New York-based company selling live kittens in tiny glass jars; the attempt to murder Microsoft founder Bill Gates; and the 'bambi women', a hunting area in which it is possible to shoot naked women instead of fox and deer. Before being exposed as hoaxes, all of these stories garnered the interest of the international media – compelling proof that the mainstream media is willing to take entirely constructed news as real. In the media system, every piece of information is given life by undergoing a standardized, mechanized process. Rather than representing the truth, news is produced and assembled according to a well established script. It is a narrative and a genre, far more conversant with the imaginary than with reality.

Combining Debord's and Boorstin's views, Francalanci states that: 'The image (aesthetically projected) is the base of any strategy of the political, the core of appearance and appearing, the soul of persuasion and publicity. Pure aesthetics.'[23] In the words of Jameson, 'aesthetic production' has taken the role of the 'dominant cultural logic or hegemonic norm'.[24] In the context of a spectacularized society, the media has no choice but to employ aesthetic strategies. As a result, any semantic or ethical interpretation is necessarily omitted.

The aestheticization or formalization of media content is notably addressed in the work of Mark Napier, a pioneer of net.art. Napier's series *Black and White* began in 2003, and was based on the Radical Software Group's re-engineering of the FBI's surveillance software using an open source platform.[25] In *Black and White - CNN* (2003),[26] Napier converts data from the popular American network website CNN into a binary format. As the application's algorithm causes a black pixel to move horizontally when a '0' is present and a white pixel to move vertically when a '1' is present, clouds of black and white pixels take shape on screen, offering a powerful metaphor for the superficiality of broadcast news.

Using the same procedure, in *Sacred and Code* (2003)[27] Napier converts the Old and New Testaments of the Bible and the Qur'an into a stream of binary figures. Converting texts of religious significance into an endless dance of black and white graphic elements, Napier produces an aesthetic experience profoundly different to that of reading.[28]

Metamorphosis of Things

Turning from media to ordinary, everyday objects, I now wish to discuss Francalanci's conceptualization of the 'metamorphization of things'. For Francalanci, it is in a domestic environment that we see the 'overflowing of aesthetics itself from the status of the formal quality of material to a phenomenology of immaterial entities'.[29] Recalling Perniola, who speaks of a situation in which 'to give oneself as a thing that feels and to take a thing that feels' as an experience that characterizes contemporary feeling,[30] Francalanci asserts that things have extended beyond their physical boundaries and have reached a level of conceptual sensibility, so that when one mentions a 'thing', this word always involves a number of semantic references. Diffuse aesthetics is evident in this shift from things elevated from a material and formal level and elevated to logical, immaterial, conceptual tools. Consider, for example, those phenomena that exist both materially and immaterially: the Web, Windows, or desktop. Yet, even common objects such as doors or chairs metamorphose into 'sensitive machines' and 'intelligent goods',[31] as, for example, the increasing application of RFID (Radio Frequency Identification) tags to common objects imbues them with a singular identity and history.

According to science-fiction author Bruce Sterling, the present 'technosociety' is characterized by the progressive replacement of machines and products with 'gizmos': highly multifunctional objects that are easily altered by the user. Usually these 'gizmos' are linked to network services providers, so that they are not real objects, but proper interfaces. Sterling provides the example of an Italian bottle of wine, with a label that also refers to a webpage, on which one might find information about the wine's production, different varieties of vines, or tips on how to organize a dinner party. In this case, a more complex interaction between subject and object takes place: apart from containing the wine, the bottle has a 'mission' to educate the user, to make them aware of the places, people and traditions involved in the production of its content.[32]

And yet, the era of 'gizmos' may be nearing its end, as we enter an era of 'spime' (a contraction of space and time), in which we find 'objects with informational support so extensive and rich that they are regarded as material instantiations of an immaterial system'.[33] The introduction of RFID tags, for example, inserts objects into a permanent stream of data, from the first stages of computer design, to the final disposal and recycling of the object ('spimes' are in fact realized with materials that can be reintroduced into the process of production). More significantly, objects with RFID tags are constantly animated: they are able to communicate, for example, their position in space, their design features, the productive process that created them, or their cost. Thus, humans find themselves confronting an object that feels and that exists whether they are present or not, so that 'our presence only gives sense to things, it does not confirm their existence'.[34] Using built-in radio tags or small computers, ordinary objects are able to give life to *self-configuring* communication networks. The immediate consequence of this is that the Internet tends to turn itself into an 'Internet of things': it becomes the pivotal point of communication among these 'intelligent' objects. Since 1999, a research team working first within Boston MIT and then working as Auto-ID Labs[35] has been studying the application of radio frequency technologies of identification to household appliances. The aim of the group's projects is to allow the appliances to talk to each other and to follow orders given remotely. The wider aim, however, is to turn the objects of everyday life, from spaghetti to cars, into devices that can be identified and controlled by computers and, through them, by human beings.[36]

From an aesthetic point of view, the most significant feature of the 'Internet of things' are the urgent expectations of greater intimacy with the technological universe. In order to achieve this, we need to become emotionally involved, and for this to happen, we need to overcome the boundary of the screen, and to create objects that 'autonomously' interact with their environments. A good example is the rabbit Nabaztag, created by the French company Violet. Founded in 2003, the stated vocation of the company is 'to develop products and services based on calm and emotional technologies'.[37] What is Nabaztag? Though difficult to define, and therefore evincing the semantic multiplicity inherent to digital objects, one convincing definition on the Web is that it is a

'Wi-Fi-enabled toy'. Perhaps it is easier to ask what Nabaztag can do: it can wake one with an alarm, after which it recites the news it has gathered overnight and the latest weather reports, before connecting to the user's favourite radio station; when away from home, it can inform your partner that you will be late home from work, or that you are thinking of them, or it can cheer them up by wiggling its ears; it can remind one's children's to do their homework, read them stories, or entertain them with a quiz; it can follow stock market trends or football scores; it can read out the topics of your favourite blogs, emails or a friend's Tweets.[38] According to Violet, Nabaztag is not merely a functional object, but an entity with its own personality. As it performs the above tasks, Nabaztag changes colour, its lights blink, its ears move and it mimics the voice of the user. When it is not busy, it might perform Tai Chi exercises; or it might 'choose' to marry another Nabaztag (in which case the two rabbits will move their ears simultaneously, even if they are millions of miles away). A Nabaztag is to be adopted, not purchased.[39]

From a strictly functional point of view, these devices merely extend the operations provided by the Internet: they allow for remote communication, and create networks without the user needing a computer in front of them. More interesting, however, is the fact that Nabaztag attempts to replace the coldness of the computer, mobile, or organizer screen interface with a warmer and more involving way to access the stream of digital data.

International research into technological development aims to surpass the limitations of the screen, with a bi-fold result. The first is the hypertrophy of the screen. Gigantic and ubiquitous, the screen no longer makes us feel we are in front of a frame; rather, the screen is all around us, and it is we who are in the frame. The conversion of domestic spaces into screens, for example, will give us the feeling of being inside the very stream, or the 'matrix' of data. The second line of research aims towards a future in which common objects become animate and interface us so completely with digital data that they encompass the whole of human existence. To some extent, we have seen all this before: literature and cinema are rich in references to machines that are capable of feeling and thinking. However, compared to the tenderness evoked by a Nabaztag, these fantasies still suffer from a mechanical coldness. Modern 'intelligent' objects are designed to involve emotionally, to seduce, and they ask to be touched, to be grazed, and – sometimes – to be penetrated. An 'intelligent' object involves us more than a screen, so that Perniola is led to speak of the 'sex-appeal of the inorganic'.[40] Yet, as Perniola states, though undeniably libidinal, 'the sexuality of the thing' is not aimed at a climax, but at the indefinite continuation of excitement 'a movement without time and without purpose, sufficient unto itself, which asks only for its continuation'.[41] 'Intelligent' objects, then, represent the latest stage of the attempt to anthropomorphize things, to make them as sensitive as living things, to assign them a singular intelligence and to imbue them with a sexual drive. And yet, as Perniola points out, the correlation to the process of creating a 'thing that feels' is the pathological care of the body: make-up, tattoos, hairdressing, aerobics, body building, plastic surgery and genetic engineering are steps on a 'catastrophic' path that leads the person to become what he terms an 'almost thing',[42] as the inorganic and the organic mutually adapt to each other.

According to Francalanci, the meeting point is to be found in the 'principle of convenience', namely 'in what regards at the same time both the subject and the object falsely balance the relationship'.[43] The classical principle of beauty and the search for the sublime are replaced by the principle of convenience, so that aesthetics becomes a 'relational and communicational' strategy, a technique that places appearance before functionality.[44] As aesthetics becomes a surplus of digital goods, the subject is placed both inside the matrix of diffuse aesthetics and of digital data. We might ask: How can we scratch the surface that humans appear to be condemned to live on? To me, the immediate answer is art: the aim of which has always been the creation of imaginary worlds in which to escape from the realities of everyday life. Yet as Francalanci reminds us, this very function has today been subsumed by technology, and in particular by technology's creation of simulated and virtual worlds. Unlike the fantastic universes created in the fine arts or in cinema, the digital dimension aims at entertainment and, as such, cannot be but spectacularized. This dimension constitutes 'a sort of surface outflowing of images, that no longer require a semantic encoding, lacking any symbolic and poetic depth'.[45]

The Spillage of the Aesthetic from the Artistic Sphere
This brings us to a phenomenon that clearly evinces the schism
between modern and postmodern culture. In modernity, art reflects
upon the everyday in order to question the view that the object exists
apart from its context, as in Marcel Duchamp's famed 'ready-mades'. As
art historian Giulio Carlo Argan observes, Duchamp removes objects
from a context 'in which, everything being utilitarian, nothing can be
aesthetic' and places them in a context 'in which nothing being utilitarian, everything can be aesthetic'.[46] In Dadaism, too, a common object
gains artistic value purely through a mental act. At around the same
time, the Bauhaus school will develop a theory of industrial design
diametrically opposed to that of Dadaism, in which aesthetic form and
practical use are the results of a single process, and aesthetic value is a
product of technological processes of production, rather than its antith-
esis. This school clears the path for postmodernism, in which aesthetics
are subsumed into the industrial process of production,[47] as Francalanci
observes:

> The world has not been changed from the revolutionary project of
> avant-gardes, but from the industrial philosophy and the neocapi-
> talistic ways of the new types of economy, that have used, for their
> representation, the cultural heritage of art, converting it into an at-
> tractive substance and hence as an extra ... to its product. The new
> 'international style' of creativity no longer creates its forms out of
> nothing, it rather collects given representations of reality by reorgan-
> izing and recombining pre-existing expressive materials.[48]

Wherever we look, we see either products that aspire to the *status* of
art objects, singular and unreproducible objects that are hence able to
reproduce the dearth that the art market proliferates upon; or serial objects, addressed to the mass market, that hide their banality and cheap-
ness behind an original and incomparable artistic intuition. This takes
place in three ways: the promotion of products to the *status* of works of
art; the erosion of the boundary between art and design; and the fusing
of the languages of artistic and commercial communication. The first
point encompasses a massive variety of objects, including household
appliances, clothing and accessories, and work tools, among many

others. As I write, for example, I have in front of me cardboard document folders upon the surface of which is a reproduction of famous Impressionist paintings. The strategy behind such objects is to surpass mere functional use – keeping documents in order – and to elevate them to what Baudrillard terms the trans-aesthetic domain. Here, every object attains the status of aesthetic banality, and art, as a separate and transcendent phenomenon, simply disappears.[49] The trend towards customized or customizable products attempts to exploit the desire of the contemporary subject to express their singular individuality in each and every object they purchase. The corollary, however, is the debasement of industrial design and the rationality of function. Most of the time, customization concerns those functions that are inessential, such as choice of colour or other decorative features.[50] Nowadays, therefore, purchasing decisions are made on an aesthetic basis rather than a functional one. I have to admit, for example, that when I made the decision to purchase the folders, I never thought to ask if the metallic rings inside them would work well. In a similar way, purchasers of Mac computers are seduced by design rather than by quality or value. Those products 'signed' by a particular designer, artist or architect belong in the same category. In such cases, it is nonsensical to speak of function or quality; the purchaser of these products is paying for the right to exhibit the sign, not the product. To some extent, this is merely a continuation of the situation in the contemporary art world, in which it is the certificate of originality that establishes the value of the work of art, rather than the works themselves. Piero Manzoni's work, in which the work of art coincides with the certificate, is a beautiful illustration of this situation. A further trend towards the debasement of both functionality and art is that of the commercialization of ordinary objects that are produced in limited series or unique pieces by famous artists or designers. In these cases, it is impossible to demarcate the object of art from the object of use. In a similar way, it is no longer possible to demarcate art from design, as designers display their pieces in museums and galleries and artists produce collections of functional objects. A good example of the merging of design (applied art) and 'pure' art is the Milan International Furniture Fair.[51]

As Francalanci suggests, modern design carries with it an 'artistic vocation' that inheres in the fact that 'every datum memorized from the whole history of art is now genetically inoculated in the process of hypervalorisation of the product'.[52] This 'vocation' – the perpetual attempt to simulate artistic products – is aided by those techniques that efface any difference between artist, designer, architect or writer; today, everybody works in front of a screen. After all, artists have given up on the attempt to represent the complexity of the contemporary world. Instead, they build alternatives to reality that, placed in competition with technology, have no choice but to disappear behind meaningless appearances. The consequence of the merging of art and design is that the 'sense of justice' evoked by the balance between form and function that typified modern design has disappeared. In the postmodern world, function is replaced by form. Deprived of both aesthetic enjoyment and practical use, the result is a trivialization of aesthetics in which everything becomes 'beautiful', 'artistic' or 'unique'.

The third point is the semantic shift taking place as the languages of advertising and marketing increasingly overlap with the language of art. This phenomenon was already apparent in the second half of the nineteenth century, on billboards by Jules Chéret and Toulouse-Lautrec (who also discovered lithography thanks to his job as an 'advertiser' and introduced it into his artistic work). A further stage in this process occurred with futurism, and in particular in Fortunato Depero's work. For Depero, artistic expression and the advertising profession were deeply connected, and he claimed, therefore, that 'the art of the future will be powerfully advertising art'.[53] As social conditions change, the relation of art to advertising changes too.

Dadaism repudiates the communicational paradigm that informs advertising, and focuses on twisting its peculiar expressive registers. Today, this attitude is expressed in the Adbusters network, and can also be found in the work of French composer Erik Satie. After Satie's death, thousands of short musical compositions were found in his house, in which he mocked and satirised advertising jingles. In many of these works, Satie pretended to be advertising nonsensical or non-existent entities, such as metal buildings or territories. A final, vital step in this process was undertaken in the work of Andy Warhol. Arthur Danto defines Warhol's work as enacting a 'transfiguration of the commonplace', by crossing the borders between 'high' and 'low' art, and between applied art or design, and pure or fine arts. When Warhol demands that the *Brillo Box* (1964), an image created by a designer paid by the hour for his creativity, be recognized as a work of art, he closes the circle between art and commercial product.[54] Compared to the present degree of osmosis between art and advertising, however, poetic action is still visible in Warhol's work: that which Baudrillard identifies as the reintroduction of nothingness or meaninglessness into the very heart of the image.[55] Warhol 'makes nothingness and meaninglessness an event that lately turns into a fatal strategy of the image',[56] whereas, for Baudrillard, contemporary artists have only a commercial strategy of nothingness. This strategy is evinced through a form of advertising that, recalling Baudelaire, Baudrillard terms a 'sentimental form of the goods'.[57]

It is in this very form that the long journey of standardization between the languages of art, advertising, and expressive modes ends. Behind diffuse aesthetics hides the nothing that both art and industrial design have become. The production of artistic artefacts and of consumer goods both aim to erase any opportunity for the spectator or consumer to express critical judgement on the work or the product. The sphere of judgment is replaced by the sphere of action: buying, taking part in the show, living the experience. One final point worthy of attention is the practice of quotation in contemporary advertising and artistic activities. Following Francalanci, I have claimed that advertisers take possession of both history and art, and produce signs, images and keywords in their stead. As Andreas Huyssen observes:

> All modern and avantgardist techniques, forms and images are now stored for instant recall in the computerized memory banks of our culture. But the same memory also stores all of pre-modernist art as well as the genres, codes, and image worlds of popular cultures and modern mass culture.[58]

Baudrillard points out that such remaking and recycling would like to be ironical, 'but the humour here is merely the transparent invocation of humour. Like the worn threads of a piece of fabric, it is an irony produced only by the disillusion of things, a fossilized irony.'[59] In such quotations and adaptations of art, the revolutionary drive is inevitably displaced by the monotonous and trivialized. Such a 'carefree' use of a slowly sedimenting cultural heritage leads finally to those banal, depthless images that typify contemporary times. Reprinting Leonardo's *Gioconda* on countless billboards in order to advertise mineral water displaces the image from its historical, social and cultural context, obliterating the depth of the painting in an instant. As the weight of the *Gioconda*'s implication slips away, the image is flattened, ready to take part in the game of commercialized communications. It is the 'lightheartedness' of these practices, as well as the break with classical artistic heritage carried out by the avant-garde, that gave contemporary artists the same freedom to move. Yet their perpetual seizing of materials without considering their expressive complexity has extinguished that interactive continuum that is constitutive of art. If every artistic act contains an implicit connection with the history of art, present artistic practices break off the dialogue, giving rise to an annoying fog of 'micro-ideas', a persisting sequence of pseudo-styles-values-rules that eliminate the possibility for art to create substantial styles-values-rules. A perpetual movement defines art, but now it seems to move only as a sequence of trends,[60] which seems to evince that which Matei Calinescu terms the 'cancerous proliferation of micro-ideologies',[61] through which mankind attempts to fill the void left by the great ideologies of modern age.

The Domestic as Aesthetic

According to Francalanci, the 'domestication of the aesthetic' represents the final stage of diffuse aesthetics. The 'aesthetics of the domestic' can be viewed in the mutation of things that are considered house furniture, the *intérieur* upon which the bourgeoisie conferred a symbolic value over and above their condition of goods (mere use value).[62] If, as Benjamin wrote, 'the interior is the asylum of the art',[63] for Francalanci that situation has today been reversed. That is, domestic objects no longer have the intimate nature of the *intérieur*, but they rather belong to the *extérieur*, 'that is to say to the places of production and commerce and the endless paths of the distribution and consumption of goods'.[64] At every latitude, one finds 'the same forms, the same substances, the same ideas'[65] on display. In such a scenario, the individual is freed from (or deprived of) the charge of turning things into symbols of something larger. Rather, things turn the house into an aesthetic model, built by accumulation, and finally include 'the tenant in its aesthetic orbit'.[66]

It is at this stage that Francalanci addresses the 'metamorphization of things'. Once the subject has been marginalized, things become animate, entities through which to form an alliance that are 'sensual rather than rational, bodily rather than spiritual, emotional rather than logical'.[67]

That same technique that has put a soul into things has the potential to turn every human being into a potential 'media amateur' in their own home. Through the use of domestic digital gadgets, the home becomes the place in which the subject feeds the illusion that they shape or control reality. Thus far, I have stated that diffuse aesthetics is the mode through which contemporary reality presents itself to human beings. I have also stated that it is through the unceasing flowing of digital data that contemporary lives become bound by this (virtual) reality. With these premises in mind, it is now possible to assert that the locus of the multiplication of simulative images is the modern home. Homes are the places in which we hear the siren's song, calling us to shape 'reality' according to our own particular taste. It is here that subjects experience the vertigo of inventing new worlds according to their own aesthetic vision; it is here that, as Baudrillard puts it, 'the object is seducing us by giving us the illusion of power over it'.[68] In those hours we spend at home editing pictures in Photoshop, building a marvellous house in a metaverse, creating playlists, editing moving images or writing on forums and blogs, one is not *only* acting as a 'tenant in the aesthetic orbit', one is also re-creating, feeding and encouraging that very aesthetic flow. Thus, human beings are not destined to be simply immersed in digital technologies, they have to commit to this dimension, in order for their movements to widen its borders.

We are far beyond the 'society of the spectacle' in which some room for critical thinking remained. As Badurillard observes, we are no longer alienated or deprived when technology allows us to own any possible knowledge, and when all human acts and events are actualized as pure information. In such a context, he writes: 'We are no longer spectators, but actors in the performance, and actors increasingly integrated into the course of that performance.'[69] For this reason, in the following pages I will capitalize on the title of the Wachowski brothers'[70] notorious film, and refer to the 'aesthetic matrix'. More than any other term, this captures the situation of the contemporary subject who is both included in, and acted upon, by the diffuse aesthetics of digital technologies. According to sociologist Manuel Castells:

> Every cultural expression, from the worst to the best, from the most elitist to the most popular, comes together in this digital universe that links up in a giant, non-historical hypertext, past, present and future manifestations of the communicative mind. By so doing, they construct a new symbolic environment. They make virtuality our reality.[71]

In conclusion, I would like to emphasize that, in a 'network society',[72] it is essential to identify the aesthetics specific to the Web in order to understand the present intertwining of social, cultural and mediated phenomena. As I made clear in the Introduction to the present work, I mean the expression 'Web aesthetics' in its widest sense, as an aesthetics of digital networks. Hence, my research into diffuse aesthetics is confluent with the concept of 'distributed aesthetics', according to which contemporary aesthetic forms are not only *disseminated in* 'techno-social networks', but are also *made of* them.[73] In summary, I support the view that the 'Web' represents the dominant formation of the present time, and that this is a formation that aestheticizes every sphere of existence. Yet, I also see in the Web the ideal breeding ground for that mode of transmission of culture that takes place through minimal units of information: memes.

Theory of Memes

Meme: an element of behaviour or culture passed on by imitation or other non-genetic means.
Oxford English Dictionary

The theory of memes[1] is usually considered to have originated in 1976, with the publication of evolutionary biologist Richard Dawkins' *The Selfish Gene*.[2] In the final chapter of this work, Dawkins develops the theory that Darwinian principles can be used to explain the proliferation of ideas and other cultural phenomena. According to this perspective memes, just like genes, have no purpose beyond their own reproduction. Just as biological replication takes place by means of DNA, spermatozoa and ova, memes reproduce in human brains via a process that, broadly speaking, can be called imitation. Some of Dawkins' examples of memes are 'tunes, ideas, catch-phrases, clothes fashions, ways of making pots or of building arches'.[3]

An important contribution to memetic theory is made by American philosopher Daniel Dennett.[4] In a number of publications, Dennett resolves some of the ambiguities in Dawkins' work, and develops the argument that the meme, just like the gene, is constituted by 'packages of information' containing the strings of symbols that constitute the mental existence of a living creature. In this perspective, ideas possess features similar to those of virus or bacteria, so that they are subject to the rules of Darwinian selection. The mind itself consists of nothing other than the cognitive and cultural heritage of the entire set of memes that human beings host, and help to replicate. 'Meme complexes' such as philosophical systems, ideologies, and religions, as well as 'single memes' including habits, trends, advertising jingles, commonplaces and urban myths are all determined by their virulence.

The replication perspective, in which memes act as Darwinian replicators, coexists with the epidemiological perspective, in which memes act as pathogens. For Dawkins, memes travel longitudinally across generations as well as horizontally as epidemics. For instance, the spreading of terms such as *memetic, docudrama* or *studmuffin* over the Internet represents a solely horizontal epidemiology.[5] After all, as Dawkins points out, most memes are nothing but good ideas, goods tunes or good poems.[6]

A final important contribution to memetic theory is made by computer programmer Richard Brodie, who defines the meme as a 'virus of the mind', and who identifies three methods of infection: repetition, cognitive dissonance and Trojan Horses. The most effective way to insert a meme into the mind is to hear it constantly. A brief glance at modern communication, from advertising to the media's obsessive repetition of keywords such as 'terrorist' and 'crisis' easily enables us to understand this process. The theory of cognitive dissonance was developed in the 1950s by psychologist Leon Festinger, to denote a process that takes place when an individual finds himself confronted with ideas and/or behaviours in contradiction with each other. In this case, one escapes from psychological discomfort by revising one's mindset or behavioural attitudes. This gives rise to an ideal situation for the reproduction of memes that are able to reduce or erase the contradiction. The strategy of the 'Trojan Horse' involves hiding a powerful, but unpleasant, mental virus in an 'attractive' package. For example, in a single slogan such as 'fighting fundamentalism', politicians are able to insert a range of different concepts, such as safety in the cities, and protection of secular and democratic values, but also the suppression of essential liberties such as privacy.[7]

The Meme Machine

In *The Meme Machine*,[8] psychologist Susan Blackmore argues that the enormous progress made by information media in contemporary times is merely a process of memetic selection. Drawing a parallel with ribosomes in cells, Blackmore suggests that the survival of memes might soon become independent of humans. The next step in memetic evolution, then, will result from developments in Artificial Intelligence that, unlike the human brain, will ensure an *actual*, digital, replication of memes, reducing transmission errors to a minimum. Furthermore, Blackmore concludes that the Self is actually just a bunch of memes, a temporary configuration of viruses nestled in the mind that drive everyday behaviours and influence decisions and tastes. Men and women might deceive themselves that they are driven by conscience or by a *deep Self,* but they are nothing but *meme machines* (made of brain, body and memes).[9] In regard to the argument I am developing, the most pertinent feature of Blackmore's theory is her vision of the modern mass media as the ideal breeding ground for memes. The Internet in particular is believed by many to be the most efficient tool for spreading ideas, beliefs and trends that spread like viruses from computer to computer, thereby infecting the minds of users. It might even seem prosaic to identify the shift towards social media as a means of creating memetic epidemics: share an idea with one's own contacts on Facebook and they will do the same, giving credit to the 'six degree of separation' theory,[10] and putting the whole world at risk of contagion. Such a contagion becomes even more likely in the case in which an idea encounters one of those replicators that studies of social networks have termed 'hubs'.

Scale-Free Networks

The concept of the hub and its relevance in social networks is elaborated in the work of Hungarian-Romanian scientist Albert-László Barabási and his colleagues at the University of Notre Dame.[11] In 1998, Barabási introduced the concept of *scale-free* networks, those networks in which a new node is established by drawing on those nodes, or hubs, that already possess a great many connections. As the number of the nodes in the network is bound to increase in time, the hub grows exponentially larger, while connection-poor nodes become poorer.[12] Examples of *scale-free* networks are metabolic networks, social networks, economic networks and electronic networks on the Internet and the Web. In particular, research into the Web has led to the conclusion that the distribution of links is subject to *scale-free* criteria, as in, for example, those websites that profit through a very good position in the search engines and a well-established presence on the Web. It is precisely these websites that attract the highest number of links; so that, applying the generative models of Barabási and Réka Albert (a principle also known as the 'rich get richer') it is clear that every webpage provides links to pre-existing pages with a distribution that is not uniform, but proportional to the actual size of the websites. The Web also exhibits the same structure of those networks through which humans exist and interact with each other: the protein reactions of a cell, public transport, social relationships, economic corporations and crime organizations. Each of these networks is based on a *power-law* that legislates that the majority of nodes will have few connections, and a few nodes will have a vast number of connections.

Some examples of memes that have used the Web as their main channel of replication might help us to understand this phenomenon:

- Google, whose popularity has not only undermined but has committed any other search engine to oblivion;
- the iPod, which has become synonymous with the MP3 player;
- the triad that is commonly considered to ratify the presence of an actual digital life: a place in Second Life, a photostream on Flickr, and a Facebook account.

Aside from restating the significance of the Web in inaugurating global epidemics in a relatively short time, all these examples allow us to understand the features of a successful meme. Some of these, such as longevity (the ability to survive in a certain environment), or fertility (the ability to generate offspring), are obvious. Others, such as the 'copying facility', require greater explanation. If the purpose of memes is to reproduce copies in order to spread in as great a number as is possible, it is crucial that the information contained in the meme is easy to copy. Chain letters, photocopies, and digital files are all examples of how the copying facility increases the chance of spreading at epidemic levels. However, if the literal meaning of 'copy' is left aside, the field widens to include the 'catchiness' of a tune or, in relation to the Web, the ease with which a user can add a website to the list of favourites on Delicious, share a media object with friends on Facebook, or publish the RSS feed on an interesting article on a blog. In all of these cases, though an identical copy is not created (as evolutionary theory would require, since according to it the replicator needs to be copied precisely), the substance of the content whose circulation is favoured does not change. At the same time, we can see that a technology dominated by the actions of 'cut and paste' provides the ideal breeding ground for memes.

Contagion, Repetition and Social Inheritance
Having introduced the memetic perspective to research into the aesthetics of the Web, it is essential to be aware of its historical premises. By the beginning of the nineteenth century, the principle of imitation had already been used in a number of fields, and was considered the common root of cultural and social development. Thus, Francesco

77

Ianneo[13] identifies the roots of Dawkins' theory in the process of 'selective imitation' offered by the sociologist Gabriel Tarde in *Les lois de l'imitation* (1890)[14] and further developed by James Baldwin in *Social and Ethical Interpretations in Mental Development* (1897).[15] According to Tarde, the role played by heredity in organisms is the same as that played by imitation in society. Moreover, every social repetition comes from an innovation: with every human invention, a new series begins. Thus, the invention of gun powder is to social science what the blooming of a new plant species is to biology, or the birth of new matter to chemistry: 'Repetitions are also multiplications or self-spreading contagions.'[16]

According to Baldwin, when an idea blooms inside a community and is repeatedly picked up on and spread, it gradually becomes a part of that community's culture. Cultural traditions therefore represent a set of ideas that have proven to be useful and so have been reproduced and imitated; this, then, is a social rather than physical heredity.[17]

Following Tarde, French sociologist and social psychologist Gustave Le Bon assigns a pivotal role to contagion in the formation and entrenchment of opinions and beliefs. Not only does contagion set the intellectual orientation, it also enables the individual to disappear inside the crowd (collective souls whose main feature is the near absolute psychic solidarity of the constituents' minds).[18] As Le Bon writes:

As soon as the mechanism of contagion intervenes, the idea enters on the phase which necessarily means success. It is soon accepted by opinion. It then acquires a penetrating and subtle force which spreads it progressively among all intellects, creating simultaneously a sort of special atmosphere, a general manner of thinking.[19]

Another significant foundation of the theory of memes is cybernetics. In fact, a cultural transmission system based on memes is supported by the tendency of contemporary individuals to *externalize themselves* in communication. As Philippe Breton states, this process has roots in the second half of the twentieth century. After the Second World War, the genocide of Jews and gypsies, Hiroshima and Nagasaki, the need for an alternative to 'humanistic man', became both obvious and urgent. In the work of Norbert Wiener, a 'new model of man', who is more universal, who inaugurates a new set of values and offers a renewal of the political utopia, begins to take shape. For Wiener, the 'new model of man' is rational and transparent, as well as separated from his biological body in order to be treated as a 'pure communicative being':[20]

> The *homo communicans* is a man who is protected from any limitations of the body, from any chance of stigmatizing his body according to his belonging, a man who is finally safe from man himself by going beyond his externalization in communication.[21]

Wiener's man possesses no inner self; rather, he is 'totally defined in terms of his ways of exchanging information'.[22] As a purely social being, he is no longer 'driven from inside', nor by the obscure force of ideology, but by external social connections and, above all, by the supreme value of communication. As Breton observes: 'Every micro-use of a machine for communication brings to an implicit communication of the values it holds.'[23] Within this modern conception of communication that Breton terms the 'utopia of communication', any machine hides its own ideological point of view, just as the Trojan Horse hides Ulysses and his comrades. When using a machine its ideology penetrates the social body and individuals without a complex inner self are left with very few means of resistance against technologies that exhibit significantly more complexity than they do. In cybernetics, it is possible to find all the constituents of a reality in which every human sphere is enslaved to the domain of communication and its modern machines.

In conclusion, the key premises of the theory of memes for aesthetics are contagion, repetition, and social heredity. I consider these concepts as a kind of bridge connecting the theory of memes to aesthetic reflections, as we become aware that forms, figures, and expressive patterns are suitable for those mechanisms of spreading by imitation that are the object of memetics. This very awareness grounds the work of the art historian Aby Warburg (1866-1929), whose research focuses on the concepts and dynamics of Western cultural memory, such as the migration of the iconographical patterns of ancient times to Renaissance art.

Aby Warburg: the Concept of Engram

With both his hands he labors at the knots;
His holy fillets the blue venom blots;
His roaring fills the flitting air around.
Thus, when an ox receives a glancing wound,
He breaks his bands, the fatal altar flies,
And with loud bellowings breaks the yielding skies.
Publio Virgilio Marone, *Eneide*, Book II (29 - 19 BC); translation
by John Dryden in: *The Works of Virgil* (1697)

Aby Warburg was born in Hamburg, into a family of wealthy Jewish
bankers. After a life spent travelling the world and cultivating his
interests in the history of art, archaeology, psychology and ethnol-
ogy, Warburg left several publications, a significant library, and the
unfinished *Mnemosyne Atlas*. Founded in Hamburg and named KBW
(*Kulturwissenschaftliche Bibliothek Warburg*), the library moved to London
in 1933 to protect it from the Nazis. In London, the library became a
kind of cultural institution known as the Warburg Institute, and is today
affiliated with the University of London.[1] One feature peculiar to this
library is that the books are not arranged in alphabetical order, but dy-
namically. The position of the books changes according to 'rules of civil-
neighbourly behaviour', the aim of which is to forge the best connections among volumes that share the same shelf. For Mathias Bruhn, this
way of ordering the books 'envisioned the idea of a library as a creative
place, a "generator" that combines objects and concepts of all kinds in a
limited space'.[2] Warburg's concept of the library clearly anticipates the
fluid and horizontal nature of knowledge on the Internet. His aim was to
allow changing sets of connections to develop between books – connections which, today, we might term links. In a very contemporary conception of culture, these connections might depend on analogies, recurring
topics or apparently random association between different subjects.

The Bilderatlas

Warburg's most important legacy, however, is the *Mnemosyne Atlas*.
The atlas is the prototype of an image atlas (*Bilderatlas*) composed of a
series of plates, each of which is itself composed of photographic repro-

ductions of different works. These include works of art, pages of manuscripts and playing cards from the Renaissance, archeological finds from Oriental, Greek and Roman cultures, and various objects from contemporary culture, such as tags and stamps. In the *Bilderatlas*, Warburg's purpose is predominantly didactic: he aims to prove the continuity of themes between the ancient past and the Renaissance, between Eastern and Western cultures, and from Northern to Southern Europe. The image atlas can be read as an attempt to build a pattern of Western cultural memory, and Warburg, true to his motto *zum Bild das Wort* (the word to the image), leaves the task of relating this history to the images themselves. He is also one of the first scholars to use photography as a medium of historicocultural memory.[3] In some ways, the *Bilderatlas* anticipates the Web, for it is a truly global work inside which one can search in order to know the world.

In Warburg's work, the concept of the *engram* is crucial. This term originates with the Greek εγγράφω, or carving, and is taken up by German scientist Richard Semon at the beginning of 1900 to describe the trace left by events in the organism's nervous system.[4] As a permanent change in the nervous system, Semon's engram retains an energetic trace of experience that is reactivated whenever the organism encounters a new experience. According to Warburg's interpretation, engrams are highly expressive images that have survived in the heritage of Western cultural memory, and that re-emerge irregularly and disjointedly. Memory is seen as a tabula rasa on which the strongest emotions leave traces that, when they come into contact with the present, are capable of releasing the emotional experiences that constituted their history.[5] In particular, *Pathosformel*[6] are engrams expressing the imagery of sacrifice, mourning, melancholy, ecstasy and triumph: emotions characteristic of the Ancient period, which Renaissance artists would later rediscover. By means of bodily and facial gestures, these images communicated powerfully across different centuries, in spite of vast cultural transformations. To Warburg, they represent the emotional intensity of the gesture at its highest level, as such they cannot but show themselves in a single form, and are always ready to reappear in cultural memory.

Warburg's studies are almost always focused on memory. One need only consider that the atlas is titled in tribute to Mnemosyne, the goddess of memory, as well as the mother of Muses and hence the inspirer of all arts. However, I believe it is worth considering Warburg's concept of the engram in light of the perspective of memetics. In fact, this conceptual procedure can be found in passages by Ernst Gombrich, one of Warburg's main disciples, as well as the editor of his intellectual biography.[7] Gombrich deserves credit for emphasizing the influence of the Italian positivist Tito Vignoli, who was among the first Italian thinkers to take up the theory of evolution, on Warburg. Although Warburg will never explicitly accept Darwin's influence, it is possible to recognize, as Cristina Bignardi states, a parallelism between Darwin, for whom emotional expression includes a fixed reactive ability, and Warburg, for whom the symbol (or engram) retains the trace of the emotions that led to the creation of the engram itself. Those feelings visible in primitive rituals, Dionysian rites and the dance of the maenads exhibit such passionate frenzy and religious fervour that they cannot but incite strong emotions in the observer, from the Renaissance to the modern age. These very images, in the form of symbols, 'turn the artistic imagery in a sort of strongbox to the emotional legacy of human civilization'.[8]

For Warburg, the images that are etched on our collective memory do not surface with a precise content. Rather, they possess a neutral charge that may be polarized. Regarding this topic, Gombrich highlights that in Warburg's theory, the energy of the past experience that is preserved in engrams or symbols may be channelled into various expressive modes. Engrams possess a neutral charge, and it is only in contact with the 'selective will of the age' that the charge is polarized.[9] Warburg's recall of the 'selective will of the age' can, I believe, be viewed in light of the concept of 'selective imitation' introduced by Tarde, and recovered by Baldwin. The engram is not transmitted to offspring, as Semon had thought; rather, transmission occurs through social heredity, and as such the reactivation of the latent energy of past ages is subject to the social, cultural and stylistic influences of a particular age.

The Memetic Contagion of Aesthetic Ideas

At this point, I wish to consider the images that have survived in cultural memory as memes, due to their extraordinary reproductive fitness. In an age of diffuse aestheticization such as the present one, the transmission of aesthetic ideas takes place through memetic contagion.

The viral idea of aestheticization spreads much as advertisements and propaganda do, through repetition. This process takes advantage of privileged replicators, such as the hubs (be they actual persons, websites or other media) at the core of extremely ramified networks. In just a few steps, the viral idea spreads across an increasingly interconnected globe. The idea, however, does not arise out of nowhere, but represents the revitalization of a symbol etched in cultural memory, and now re-activated and re-polarized according to contemporary styles and modes of communication. According to this scenario, the Web retains the cultural memory sedimented over the centuries, representing a global and ever-changing *Bilderatlas*. The Web is the privileged site of the imitative practices that are paradigmatic of the contemporary age, and, for an increasing number of individuals, it is the medium through which aesthetic experience takes place.

Meme Gallery

The idiot for whom I endeavour to formulate a theoretical point as
clearly as possible is ultimately myself.
Slavoj Žižek, *The Metastases of Enjoyment* (1994)

Before analysing specific aspects of aesthetic experience on the Web,
I would like to briefly focus on several works that provide us with an
artistic reading of the concept of the meme.

Santo_File
   The first reference is to the Spanish collective santo_file (santofile.
org). Santo_file calls itself a memegenic guerrilla group, and dedicates
its artistic production to the attempt to develop a view of life 'as a fight
between memes and genes'. In a multi-subject approach to the topic,
David Casacuberta (alias da5iv) and Marco Bellonzi (alias marco13) exhibit a clear preference for low-tech aesthetics typical of pioneer net.art
experiments. In this sense, the project *Versus* (2005),[1] in which the processes by which images of sport become memes is analysed, is emblematic. The graphic set up, which resembles the very first webpages, displays
images as ironic mediations between antonymic terms. An image of the
disaster that took place at the Belgian football stadium Heysel, for example, is placed between the words 'fun' and 'death'; and the image of a
famous cyclist disqualified for doping is placed between the terms 'natural' and 'artificial'. Clearly, the purpose is to unveil the hypocrisy in the
slogans utilized by the mass media in relation to sport. In my opinion,
the most interesting of santo_file's projects is *X-reloaded* (2005).[2] After
the celebration of the 400th anniversary (1605-2005) of Cervantes' *Don
Quixote*, santo_file explored the ease with which memes related to the
novel may be spread by drawing on suitable flows of mainstream communication. In order to take advantage of the 'memetic coincidence'
of the anniversary and of search engines, the Spanish group gathered
together a number of media artists and asked each of them to interpret
a portion of Cervantes' text in the light of concepts such as copyleft,
appropriation and piracy in relation to digital art. The artists involved,
including Jodi, Olia Lialina, Adbusters and Alexei Shulgin, took cultur-
ally renowned symbols out of their context, thus imbuing them with

new forms and meanings. As this is analogous to the way that writers use language, it is not surprising that santo_file quote Jorge Luis Borges' statement that, from a literary point of view, *Don Quixote* is more interesting in its English translation than in the original Spanish version.

Memetic Simulations

Another artist in this little gallery is Joseph Hocking (newarteest. com). An American of Korean origin, Hocking firmly believes in the ability of computers to give life to thought, as he explains in his artist statement: 'The code reflects my mind in a very direct way, so when I program I am putting a piece of my brain into the computer.'[3] In the unfinished series *memetic simulations*, Hocking explores the topic of memetic propagation. In *memetics simulations no.1* (2005), a touchscreen mounted on a stand functions as both the environment in which imaginary creatures move and the interface through which users interact with a system (created with 3-D models) that simulates artificial intelligence. Each little creature holds a meme in the form of a package of information, and when the memes meet each other they recombine. All memes have been collected from the Web, using search-terms such as 'urban legend' or 'medical news'. The nature of the meme justifies the graphic used for its host. For example, a creature holding the meme of a feature from religious mythology has cross-shaped legs. By touching the screen, the user can either kill the little creature or read the information it holds, so that the interactive level overlaps with the underlying narrative of recombination. Hocking's work offers an effective representation of the dynamics of memetics, in which a community attains and builds up a storehouse of knowledge, and is eventually shaped by the ideas that traverse it. In the sequel to this project, *memetics simulations no.2* (2006), it is the metaphor of the community that evolves. In place of the little creatures are human figures, surrounded by a halo. As memes combine with other memes, the colour of the halo changes accordingly. As in a typical shooter video game, characters shoot one another by ejecting words that resemble flames. As they come into contact with the flow of words being ejected, other characters assimilate the idea expressed into their background of knowledge. Eventually, as every member of the community comes to use the same words, the screen fades to black. The system then places an idea back inside the community randomly so that the 'game' can start again. In this second version of *memetics simulations*, Hocking provides an even clearer representation of the contagious, viral nature of the meme. The unifying vision, as Valentina Culatti observes,[4] tends to relate to the standardizing effects of mass communication and does not consider the differences that are introduced by each individual in the repetition of the virus-ideas (an evolutionary process that has appeared to be crucial in the memetic propagation as well as in the genetic one). Nevertheless, I believe that Hocking's work offers one of the best metaphors for meme action within a community. The interactive nature of the installation also offers a chance to quite literally touch the memes. This simple gesture, it seems to me, is more helpful than any theory in developing an awareness of the reality of memetic transmission.

The Relational Element

I will end with a well-known project by Victoria Vesna and Josh Nimoy. *n 0 time* (2001)[5] is a network screen saver that explores the concept of time *to waste* – time that, according to the authors' statement, becomes increasingly rare in a world of globalized networks. It is well known that screensavers are activated when the computer is not in use. The 'wasted time' of the machine, or *n 0 time*, rises along with the time that is spent away from the computer, and this amount of time is constantly transmitted to the central database of the project (the essential requirement of the network is that *n 0 time* aims at building an Internet connection of the involved computers). Vesna and Nimoy represent the amount of this time through the 'body' of a tetrahedron, which is a polyhedron with four triangular faces, four vertices and six corners or segments. Each of the six segments coincides with a colour, a sound and a basic meaning, so that, for example, red = family, green = love and yellow = creativity. The length difference depends on the importance that each corner is given, and determines the starting shape and the way it evolves. The four vertices represent the position of the memes and in the original setting they correspond to the first letters of the genetic alphabet: A, T, C and G, which here stand for Asynchronous, Time, Communication and Generation). The evolution of the *body n 0 time* depends on the interactions that take place in both virtual and physical space. In the actual installation, a user can explore the shapes of the original tetrahedron, thus triggering a replication of the sides/ segments and vertexes, and clearing a path to the introduction of new memes. These, however, can only be added by persons who have been invited by the instigator of *body n o time*, who gave life to the initial tetrahedron, via email or using special donor cards. This process continues until the body reaches such a high number of segments that it implodes and returns to its earlier state, an event that is announced by email to the whole *n o time* screensaver community. Apart from the theoretical complexity of this project, looking at an *n o time* screensaver involves one in a state of genuine aesthetic rapture. It is a *rêverie* in Ingarden's sense: a vision of the constant mutation of a geometric shape, capable of building a connection between the chaos of natural phenomena and the perfection of Hyperuranium, the place where ideas reside.

The project *n o time* highlights both the rational element in the spreading of the memes and the pivotal role of networks in the proliferation of viral ideas by crossing spatial, temporal, physical and linguistic borders. In *n o time*, a new meme appears simultaneously in the screen savers of all the users connected to the network, regardless of their location, gender or culture, just as a meme uses the global networks of communication to spread ever more quickly across the 'digital village'.

Chapter III

Aesthetic Experience on the Web

To Flow or Not to Flow

- I started to follow people.
- Who?
- Anyone at first. I mean, that was the whole point: somebody at
  random, somebody who didn't know who I was.
- And then?
- And then nothing.
- 'Nothing?'
- Nothing. I'd just see where they went, what they did . . . and go
  home afterwards.

Christopher Nolan, *Following* (1998)

Aesthetic experience on the Web begins with that act of travelling across images that characterizes diffuse aesthetics. It is well known that the Web is based on a hypertext principle, and that this confers upon users the sense that they are in the driver's seat: it is they who choose which direction to take, which options to activate, which language, version or template to select. Users may also contribute to the Infosphere by constructing a personal website, starting a blog, organizing a personal profile or a newsgroup in a social network, posting photographs or videos, or simply offering feedback. The multiplicity of ways to interact with the Web has led theorists to contrast this medium with broadcast media such as radio and television. Indeed, the analyses that have developed over the last 15 years have emphasized interactivity to such an extent that it is possible to state that interactivity is the founding myth of the Web, and of digital media as a whole.

Interactivity: A Founding Myth

Freed from the slavery of the broadcast model, it has not taken people long to turn themselves into autonomous sources of broadcast media, according to the motto 'be your media'. As the rich array of new digital tools have begun to be enjoyed in full, we find ourselves taking part in a true feast à la Rabelais, in which it becomes increasingly difficult to make any final distinction between mainstream and alternative, 'high' and 'low' culture, professional and amateur, and original and copy. In his criticism of the 'interactivity myth', Manovich observes that, by applying this concept exclusively to new media, we risk privileging the concept of 'physical interactivity', such as clicking with a mouse, or using a keyboard, over the 'psychological interaction' that characterizes so-called old media.[1] For example, the descriptive strategies of both classical and modern art force viewers to assemble disparate pieces of information; the composition techniques within a play shift viewers' attention towards different parts of the work; and cinematic editing techniques lead audiences to fill the gap between disconnected images. To Manovich, such a literal interpretation of interactivity forms part of a larger tendency in the way that we represent mental life; a tendency in which media such as photography, cinema, and more recently virtual reality, have played a crucial role. Recalling Galton's, Ejzenstejn's, and Lanier's theories, according to which technologies give shape to and objectify human minds, Manovich states that shifting private thought into the public sphere is a consequence of the demand for standardization that typifies mass society. Once objectified, internal mental processes can be matched to external visual forms, so that they become easily modifiable and serially reproducible. With interactive digital media, this process becomes complete. On this point, Manovich's reasoning is so compelling that I will quote him at length:

> The very principle of hyperlinking, which forms the basis of interactive media, objectifies the process of association, often taken to be central to human thinking. Mental processes of reflection, problem solving, recall, and association are externalized, equated with following a link, moving to a new page, choosing a new image, or a new scene. Before we would look at an image and mentally follow our own private associations to other images. Now interactive computer media asks us instead to click on an image in order to go to another image. Before, we would read a sentence of a story or a line of a poem and think of other lines, images, memories. Now interactive media asks us to click on a highlighted sentence to go to another sentence. In short, we are asked to follow pre-programmed objectively existing associations. . . . This is a new kind of identification appropriate for the information age of cognitive labor. The cultural technologies of an industrial society – cinema and fashion – asked us to identify with someone else's bodily image. Interactive media ask us to identify

with someone else's mental structure. If the cinema viewer, male and female, lusted after and tried to emulate the body of the movie star, the computer users are asked to follow the mental trajectory of the new media designer.[2]

Let us now try to establish several points regarding aesthetic experience on the Web. First of all, since it forces us to *look*, it expropriates the opportunity to *imagine*. This, then, is a true Lacanian short circuit – a dynamic in which the imaginary becomes the real, and the real in turn becomes virtual. We can ask, however, if Web users direct their own journeys, or if we should consider their movement on the Web as the following of a trace. The first point to clarify is that Manovich is referring to new digital media, and not specifically to the Web. According to a scholastic distinction, a digital medium like a DVD gives users an infinite number of finite options (precisely those pre-set by the author), while on the Internet the options become endless. However, it is also true that the Web is the result of a pre-set logic, and that it actually results from the mental trajectories of a finite number of new media designers, and that the interaction between these trajectories does lead Web users to follow one direction rather than another. The image that comes to mind is that of miniature car rides at an amusement park: the child has the feeling of steering a car that is actually moving according to pre-set trajectories. It might, however, be more appropriate to describe the journey of a Web user as analogous to a bird flying in a flock. Unlike the car, the bird has the 'freedom' to fly apart from the flock, and yet it ends up being stuck in the trajectories of the flock as a whole. Similarly, Web users are free to explore and to trace new and surprising paths through the Web, and yet they usually end up following well-worn paths.

Consider the social networks of Web 2.0: users view and subscribe to groups preferred by their friends and contacts; visit the websites that have been added to the bookmarks they share with other users; watch video clips and listen to songs at the top of the 'most viewed' and 'most ranked' categories; click on the words with the biggest font size in tag clouds; enter the chat-rooms with most guests; contribute to topics with the highest number of posts in forums; constantly make use of 'related' contents; and navigate to pages within the first ten results of the search engine. I could list many more examples of self-referentiality; as Lovink observes: 'The coded maxim here is: I want to see what you see.... Those who seek depth are simply barking (up) the wrong tree.'[3] These flows are characterized by a diffuse aestheticity; the contents are perceived solely at a formal level and any semantic interpretations are simply excluded: this is the final victory of the signifier over the signified. Within these flows, the recurrence of worldwide standardized forms guarantees the supremacy in the fight for getting the attention (and the clicks) of the internaut masses.

The Meme of Usability

I have referred above to Web 2.0, but I am speaking of a phenomenon that arises with the medium itself, and of a form of standardization already evident in the dot-com era. A good example is Jacob Nielsen's popular book on the usability of webpages.[4] Published in 1999, this text instantly became the Bible of Web designers, who preferred to follow the prescriptions of a Danish computer scientist than to experiment with different means of communication. Having rapidly spread across the globe, the 'usability of the Web' meme instantly flattened the form of the website, and websites rapidly began to exhibit similar structures and layouts. Following the motto 'Jacob Nielsen said it', menus were placed at the top-left hand of the page, links were labelled and coloured, and creativity was effectively numbed. It was as if a painter had placed Rudolf Arnheim's *Art and Visual Perception* among their paints and brushes, and consulted it before every single brush stroke. Rather than viewing websites as semantic frames (or cultural interfaces, in Manovich's words) to be filled with contents, from the very beginning of the Web's commercial development attention was focused on finding those archetypal forms capable of turning e-business into reality. In the history of Web design, websites used for business or political messages have brought out the worst side of the Net. The scene during the dot-com era was particularly boring – an endlessly reproduced copy of a few standardized models, with negligible variation. The navigation experience was also standardized, leaving nothing to improvisation or to creativity.

From a humanistic point of view, the codification of websites' usability was a true abomination. I will provide one example. That the placement of the object on the monitor surface catches the eye of the users according to its position on a harmonic (/) or disharmonic (\) diagonal is a fact supported by a massive amount of scientific literature. Of course, most attention is focused on the top left-hand corner of the page. What is worth contesting, however, is that every single designer must place the website menu in that area. Might a more gripping interaction be achieved by hiding the menu? Might a higher level of attention from users be achieved by forcing users to face the interface, and to overcome difficulties in order to find what they want? For a traveller, it is natural to stop and ask for information from passers-by. These difficulties do not prevent us from visiting new places – indeed, they can become stimulating experiences. According to Matthew Fuller, Web designers often possess an idealized image of Web users. By creating software for these idealized images, designers impose a one-size-fits-all model upon what is, in fact, a chaotic mass of non-aggregated users.[5] The search for formal standardization and the effort towards the homogenization of interfaces have produced 'castrating forms', which bridle the individual's creativity as they interact with different interfaces. No matter how efficient the navigation, where is the pleasure in visiting websites that look like each other and that work in the same predictable way?

The most surprising irony is that, particularly after the dot-com crash, the very entities that pushed for the adoption of usability standards in order to sell their products online found themselves with the need to make their websites look different from their competitors. Branding needs have turned the interface into one of the main features of the coordinated image, so that it is absolutely essential to attain the desired look and feel. With the bursting of the dot-com bubble a new stage begins, in which marketing research into website design focuses on *form*. Web design is reduced to style. As I have claimed above, this reflects a tendency within society more generally to shift away from functionality and towards aesthetic surfaces.

Social Networks and the Expropriation of the Philosophy of Community
As Francalanci states, the immaterial and virtual status of contemporary objects is evident in the marginalization of 'function' in favour of 'taste'; a diffusion of aesthetics that deprives object-goods of any judgment of sense and value. A Net ruled by the signifier is certainly

functional in regards to the goods that are advertised on it – from this point of view, the new medium is exactly identical to television. However, the Web is crossed not only by flows of goods and ideologies, but also by the relational flows of social networks. The 'myth of interactivity' finds new life in discussions of sociality on the Internet, in which interactive tools are seen to encourage the formation of new social relationships. Compared to previous forms of media, the Internet is also seen to offer different models of communication, such as one-to-many or many-to-many. Furthermore, a single tool might be used for different tasks: I can send an email to a single person or to a group, I can chat or talk via Skype with one or dozens of people at the same time. Along with the erasure of geographical and temporal barriers, these features certainly favour interaction. Yet, the Internet's community culture does not derive solely from the technical specificity of its tools; it has its roots in the anarchist and libertarian features that characterized the pioneering stage of the development of the medium. In the cyberculture of the late 1980s and early 1990s, we find the seeds of a utopistic community, in which a 'bottom-up' model would replace dominant hierarchical structures of communication. This is the ethics of creative involvement that the hacker scene takes from the punk and cyberpunk movements: the idea that reality can be shaped through the sharing of tools and skills.

Today, that communitarian philosophy has been expropriated by commercial social networking sites, and 'community' has become the flag behind which Twitter, Facebook, MySpace, Flickr, YouTube, LinkedIn, QQ in China and Cyworld in South Korea hide the fact that millions of unpaid users are increasing their own economic value through the generation of content.[6] Of course, the phenomenon of social networking is in line with the immaterial shift of post-Fordist economics and with that resurgence of late hyperglobalized capitalism known as 'cognitive capitalism'. I am speaking of those processes that, according to Yochai Benkler, are at the heart of *network society*, in which economic considerations enter into human activities previously unrelated to profit, such as social networks and the exchange of contents within them, and incorporate those activities into the core of the networked information economy.[7] The winning strategy of international capital has been to take hold of habits and practices belonging to the counter-culture, *in primis* freeing cultural production from the 'job-employment' paradigm. As Lovink observes, however, this has ended up making the rich richer. Thus, Lovink advises us to remain outside of the logic ruling Web 2.0, according to which giving one's own contents for free is the only option.[8]

Although in agreement with Lovink, I am sceptical of whether this is a realistic possibility, for I believe that the processes of capture used by social networks are too powerful. In the context of total self-referentiality and monolingualism, users of social media on the Web come to speak one single language, and give life to the development of monolithic blocks of beliefs and desires. If everything emerges and develops within the context of the group, it is difficult to envision any way in which the group might be opened up to an exterior. It is precisely those technologies viewed as participative and freedom-giving that encourage the building and the maintenance of 'monolingual blocks'. This is, perhaps, the Web's most significant paradox: those technologies supposed to mobilize users actually direct them into pre-existing flows. Rather than conversing, one is constantly invited to subscribe to ideas, modes and images through procedures that the software makes pleasantly easy. It is lovely to link to someone in one's own blogroll, to reply 'attending' to an event invitation, or to 'follow' someone on Twitter. The ease with which these actions are undertaken ensures the erasure of any critical level, for any expression of dissent or difference requires one to confront massive technological complexity, vastly out of proportion to the ease of 'going with the flow'. Anyone can use these technological tools to express dissent, but the question remains: Why would I do such a thing when it is so nice to linger in this oasis of happiness with my (ever-increasing number of) friends?

A conversation or dialogue creates a space in which differences might come to light – for this very reason, techniques must be developed that make such conversation possible, but difficult and unpleasant. Contemporary individuals have a great deal of trust in technology's capacity to be a sentinel or watch dog; a protector of the carefree nature of their *being digital*. In a similar way, critical thought is to be encouraged as long as it is 'mainstream'. It is banal, but instructive, to point out how much easier it is to be against George Bush than in his favour. On the Web, critical thought must always be 'trendy'. It is cool to create a

Facebook group against the slaughter of whales, and rewarding to count the number of friends allied in the name of a shared environmentalist indignation, but can it really be called an expression of dissent? This is a form of rapture, an appropriation of brains that Lazzarato views as a concatenation of subjectivities, a device capable of creating both junctions and disjunctions of flows.[9] Speaking of blogs, Lovink himself cannot help but realize that the price paid for closing the gap between society and the Internet has been a trivialization of that push for change that had first given life to the phenomenon.[10] Normalized in the recurrence of a daily self-celebration, aestheticized to the nth degree, the antagonistic drives of the Web have become inoffensive. Today, starting a blog intended to host political content is about as revolutionary as wearing a Che Guevara T-shirt.

Flow and Process

To recap: aesthetic experience on the Web, both in commercial websites and social networks and the blogosphere, is characterized by three forms of expropriation: a kind of 'travelling with eyes wide open' that expropriates the imaginary dimension; a following of pre-established flows and trajectories that expropriates the subjective dimension; and a making public of one's own mental processes, in an expropriation of the private dimension. The Web, in fact, becomes increasingly exemplary of postmodern communication, holding within itself every theory and its contradiction, every ideology and the most radical denial of the need for ideology itself, every image, every polarity, and both the realization and castration of every desire. It is the dream of every material good in the same place and at the same time; it is the breast that feeds us as television had done for decades. But since the Web is already everything before any action of mine, I no longer interact, I only jump from one flow to the other. Finally, I end up not going anywhere, I remain inside this welcoming womb. Rather than interacting with the Web, one undergoes it. One is constantly titillated, and one responds in ways that are interpreted by theorists as interactions: leave feedback, add to cart, subscribe to feed, add to friends, search, get link, copy, paste, share, skip, reply. Here is a grammar of gestures that creates a sense of boundless creativity and excitement. Yet this is a simulacrum, one image among many others and, just like them, at once true and false.

97

We are persuaded that we are in control of our journey, without realizing that some paths will lead nowhere but to surrender. The citizens of the network society believe that they are acting, but they are being acted on. They take the memes they transmit as ideas shaped by their own minds, but they are shaped by the tools required for the spreading of the meme. It becomes impossible to find alternatives to the aesthetic paradigms whose specific purpose is to erase any residual difference in the minds of the individuals, whose thoughts become sterilized and inoffensive. If, then, the plurality of data flows are constitutive of the digital contemporary age, what does the future hold? The thesis of *Web Aesthetics* is that these flows lead to the plurality of processes, that series of temporary configurations that in fact make up daily experience. This process, which is never autonomous but always induced, is constituted by all the actions/interactions performed within the mediascape; all the events that beat the time of a network society; all the objects that do take shape and all those that remain nothing but projects; all the possible intellectual speculations that surround the Web (including this book); and all the forms that offer themselves to human senses as the illusory possibility of fixed representations of the flowing. Sometimes these expressions of process are linked to each other, and give life to series in the form of imitations and remixes. At other times, they enjoy a certain 'innovative' independence, but this lasts only until they begin to be imitated, thus becoming the beginning of a new series. In both cases, the responses depend upon, are induced by, and provide an ephemeral representation of the flow itself. One might experience the vertiginous sense of removing an idea or a form from the flow, so that it seems to possess a kind of autonomous existence, yet one is only assisting in the propagation of the flow. Any attempt to subjectify, or more generally any attempt to resist, can only lead to a disjunction of flows, hence contributing to the plurality that is irreducible by its very nature.[11] In this view, it is mistaken to consider the ideas, actions, events and forms that appear in the frame of the media chain as giving back, or as putting back into the flow the elements that have been taken; being sucked into the media system means being inside the flow, and in this condition nothing is taken and nothing is given back.

If this is true, one must conclude that the whole of existence, and every aesthetic experience, takes place within the flow, and becomes an experiencing of the flowing. Interacting becomes ineffectual and futile or, more optimistically, a means of learning to live alongside the elements that make and nurture the flow. In the same way, any attempt to represent the flow is bound to remain ephemeral. In conclusion, the flowing and the expressions of the process triggered by the flowing can be witnessed and somewhat explained, but can never be experienced as such.

Fictions

> Reality itself... is entirely captured... in the world of make believe,
> in which appearances are not just on the screen through which
> experience is communicated, but they become the experience.
> Manuel Castells, *The Rise of the Network Society* (1996)

Two antinomies are particularly relevant to aesthetic experience on
the Web: between form and content and between the optical and the
haptic. Within the history of aesthetics, at least five different meanings have been given to the term 'form'.[1] The first conceives of form
as an 'arrangement of parts', such as the positions of the columns in a
portico, whose balance and proportion confers beauty upon the object.
In this view, form is an abstraction, so that if it is true that a work of
art is nothing but a composition, it is nevertheless composed of parts
organized in a certain way. A more concrete definition of form is that
it is what is 'directly given to senses'. In poetry, for example, the sound
of the words is part of the form, whereas the meaning of the words constitutes the poem's content. Although these two definitions of form are
often combined in order to denote a certain composition given directly
to the senses, I will refer in the main to the second definition, in order
to explore the form/content dyad with more clarity. Form can also be
defined as the contour or boundary of an object, as opposed to the material of which it is composed. In addition, Aristotle defined form as the
'conceptual essence' of an object, against which he opposed the object's
accidental features, and Kant defined form as the 'contribution of the
mind' to the knowledge of an object, as opposed to what is not produced
by the mind, but comes from external experience.

In ancient times, form was referred to as poetics, as the sound of a
word (the form) and its meaning (the content) were easy to distinguish.
For similar reasons, in the Middle Ages and in the Renaissance, this
definition of form was believed to be more applicable to verbal art, in
which there are two distinct layers: in the Renaissance these are *verba*
and *res*, or words and things. In the visual arts, the concepts of form as
an exterior feature and as composition tend to overlap. Moreover, in the
nineteenth century, and to an even greater extent in the twentieth, form
and content are in active competition with each other. In this period,

schools such as formalism, suprematism and purism, in which form is the only significant feature, develop. Supporters of this tendency are Malevič, Le Corbusier, Mondrian and Focillon; Kandinsky is a kind of mediator for, in spite of everything, he recognizes content as crucial to the work of art. 'Form' is clearly a polysemous term. Yet, as Tatarkiewicz observes, if one is clear about which sense of a polysemous term one is referring to, the plurality of meaning is no longer dangerous.[2] Once I have clarified the concept of form I intend to refer to in the following section of this chapter, we need no longer be too concerned by the term's ambiguity.

The Interface

The first point to clarify is what form means in relation to the Web – in other words, what is directly given to the senses. In order to identify this, it is necessary to introduce the concept of *interface*. As Frieder Nake and Susanne Grabowski state:

> Software never appears without its interface. The human-computer interface is, first of all, the face of its software ... [and] software cannot exist without face. The face of software is its appearance at the periphery of the computer; without its face, it does not exist at all.[3]

The beginning of the 1980s was a crucial period in the development of the interface, and 22 January 1984 is an especially significant date. On this date, during the Super Bowl,[4] a commercial entitled *1984* is broadcast for the first time. Directed by Ridley Scott and inspired by George Orwell's novel of the same name, the commercial signals Apple's intent to liberate computer users from IBM's PC, which represented the standard in computing at that time. Embodying Apple's nonconformist image, the commercial presents the computer as a source of freedom, rather than as an alienating and complicated tool. The commercial opens with a shot of a murky tunnel, traversed by a row of pale-faced and hollow-eyed people, whose bodies are covered by pale, ash-grey uniforms. The group marches slowly, their feet beating the iron-grilled floor simultaneously, while three screens on the right show the grim and harsh face of Orwell's Big Brother. This scene alternates with another: that of a fit, young and blond female athlete, wearing a top with a stylized version of the Mac computer and the Apple logo. She holds a hammer in her hands, and is being chased by guards holding truncheons. Meanwhile, the dismal march proceeds until the people reach a room in which a gigantic screen broadcasts images of the Leader. Quiescent and near-unconscious, a great number of people stare up at him as he states:

> Today, we celebrate the first glorious anniversary of the Information Purification Directives. We have created, for the first time in all history, a garden of pure ideology, where each worker may bloom secure from the pests of contradictory and confusing truths. Our Unification of Thoughts is more powerful a weapon than any fleet or army on earth. We are one people, with one will, one resolve, one cause. Our enemies shall talk themselves to death and we will bury them with their own confusion.
> We shall prevail!

As the people listen, hypnotized, the young woman enters and hurls the hammer at the screen, which explodes, destroying the image of the Leader and bathing the audience in light. The people appear to wake from a nightmare, and the commercial ends with the prophecy that 'on January 24th Apple Computer will introduce Macintosh. And you'll see why 1984 won't be like 1984'. Two days later the Macintosh, a light and relatively small computer is launched onto the market; and it seems, for once, that a commercial's dramatics are justified. The Mac actually represents a crucial turning point in the history of information technology: the first personal computer with a GUI, or Graphic User Interface, that allows users to access content much more easily. The GUI uses icons and windows to enable users to feel and act as if they are sitting at their own desktop. They can, for example, organize their materials in 'folders', or discard them in the 'bin' if they are not needed.

Recalling Peter Lunenfeld, media theorist Lev Manovich writes that the commercial, together with Ridley Scott's *Blade Runner* (1982), 'defined the two aesthetics that, twenty years later, still rule contemporary culture, miring us in what he (Lunenfeld) calls the "permanent present"'.[5] Manovich observes that, despite the fact that *Blade Runner* has been quoted in an enormous number of 'films, computer games,

novels, and other cultural objects', and despite the aesthetic models
proposed by many artists and by commercial culture in general, none
has really weakened the influence of Scott's film on the image of the
future of the last decades.[6] To this combination, I would add that one
final cultural product makes a critical contribution: William Gibson's
Neuromancer. Published on 1 July 1984, Gibson's novel features the following famous definition of cyberspace:

> A consensual hallucination experienced daily by billions of legiti-
> mate operators, in every nation, by children being taught mathemati-
> cal concepts ... A graphical representation of data abstracted from
> the banks of every computer in the human system. Unthinkable
> complexity.[7]

Gibson's description is critical, for it replaces a geometrical conception
of space as depth with a conception of space as a flow of data. The image of space as infinite depth, a conception that extends from Euclid
to Stanley Kubrick's *2001: A Space Odyssey* (1968) as well as to all the
works inspired by Kubrick's film, is replaced, now, by the image of data
as the infinite: a matrix, as Gibson will presciently define it.

In Manovich's view, the dark, decayed and postmodern aesthetic of
Blade Runner contrasts with the Mac's GUI 'modernist values of clarity
and functionality'. In fact, the Mac embodies a vision of the future in
which 'the lines between the human and its technological creations
are clearly drawn, and decay is not tolerated'.[8] This opposition between
modernist and postmodernist values allows me to introduce my argument concerning the antinomy between form and content in relation to
the Web. The key point is that when one views a webpage one does anything but directly relate to the flow of data.[9] In this view, the interface
given to the subject's senses is nothing but a contingent, momentary
form, a form that in that very moment seems to fix a more or less well-
defined set of data. In actuality, the data are always flowing. The interface is a fiction, a form that *pretends* that data can be held steady: a quality that is crucial for humans to be able to interact with it. The forms
given to the flow cannot be but fictions, for it is impossible to crystallize
the flow into a form. When one believes oneself to be representing the
flowing, one is actually only giving shape to the *flown*.[10] At this point,

we might recall Heraclitus' famous aphorism, according to which it is not possible to bathe twice in the same river. The aphorism reminds us that the concepts we are dealing with are not specific to digital technologies; they have, in fact, been recognized for a very long time. Thus, Manovich's statement above might be completed as follows: Mac's GUI and all the interfaces that software designers have realized (and will realize) express the (still) modernist project of imposing human power upon technology (in particular, the project of imposing a hierarchical system for the files and other resources processed by a computer).

To these attempts, postmodernity opposes the powerlessness of humans who have lost control of their machines and have become secondary to them, as in *Blade Runner*, as well as the impossibility of relating to the liquid, relentlessly flowing data that give life to Gibsonian cyberspace. Manovich himself believes that the GUI and the Web represent the world in different, and perhaps opposing, ways:

> A hierarchical file system assumes that the world can be reduced to a logical and hierarchical order, where every object has a distinct and well-defined place. The World Wide Web model assumes that every object has the same importance as any other, and that everything is, or can be, connected to everything else.[11]

Since our computers began to be constantly connected to the Internet, and since the spreading of broadband and public Wi-Fi hotspots, this distinction may be losing its power. When a computer is connected to the Net it is in fact within the flow of data; when 'everything is ... connected to everything else', any effort to rationalize and order resources is bound to be overwhelmed by the next wave of data that will strike the computer itself.

The Separation of Form and Content

In order to understand the form of the Web, one needs to remember that the Web is composed of a network of heterogeneous media objects, each of which can be interpreted and viewed in infinite ways. The Web and new media in general are characterized by what Manovich terms a 'principle of variability', which gives life to a mutable and liquid landscape. One of the consequences of this principle is that it is possible to keep levels of content (data) and form (interface) separate so that, as Manovich observes, 'a number of different interfaces can be created from the same data'.[12] This feature has characterized the Web since its inception. However, HTML, the language this new medium was born in, is made of tags that make the separation of form and content difficult, as in a HTML file there are also instructions about how the file will need to be displayed. In contrast, the newer language XML, upon which Web 2.0 is based, allows data to be exported with no connection to its formatting. In fact, XML tags describe only the content, and do not specify which style to use for its display. On the one hand, this radical separation of form and content allows every user, even those who are relatively unskilled, to create Web content.[13] On the other, it allows content to be freely exported: not only links, but an entire blog post can be exported and displayed according to the style of the website that imports it. This is true not only for text, but for multimedia. For example, videos and images can be placed on a geographical map related to the place where the shooting took place.[14]

The Web is at a stage on which the separation of form and content has reached its full flowering. It is obvious that content exported from one website to another tends to take a different form, yet it is important to note that this variability of output also takes place when content (literally, the same file) is displayed on computers with different operating systems or browsers. As there are no universal standards or specifications common to the major software companies, it is not unusual for the same website to look very different on two computers using different forms of software.[15] In addition, many websites (according to the 'principle of variability') give users different modes for the same content, and the chance to skip from one to the other in a click.

On the Web, videos are always displayed along with a series of other videos, related by content or by keywords. At least until the 'full screen' option is selected, one is never alone with a single video, so that the video never has a meaning in and of itself, but is related to other videos and therefore to wider flows of data. We might say that the 'full screen' option allows users to become a kind of demiurge, to shape the world by making a single video's meaning absolute. In doing so, the user operates directly on the page composition, and hence on the form through which contents are conveyed. For example, the layout of pages in YouTube relates the video one is interacting with to the others included in thumbnails, small images representing a single frame. As the thumbnails explicitly recall the relativity of the video being played to the Web's endless content, this form ends up dominating the contents of any one single video. Choosing the 'full screen' reverses this relationship, and leads content to dominate over form. The specific content is no longer relative to other content; yet the sense that the video has a meaning in and of itself and not merely as part of a fluid plurality remains a fiction. After all, the 'full screen' mode is temporary – at the end of the video, a series of miniatures of videos with (presumably) similar content will return. Here is a quick, but revealing glimpse of the unsteadiness of the relation between form and content that characterizes the Web, which also reveals that the peculiarity of this dyadic relation cannot be quickly resolved.[16]

The Web is also characterized by a permanent tension between pre-imposed forms and editable forms. Three examples of popular platforms should suffice to demonstrate this point. Consider the website of the popular American broadcaster CNN: one can jump from one section to the other as well as from one article to the other; or one can choose between textual and multimedia contents, lingering in an image gallery as well as listening to streaming audio files. None of these options, however, allows the user actually to modify the interface. As opposed to this 'classical' Web 1.0 setting, a website such as MySpace allows users to act directly upon the code underlying their profile pages. In doing so, the site allows a virtually infinite level of customization[17] (interventions into page backgrounds gives rise to the most surprising, and often baffling, results). Furthermore, the development of applications that provide widgets through which it is possible to generate MySpace-compatible codes without any knowledge of HTML or Java allows an army of amateurs to express the uniqueness of their own personality. Even if a lack of expertise decreases the quality of the content – when, for example, the text becomes indistinguishable from the background – this is a price that the community of MySpace users is happy to pay, as the usability of contents is necessarily secondary to the freedom to customize the look of one's own page. The third and final example is Facebook. Here, the recurring order of the elements and the fixed white background give rise to a flat and tidy interface. The customizing options are restricted to which applications to retain on one's own page, and sometimes in which order they will appear. In this setting, users are able to express their personality through selecting the contents to be displayed on the wall, and hence to be shared with all of one's contacts. In this case, in a way, attention shifts from the interface to the contents.

The three websites examined are all real-time displays of a constant stream of data. However, each offers users a different degree of scope to alter the form: the lowest possible grade is represented by CNN, in contrast to which MySpace offers an almost baroque excess, and Facebook occupies a midpoint between the two. If we now try to imagine the total number of websites, each of which offers different opportunities for formal intervention, the degree of complexity involved in discussing the form/content antinomy on the Web becomes clear. Obviously, the history of aesthetic philosophy makes no mention of this issue, firstly because the active (or interactive) role of users only became an issue with the birth of new media, and secondly because it entails a shift away from classical aesthetical reflection and towards commercial communication and 'non professional' sectors of creativity. In order for contemporary aesthetics to be able to deal with these issues, at least two stages were required: the erasure (from the postmodern perspective) of the distinction between high and low culture (and between professionals and amateurs) and the quantum leap represented by diffuse aesthetics, that is the shift from a specific and marked sphere of the aesthetic to the all-encompassing aesthetics of the present day, with the consequence that it is now impossible to apply a specific, *higher* status to the work of art compared to other forms of expression or communication.

If the arrival point of contemporary aesthetics can be said to be the inseparability, in artistic expressions, of form and content – even with different views from Francesco De Sanctis to Benedetto Croce[18] – digital media, and the Web in particular, give rise to forms that emerge regardless of the content and, conversely, to contents that can be expressed by a variety of forms, with a rapid shifting between experiences in which the form tends to prevail and experiences in which the contents dominate.

An Impossible Task

The problem, then, is how to explain the Web's complexity through traditional categories of aesthetic thought. This, in my opinion, is a problem without a solution, because the specificity of experience on the Web represents the 'debasement' of classical concepts of form and content, in favour of what is ostensibly the most meaningful premise of contemporary times: the flowing of digital data. So, rather than repeating formula such as 'the form is the content', we need to realize that it is the flow of data that takes precedence over any distinction between content and form. The flow represents the potential for an endless plurality of forms, and every possible content. To refer to the content as an entity in itself, separate from the flow, is analogous to referring to an individual separate from the ceaseless flowing of quantum particles. Doing so means to place oneself in the world of observable and measurable physical phenomena, covering over a dimension in which the behaviour of matter is much more complex, and where certainties are replaced by probabilities. If, as quantum mechanics seems to prove, everything is part of a continuum, separateness must always be an illusion. In the contemporary age, every single datum, every single phenomenon, and every single event will only find its *raison d'être* in its relation to the liquid flowing of all the other data, phenomena and events. Perhaps the only consolation for this cosmic relativism is that one no longer risks being accused of heresy.

Form as Fiction

I have said that the sense of giving shape to the flow of data is a kind of fiction, and I would like, now, to elaborate this point. From an etymological point of view, the Latin verb *fingere* has many meanings: to pretend, to model, to conceive, to imagine, to invent, to distort, to shape, to carve and to forge, among others. As an action that creates something new, it could be considered fiction. In that case, we need to ask: What are the truth claims of those who shape the new? and, concomitantly, the question to pose for every new creation would be: What is its relation to a pre-existing reality? If it is true that every deceit requires a fiction, it is also true that not every fiction is based on a lie. Consequently, a clear distinction is needed, in order to distinguish between commercial communication, which takes advantage of established fictions not always recognized as such, and artistic expression, which is meant to be a declared fiction with an end in itself.

When I state that the forms given to the senses in the Net are fictions, I do not necessarily mean that they are deceits, with purposefully hidden intentions. Rather, they are necessary fictions, for the banal reason that if binary code was not translated into text, images and sound, it would remain a machinic language and would only be comprehensible to other machines. Secondly, these are necessary fictions because no human subject is capable of managing a liquid and constantly changing reality; for humans, it is necessary to pretend that reality takes stable, established or intelligible forms.[19] The forms of the Web function as do the images of celestial constellations: they allow humanity to process, through familiar forms (the bear, the cross, the crown) a reality that is otherwise too complex and threatening. It is also worth noting that the radical novelty represented by the Web and by other digital media has not failed to weaken the atavistic need to know and define reality through its representations, that is to say, through forms. For humans, reality comes into being along with form; prior to that there is only something that our mental faculties cannot grasp, which some term chaos.[20] John Dewey has written that:

> All interactions that effect stability and order in the whirling flux of change are rhythms. There is ebb and flow, systole and diastole: ordered change. The latter moves within bounds. To overpass the limits that are set is destruction and death, out of which, however, new rhythms are built up. The proportionate interception of changes establishes an order that is spatially, not merely temporally patterned: like the waves of the sea, the ripples of sand where waves have flowed back and forth, the fleecy and the black-bottomed cloud. Contrast of lack and fullness, of struggle and achievement, of adjustment after consummated irregularity, form the drama in which action, feeling and meaning are one. The outcome is balance and counterbalance. These are not static nor mechanical. They express power that is intense because measured through overcoming resistance. Environing objects avail and counteravail.
> There are two sorts of possible worlds in which aesthetic experience would not occur. In a world of mere flux, change would not be cumulative; it would not move towards a close. Stability and rest would have no being.[21]

Form exists, then, in between the 'whirling flux of change' and a world that is finite and unchanging. Form exists within a moment of temporary balance; it is the fiction that what is observed is steady, and still, while it is in actuality always flowing. Without form, there can be no knowledge, nor can there be aesthetic experience. Aside from in linguistics, in which the centrality of the symbolic dimension is so obvious that I have nothing to add to a discussion about it,[22] support for this statement comes from physics. A central assumption of quantum theory is that of the intrinsically probabilistic nature of physical processes. Known as the principle of indeterminacy, this theory led the Nobel Prize-winning physicist Niels Bohr to advance, in conflict with Einstein, the paradoxical statement that reality, from a physical point of view, exists or reveals itself only when it is observed. If, for humans, reality exists at the moment that we give shape to it and before that moment is not recognizable because it is too complex or chaotic, this becomes even more true for those matrices of digital data that William Gibson describes as characterized by 'unthinkable complexity'.

Representations of the Web

The streams of digital data, the endless connections among nodes in the Net, the constant *movement* among interfaces and databases, are simply beyond human understanding. In order to relate to this reality, it needs to be given a shape, although we need always to bear in mind the arbitrary and fictional nature of this process. Hence the difficulty of representation, of which Matt Woolman writes:

> Functional visualizations are more than innovative statistical analyses and computational algorithms. They must make sense to the user and require a visual language system that uses colour, shape, line, hierarchy and composition to communicate clearly and appropriately, much like the alphabetic and character-based languages used worldwide between humans.[23]

The above quote appears on the 'About' page of the website visualcomplexity.com, and it summarizes the methodological principle of the website's creator, Portuguese designer Manuel Lima. Lima's research into the modes through which complex networks are displayed began while he was attending the Parsons School of Design in New York. The lack of an organic reference system, which Lima experienced throughout his studies, prompted him in 2005 to launch a website that collected together projects concerned with the display of complex systems. Surfing visualcomplexity.com, one becomes aware of the molecular structure of contemporary realities, whether biological, musical, political, artistic, economic or Internet-related. I have already introduced Barabási's crucial concept of scale-free networks; here I would emphasize that, whatever view one takes of the relationship between art and reality, it is impossible to discuss Web aesthetics without referring to widely shared forms of visualizing its structure. Models such as Barabási's are essential, for they help to define the archetypical image of the Web, and the infinite net of connections of which it is composed. This archetype is not only crucial for artists, who without a fixed reference would not be able to give life to representations at all.[24] The capacity of men and women to benefit from representations is conditioned by the sharing of the symbolic apparatus activated by the subjects who gave life to those very representations.

What, then, is the image of the Web? Reviewing the representations on visualcomplexity.com, a frequently occurring image appears to be a multi-pointed reality in which links between different (usually spherical) nodes are represented by straight or curved lines. However creative and kaleidoscopic are the representations of this figure, it is so ubiquitous that it seems difficult to find alternative representations. Ideally, the branches in these images tend to the infinite, even if some visualizations graphically emphasize a subsection of the total number of relations in order to point out specific connections. The relative size of nodes is nearly always rendered by using a scale that makes their weight clear, a perspective that can be appreciated in both 2-D and 3-D representations. There are, however, representations that ignore size and display all nodes on a single level, in order to highlight the non-hierarchical morphological structure of the Internet, instead of the 'rich get richer' dynamic. As is well known, every computer connected to the Internet is not hierarchically subordinated to a central node, but can act either as a *server* (the computer providing services) or *client* (the computer receiving services). The ease with which nodes can shift between the role of server and client are central to those representations of the Web that render it as a horizontal, de-centred space. From a philosophical perspective, this view reflects the repudiation of frames of reference imposed by a centralized power, such as the oppositions between classes, genders and ethnicities, as well as resistance to the binary nature of social relationships (masculine/feminine, active/passive, beautiful/ugly, rich/poor, strong/weak, useful/useless etc). In opposition to this, the use of size as a scale replaces the ideal of equality, with a *realistic* interpretation of the forces involved in a system of values that creates differences, inequalities and disproportion comparable to those that characterize the social body. There are, however, a multitude of intermediate and alternative representations to these two, such as those that highlight the similarities among the nodes of the Web and choose a representation of the Web (or parts of it) as parallelisms and contact points between lines of meaning. Some of the most effective are those that employ the global standard of the subway map as a metaphor, depicting similarities with different colours, and the websites as the respective stops on the line. The merit of these projections is that they highlight trends within the development of the Web, rather than imaging its overall morphology. Emblematic in this sense is the experience of Information Architects Japan Inc.,[25] a group of architects who produce, on an annual basis, a graph that maps the Web's trends and innovations based on the Tokyo railway map.

As products of designers or artists, the visualizations of the Web displayed on visualcomplexity.com all have a highly refined graphic nature. It is worth mentioning, however, Martin Dodge's and Rob Kitchin's incredible *Atlas of Cyberspace*.[26] In this work, the authors state that the difficulties in mapping cyberspace are due to the crumbling of two of the cornerstones of Western cartography: namely, that space is continuous and stable; and that the map is not the territory, but its representation. Cyberspace is purely relational, the result of infinite media that are not elements of a natural environment, but the result of work done by designers and through the interactions between users. Many of these media have low spatial quantities (an email, for example), while there are countless entities, including blog entries, avatars and websites, that appear and disappear in a second, leaving no trace behind. According to Dodge and Kitchin, the lack of measurable space-time geometry does not mean that the Web lacks any form or structure at all. Rather, these are dematerialized and created through the interactions between users. Space and time on the Web are hence nonlinear and dynamic, subject to change, from media to media, from website to website, as materials are constantly added, modified, updated or erased. In Dodge and Kitchin's work, a single website may be interpreted from two points of view: one can highlight the connections between the node and the other entities of the Net, in which case the node is considered as the central point of the network that is being examined; or, one can investigate the connections within the pages or media objects that constitute a website. In the latter case, the hierarchical, tree-like structure – such as we might see, for example, within a company's organization chart – returns. To state that the fluid and acentrical sea of the Web is inhabited by hierarchically organized entities might seem a contradiction in terms. Yet, what appears on the surface does not always coincide with the reality of the Web; as evinced by the fact that the hierarchy is easily eluded if, for example, one accesses a website from a sub-domain rather than from its front page. On the other hand, the horizontal nature of the Web also appears to be contradicted by the actual centres, which tend to concentrate the vast majority of clicks in the direction of a minority of websites.

The internal structure of a website follows a hierarchical, tree-like logic due to the needs of designers, who must plan the ideal navigation paths through which users can intuitively access the resources they need. Rather than bringing into question the fluid nature of the Web, these structures are an expression of that which Manovich terms 'branching-type interactivity' (or else 'menu-based interactivity'). These terms refer to modes of content display and use that reflect the 'the logic of advanced and post-industrial societies, where almost every practical act involves choosing from some menu, catalog, or database'.[27] In order to make the decision procedures easier, designers create menus that branch on different levels. The presence of this hierarchy of levels is purely formal, and is often circumvented by a practice known as deep linking, which is the result of the tendency to build links that lead to a specific page (or a specific media object) of a website rather than its homepage. A search term using a search engine, for example, results in links to the webpage on which the specific search term appears, rather than to the website's front page. From a functional point of view, HTTP (the transfer protocol that rules the Web) does not differentiate between a deep link and other types of links. Furthermore, the organization that sets the standards of the Web, the W3C or World Wide Web

Consortium, has repeatedly stated that the practice of banning the deep links to one's own website demonstrates a misunderstanding of the technology, which risks undermining the functioning of the Web as a whole. The inventor of the Web, Tim Berners-Lee himself, states that hypertext would have been much more powerful if every node and every document was intrinsically equivalent. Everyone would have had an address and they would have existed together, in the same space: the space of information.[28] If it is an unquestionable fact that the pages that give life to the Web are all on the same level, it is nevertheless necessary to avoid some potential misunderstandings emerging from representations of specific websites that privilege a hierarchical vision of their contents. A hierarchy defined as such 'on paper' becomes misleading when it is simply transposed into the search for shared standards capable of giving rise to an archetypical image of the Web.

What is more interesting is the practice of representing the Web, or its segments, by beginning from a specific node, or from 'clusters', which are circumscribed groups of highly interrelated nodes. That these types of visualizations are in the majority evinces a need commonly manifest in the history of human thought: when humans face immensity, they react by circumscribing their perspective; clutching to a few, limited elements so as not to give in to vertigo. Similarly, examining a single node and its connections is analogous to focusing on a star within its galaxy; attempting to contemplate cyberspace would mean becoming lost in unfathomable complexity. Communication media has always been characterized by the circumscription of experience within a physically delimited form: the surface of papyrus, the page of a book, the frame of a picture, the width of a cinema screen, the length of a monitor. All these interfaces are based on the same convention: the experience goes beyond the 'onscreen space'.[29] When we face the 'internal space' of a small portion of the Web, the mind automatically implies the 'external space' – the vertiginous infinity of the connections of the Net. No wonder, then, that artists and designers prefer partial representations of the Web to those that seek to represent the complexity of the whole.

The Search for a Centre

In the attempt to give life to images of the Web, there is a tendency to search for a centre – not, however, in the Euclidean sense, but in the sense of the semiotic dance which is, in the words of Deleuze and Guattari, a 'black hole of subjectivity'.[30] In Deleuze and Guattari's interpretation, the face is a 'condenser of significance'. It is the most pregnant part of the body, providing the highest number of meanings, and 'the Icon proper to the signifying regime'.[31] Recovering traits of 'faceity' means, then, to fall into the black hole of subjectivity: the place where we live with our conscience, our feelings, and our passions. In a comparable way, constructing representations that reduce the complexity of the Web to an arbitrary centre upon which to focus leads us to become sunk within the black hole of our subjectivity. Most representations of the Web, I contend, are ruined by the often unconscious attempt to recover a sort of 'faceity' – a face to recognize.

Megan Gould's *Go Ogle* (2005)[32] emphasizes this tendency. The project is constituted by a series of composite images representing the mathematical averages of the first 100 images retrieved from a Google search engine query for a specific word or phrase. The results, 'a visualization of intersections between Boolean logic and the popular imagination', appear mostly as a bunch of unidentifiable pixels, although a recognizable form does emerge occasionally: the Linux penguin, a can of Coke, or a butterfly, to give a few examples. These last two images evince the innate desire of humans to provide a subjective visual synthesis, an intelligible form for an otherwise overwhelmingly complex reality. Just as in the majority of the representations of the Web, these images evince the attempt to put a face to, or to recognize ourselves, within an abstract reality, to unify an *irreducible plurality*. In Deleuze and Guattari's interpretation, the plural cannot be reduced to unity, it cannot become part of a totality, nor follow any subject. In this interpretative frame, it could be assumed that the pluralities in the Web have to be put on a level of consistency, or immanence: that is, a field that ignores the differences of level, size and distance. In other words, the Web should be represented as giving up on any individual consciousness in favour of a collective consciousness subject to a perpetual becoming.

The hypothesis of a 'search for a centre' can also be explored through projects that have emphasized features that might be missed when navigating with the usual browsers. In this sense, the project *The Web Stalker* (1997)[33] by the collective I/O/D (Matthew Fuller, Colin Green and

Simon Pope), is paradigmatic. In order to oppose the forms of navigation imposed by the browsers of that time, the collective replaced the
tired metaphor of the page with the display of links as circular lines.
A further example is *Web Tracer* (2001)[34] by NullPointer (Tom Betts),
which featured software aimed at displaying the structure of the Web
through 'a three dimensional molecular diagram, with pages as nodes
(atoms) and links as the strings (atomic forces) that connect those nodes
together'.[35] Both these projects can be said to *centre the point*, meaning
that they build their representations of the connections among nodes
starting from a specific URL that, in both cases, is put at the centre of
the display. A final successful project is *Social Circle* (2004)[36] by Marcus
Wescamp. In this case, the focus is on the networks that exist within
mailing lists. Here, a display through lines and circles is chosen, while
the maps that are highlighted show which participants and which topics are central within the examined group.

I chose these three projects for their 'historical' importance and for
their influence. However, one might analyse any of a number of recent
applications – for example, TouchGraph,[37] which is a popular means for
Facebook users to display a map of their own social network – to demonstrate that, in the attempt to give form to images of the Web or its
specific nodes, the tendency to search for a centre is constant.

Invisible Processes

Apart from this centralizing tendency, it is worth noticing that as
data spread, 'they also need to be managed, regulated and interpreted
into patterns that are comprehensible to humans', as Australian artist
and theorist Anna Munster points out. Munster's thought is based on
the distinction between recognizing, 'to see something already seen',
and perceiving: 'what we see as patterns, visualisations and diagrams
are the perceptible end of data'. 'To make something perceptible as a
data visualisation is to make it recognisable, which is not in the least
similar to perceiving a thing.'[38] Recalling recent research on perception
in work by Brian Massumi and Erin Manning, Munster points out that
what human beings cannot perceive within the constant displays of
data are the 'processes, both conceptual and computational, that render
pattern and relationships among the data'. Activities such as conduct-
ing a search using Google or collecting RSS feeds, for example, 'increas-

ingly makes this *manipulation* of data *invisible*'. In other words, the forms through which flows of data give themselves to human senses hide the very processes through which the data come into relation with each other, are structured into wholes, and finally displayed. It is banal to note that the logic ruling the way data are presented to users are never neutral, but reflect the strategies and economic interests of those groups with the power to enforce them. Paraphrasing Eyal Weizman, we might state that economic interests (politics) leave their marks in the forms that the Web (space) takes.[39]

In any case, 'these nonvisualised processes have become the imperceptible of data visualisation'; that is to say, what human subjects cannot recognize. However, those very processes that cannot be perceived by humans happen to constitute the natural environment for machines and the techniques of information analysis. Discussing that which she terms the 'disjunction-inversion between the perceptible and the imperceptible in humans and computational machines', Munster identifies an interstitial space in which fascinating artistic practices and aesthetic investigations may take place, as demonstrated by works such as *ShiftSpace* (2006),[40] *MAICgregator* (2009),[41] and *Traceblog* (2008).[42] Following this reasoning, we can see that the path beginning with the introduction of the GUI and leading up to its 2.0 version can be seen as progressively blurring the machinical processes underlying the flow of data, as well as blurring the distinctions between game and work, and users and knowledge corporations. By quoting Olia Lialina and her research on the 'vernacular Web',[43] Munster emphasizes that in Web 2.0 it is 'the search engines, the blogs, the social media that provide an already scripted space for users to play around in and have a good time'. Munster compares this to the experiments that took place during the 1990s, in which artists such as Jodi or Heath Bunting manipulated deep layers of code, hence touching the modes that allow the users to visually display networked information:

> During this early phase of web design there were no pre-packaged methods for formatting the way a web page was displayed. All graphic and stylistic elements had to be laid out in HTML script that 'told' the web browser how to format the page for on line display. For a relatively short period, both artists and designers had a measure of

access to the 'source code' of the web and this resulted in a lot of play with HTML aesthetics.[44]

In Munster's theory, the systems of automatic collection of data that typify Web 2.0 platforms play a crucial role:

> Users deploying such aggregators are usually not aware of what the parameters are for extracting and determining the stream or 'pattern' of information brought together. The processes of making the data meaningful – that is, what holds this data together in an aggregate is not immediately available to us. Automatic aggregation tends to perform operations that reduce the relations between data to commonalities rather than differences. This may be of crucial importance in the aggregation of news data where conflicting rather than similar perspectives about an item actually comprise what is meaningful about it. But techniques such as aggregation smooth out these differentials and present us instead with a flattened landscape of information. The sources, processes and contexts, which make information meaningful, are rendered imperceptible.[45]

This very situation (which anticipates an 'Age of Imperceptibility') requires, according to Munster, that networked arts and critics move without hesitation towards research that unveils the *hidden* processes of 'data undermining', in order to provide 'arenas for generating data differently', that is to say 'alternative social-political spaces for knowledge generation rather than mere knowledge discovery (the goal of data mining)'.[46] Taking up Munster's theory, we might also speak of fictions as those forms of the Web that hide the level of process, and provide a false reality by pretending that data are derived from the users' interaction with the flows, rather than as a consequence of decisions made by those who rule the processes themselves. The Google page on which the user is provided with the results of their search encounters a double fiction. First, that it is possible to provide a stable representation of the pages of the Web containing the search term, for just as the user is reading those results, more pages are being added, just as others are disappearing. The second fiction is that the result of the search is objective, rather than the result of processes instantiated by the algorithm that rules the search engine, as well as by other variables related to the interaction between human beings, hardware and software (not to mention that the geographical position of the IP assigned to the computer connected to the Internet changes the modes through which Google *lets itself* be interacted with by the user).[47]

Form and Function

I would like, now, to focus on the specific function of form on the Web. Media theorist Alexander Galloway proposes that the purpose of the Web's form is to charm users, just as cinema and television attempted to do, by 'dragging them in'. Galloway asks: How can a *medium* that is not based on narrative or time succeed in this aim? If it is actually anarchical, how can it give rise 'to such a compelling, intuitive experience for the user'? Taking up the concept of *continuity* from film theory, Galloway explains that 'a decentralized network composed of many different data fragments' makes use of a 'set of techniques practiced by webmasters that, taken as totality, create this pleasurable, fluid experience for the user'. These techniques – for example, 'conceal the source', 'eliminate dead links', 'true identity', 'remove barriers', 'highest speed possible' – represent 'a set of abstract protological rules for the application layer', that is, the level at which content is produced. Thus, it is through form itself that it is possible to assemble the fragmented contents of the web into a continuous experience, as pleasurable as cinema or television. In summary, the Internet functions according to formal techniques, or 'techniques of continuity', that are the standards for the production of contents. By applying these protocols, a heterogeneous and fragmented plurality of contents presents itself to the user as a fluid and rewarding experience, hence the term 'Web surfing'.[48] To Galloway's theory, I would add that the aesthetic experience is only one of many potential ways of experiencing the flow of digital data. Perhaps Web surfing is the most pleasurable, yet one is also in contact with these flows when withdrawing money from a cash machine. Whatever the mode of contact, the flow, before and after this contact, will keep on flowing and none of the forms, strategies or fictions used to fix it will ever contain this unrelenting reality.

In addition to the interfaces through which individuals access digitally transmitted data, form can also be examined in relation to databases. The form of a database, as the modality in which data are classified and organized, is crucial to network society. As most of the Web's contents are organized within more or less complex databases, the form that designers and programmers have given to these digital archives becomes central to building the experience, including aesthetic experience, of this medium.[49] As Lovink points out, 'allowing oneself to be led by an endlessly branching database is the cultural constant of the early 21st century'.[50] Indeed, shortly after the birth of the Web, scholars began to wonder about a *database aesthetics*. In 1998, Manovich wrote an essay entitled *Database as Symbolic Form*,[51] in which he states that the database can be considered 'a new symbolic form of a computer age'. Manovich contrasts the database with narrative, as the form that has traditionally dominated human culture, and which places elements into a sequence. In contrast, the database no longer functions sequentially, no longer possesses a clear beginning and end; rather it places its elements on a single plane.

Due to the extraordinarily rapid growth of a constantly expanding and changing information cloud,[52] more recent research has focused on the activity of *searching* that has become the predominant way in which individuals relate to information and culture. The romantic activity of *surfing* is increasingly less appropriate – like wandering in the desert without a compass, it offers the possibility of adventure, but is not really amenable to the purpose of finding data in the shortest time possible. The present hypertrophic growth of the database, then, gives rise to a *search culture*, or a 'Society of Query'. As Lovink observes, this is a culture in which any distinction between 'patrician insight' and 'plebeian gossip', or between high and low, disappears. The fundamental value becomes the popularity of the contents and not their intrinsic *truth*.[53]

'Search is the way we now live',[54] states Lovink, and it is clearly this new cultural orientation, more that the form that is given to databases, that hegemonic players such as Google are able to strategically capitalize on. That which Siva Vaidhanathan terms the 'Googlization of Everything',[55] is obviously a highly complex issue requiring a more thorough analysis than I can provide here. I will leave this for future analysis, in order to complete my reasoning on the way the fiction of form works on the Web.[56]

The 'Communicating Block'

To my mind, Mario Costa's 'flow aesthetics' offers one of the best theorizations of the specificity of digital networks. To Costa, the way that contemporary media interact with each other can be described by employing three central concepts. The first is *multimediality*, which implies a 'strong subject' who 'puts together and activates different sources of information in order to put the meaning into effect', but which in actuality offers a mere juxtaposition of media, ultimately reducing the technology to the role of mere scenography.[57] The second concept, *hybridization*, dates back to McLuhan. Compared to multimediality, hybridization produces new sensory configurations and opens up new forms of experience, 'free from the somnambulism brought by the prolonged action of a single *medium*'.[58] Costa's third concept develops from that of the 'image block', which Paul Virilio uses to describe the necessary relations of interdependence between images.[59] With new communication technologies, Costa sees the 'image block' replaced by a 'communicating block': technologies 'that work, or end up working, the same way and that have, or end up having, the same essence'.[60] As opposed to the hybridization process, the communicating block 'derealizes', because it deprives the 'thing' of its reality and turns it into an 'image'. It accumulates 'energy of the same kind and draws any mode of experience into itself'.[61] In other words, any other energy is only aimed at fuelling the machinical energy of the 'communicating block'.

In regard to new communication technologies, Costa writes that 'the construction of the form is neglected in favour of the *communicational flow* and the *events* it reflects. It is these elements that are the form and that are to be considered the new *material* of the "art"'.[62] The destruction of form is a result of the nature of the technology. And yet, it is the very awareness that aesthetic research is unavoidably turned away from form that leads Costa to refocus on the communicational flow, and how to prevent that flow from becoming the 'communicating block'. The practice of hybridization needs to be reactivated, in order to establish 'non pertinent relationships for a communication that is content free but aimed at aesthetic intentions'.[63] To do so, one has to disappear as emitter in order to serve as the 'creator of intra-technological relationships'; in a direct relationship between human beings and media the logic of media inevitably ends by making the human accede to the media's requests. However, the relationships between media must be kept 'non pertinent', meaning that they must be put in contradiction with each other, and made to work inconsistently. This communication must also be 'shallow, tautological and self-referential': a pure exchange of signs that is not subjected to the search for meaning. Aesthetic value will be given, finally, by the simple and inconsistent operations of media working without recourse to the symbolic or to meaning:[64]

> Only then will it be possible to talk about an aesthetics of the communicating block, of a flow that is then purged, removed from the 'communicating block' and actually different from it: there, in fact, the technologies take part in dialogue among themselves by means of human intermediation and in doing so they mix and mess everything up, while here they take part in dialogue among themselves without any intermediation and without saying anything. It is only in this apparent receding of the technologies, in this letting them be and allowing them to speak among themselves in the form of aesthetics, that we can still stand separated from them and keep them at a distance.[65]

In this sense, John F. Simon Jr's *Every Icon* (1997)[66] comes to mind. Simon Jr's work is an applet Java, a form of software executed by a web browser that executes the following algorithm:

> Given: An icon described by a 32 x 32 grid
> Allowed: Any element of the grid to be colored black or white
> Shown: Every icon

The applet calculates the speed of the computer processor and, beginning from a grid in which all the squares are white, shows every possible combination of black and white squares until the whole grid turns black. During this process the applet will draw every image that can be composed by a grid of 1,024 squares, which means that, processing 100 icons per second, it will take more than one year to complete all the possible combinations of the first line and over five billions years to complete the second. As the artist himself writes:

While *Every Icon* is resolved conceptually, it is unresolvable in practice. In some ways the theoretical possibilities outdistance the time scales of both evolution and imagination. It posits a representational system where computational promise is intricately linked to extraordinary duration and momentary sensation.[67]

In *Every Icon*, a computer is programmed to carry out a task that it will never be able to fully accomplish. The process takes place with no human interaction and the technologies – the computer processor, the applet Java, the browser – are engaged in a dialogue that ends in itself. Thus *Every Icon* evinces all the elements prescribed by Costa in order to prevent the communicating block, leaving them to exist in and for themselves, and revealing themselves as pure exteriority.

An Unconcerned Interest

The path recommended by Costa appears, however, to be open only to artists. Is there, then, any hope for salvation for the 'common people'? Are all of those who are unable to activate aesthetic registers merely victims of the flows and the resulting communication blocks? To be honest, it is unrealistic to imagine any other fate. And yet, we can perhaps envision one possible mode of escape through the work of Milanese artist Marco Cadioli.[68] Cadioli, a photographer, takes pictures of landscapes, faces, gestures – of all that which one might term 'everyday life'. What distinguishes his work, however, is that the subjects of his pictures live inside the Web.[69] If we think of the Net as constantly moving, the attempt to fix it that appears to be expressed within Cadioli's work might seem somehow strange, if not futile. However, it is the very ephemerality of the forms of the Web that allows us to appreciate the gesture of fixing upon one unrepeatable moment in the liquid flowing of cyberspace, and replacing it in the physical, immutable world of photography. This is an eternal artistic gesture – an attempt to fix what cannot be fixed, like closing one's hand in a fist in the flow of a river. In Cadioli's recent project *Remap Berlin* (2009),[70] Cadioli hacked Google Earth. Having taken pictures in Twinity,[71] a realistic 3-D replica of Berlin, Cadioli geo-localizes them in Google maps, and uploads them on the photo sharing community Panoramio, which is linked to Google Earth. Once they have been reviewed and accepted for inclusion,

Cadioli's photos of a 3D replica of Berlin can be found as 'Popular photos' in Google Earth. Thus, Cadioli's pictures appear side-by-side with those of hundreds of tourists and amateur photographers, thus proving that, at least to Google's algorithms, net photography and traditional photography are equivalent. A series of pictures entitled *Temporary End of the World* feature images of the limits reached by the programmers in the development of the virtual Berlin. The images of these borderline spaces are emblematic of the fluid nature of the medium itself: the *end of the world* immortalized by Cadioli's photography will simply no longer exist tomorrow; in the same way that each form taken by the Web represents a snapshot of a reality that is already mutating even as it is given a fixed shape. The act of framing an image in the constant flow of data appearing on the monitor is an apparently aimless action that fulfils only the artist's personal need; yet, this characteristic aims at removing Cadioli's gesture from the filter of creativity on command, a filter that kills any form of artistic expression and turns the artists themselves into employees – as Manetas would say: 'freelance employees of the other employees, the curators of the exhibitions'.[72] The immediacy of the gesture gives a well-rounded artistic dignity to Cadioli's work and – at the same time – it removes his work from the sphere of communication, the true enemy of art.[73] In the Milanese 'net reporter's' work, I think I see the only possible escape from the tunnel in which the forms of the Web seem to be imprisoned.

We might define this as that which Perniola, in *Contro la Comunicazione*,[74] terms 'unconcerned interest'.[75] In his discussion of the effects of mass media communication, the Italian aesthetologist Perniola emphasizes that present society has become, though communication, the place of a *pensée unique* that claims to flatten the whole of existence under its own weight. Mass media communication escapes every determination, aspiring to 'be at the same time one thing, its opposite and everything in between'.[76] By exposing the message to all its possible varieties, it ends by erasing it – its aim is always, in fact, the decay of all the contents. For Perniola, the only alternative to the effects of communication is an aesthetic feeling of things, a factual aesthetics capable of reintroducing certain qualities into society and culture: feelings such as economic unconcern, or an unconcerned interest, 'an unconcerned *habitus* that stimulates a recognition just because it is not connected to an economic interest', along with discretion, moderation, the will to challenge, wit and seduction.[77]

Following Perniola's reasoning, I believe that the only way to rescue the Web, its 'inhabitants' and its forms from the sad fate for which they seem destined is a combative, rather than a contemplative and conciliatory aesthetic approach. Aesthetics must provide the conceptual premise for a global strategy of 'resistance' to mass media communication. After all, how else can one escape the marketing logic pervading the Web than through a feeling of 'unconcerned interest'? I do not mean that the need for an economic return must be refused, but I do believe that the approval and admiration of a community of peers must be placed before commercial interests. In his conception of aesthetics and 'the unconcerned nature of the behaviours, actions, life-style that leads it'[78] as an alternative economy of symbolic goods, Perniola explicitly recalls the French sociologist Pierre Bourdieu. In my own interpretation of unconcerned interest, Pekka Himanen's theory also has a crucial role. Himanen is concerned with hacker ethics, and the way that it is guided by values such as passion, play and freedom, as opposed to the 'capitalistic' ethics that place economic interests before everything (and everyone) else. Social values such as the sharing of work and the activity of caring for others in active resistance to the perspective of Social Darwinism can support the creation of an aesthetic conception of existence. This existence is not aimed at the mere consumption of goods, but at creating *a life that is worth living* and – simultaneously – at attaining the appreciation of one's own community.[79]

In conclusion, if the strategy of capital is finally realized through form, we must fight the war on this very field. I can no longer consider resistance as separate from relationships of power;[80] I would rather formulate strategies that allow the expression of difference. In this direction, an unconcerned interest represents that which Michel de Certeau terms 'uncodeable difference';[81] that which disturbs the functioning of the system. The only way to free the forms of the Web is through becoming aware of its fictions; an awareness that allows us to construct aesthetic strategies not reducible to their 'unregulatable and constructable surface'.[82]

Optical and Haptic

The objects bathe in the dream ... and however they are painted with
a matter that returns them ... nearly tangible.
Federico Fellini, *La dolce vita* (1960)

In the 1930s, in the early stages of visual culture, Walter Benjamin
published a now-famous essay on the reproduction of art that I believe
may be useful to introduce the antinomy between optical and haptic
experience.[1] For Benjamin, one paradox of the 'society of images' is the
fact that, in both the production and the experience of images, there is
a tendency towards tactilization. For Benjamin, this was evident in the
Kunstwissenschaft, a historical and scientific school of thought concerning art that developed between the nineteenth and twentieth centuries,
and whose key protagonists were Heinrich Wölfflin and Aloïs Riegl.

Theoretical Premises

Wölfflin is to be credited for one of the most accurate theorizations
of the 'classical' dualism between linear and painterly art.[2] Wölfflin
links the linear figurative style of painting to tactile perception, to the
eye that works as a hand, touching the contour of the things; and the
painterly style to optical perception, to vision working as does the eye,
identifying shadow and chiaroscuro. Wölfflin does not, however, give
enough weight to the way that the linear works through lines, as a border that guides the eye, and the painterly through colours, whose chromatic varieties draw attention to tones regardless of their boundaries.
Wölfflin views the Renaissance as the art of quiet beauty, of full being,
and of haptic space, whereas the Baroque period is associated with the
unsteadiness of the event, and with the art of optical space.[3]

Riegl's name will recall his famous conceptualization of *Kunstwollen*,
an 'artistic will' aware of its purposes, and capable of dominating over
individualities and setting, in every age, the formal characteristics of
artefacts. In late Roman decorative art, Riegl sees a shift towards an
optical mode of perception, in which figures transcend the materiality
of the support and give the illusion that they are floating in space. The
tactile vision typical of the Egyptian style leaves the ground to the chi-
aroscuros and the image in the distance, and this happens right when

the barbaric invasion of the Roman Empire questions the conception of the body as a means of grace and introduces a view of spirituality based on the transcendence of the body.

To Riegl, then, the history of art evinces a shift from haptic to optical modes of perception, proceeding from ancient art's entrapment within a flat dimension to an intermediate stage in late Roman style, leading to the representation of endless depth in modern art. The first stage is characterized by a sensible-objective conception, as in Egyptian statues that appear from afar to be flat but that take on life as one gets closer, and only reveal their true refinement when touched. The second stage evinces a vision somewhere between near and far, as in the 'half shadows' that do not disturb the smoothness of the tactile surface. An example is the classical Greek temple, best enjoyed from a moderate distance, which elicits both tactile and optical perception. The third stage, in late Roman art, breaks with tactility through the use of deep shadows and balances the blurry (excessive) chromatism by emphasizing contours, and this is the age of late Roman art.[4]

Riegl considers these simultaneously as shifts of style and of world-views (*Weltanschauung*). In ancient Oriental cultures, he identifies an objective view of the world and a tactile mode of perception, whereas the Greeks and Indo-Germanic peoples are associated with a subjective worldview, an optical mode of perception and a distanced form of vision. In modern art, Riegl identifies a comparable difference in the tactility of Romance cultures and the optical orientation of Germanic cultures.[5]

From Riegl (and Wickhoff), Benjamin adopts the belief that perception is not static but historical – that styles of perception and of figuration develop together. In the partial return to tactility that characterizes late Roman art, Benjamin sees this evolution breaking apart and re-forming. In the art of the late nineteenth and early twentieth centuries, Benjamin sees a recovery of the tactile, and of archaic and expressive modes that are in closer contact with the object. Benjamin credits this shift mainly to the Dada movement, which made the pictorial image tactile.[6] The most significant influence, however, is that of photography and cinema. For Benjamin, as opposed to Riegl, the evolution of styles of perception is bound up with technical and social conditions. In the famous example in which the cathedral leaves its place and ends up in the studio of the art lover, Benjamin conceives of photography as a 'coming forward' (*entgegenkommen*) towards the user, a coming 'at hand' of the work that has lost its auratic uniqueness.[7]

According to philosopher of aesthetics Andrea Pinotti, the phenomenon in which the image becomes tactile is more overt in relation to cinema. According to Benjamin's theory of shock, art and literature revisit shocking experiences and create shocks themselves. Pinotti, however, contends that cinematic technique presents the viewer with jerky, disjointed images that reflect the abrupt gestures of the modern age – taking a photograph, phone calls, assembly lines, crossing a busy road – all those activities that characterize the age of the 'aura' can be included in the category of the 'tactile'.[8]

Among many important contributions to the issue of the antinomy between the optical and haptic,[9] I will consider Deleuze's essay on Francis Bacon.[10] In the essay, Deleuze discusses the complex relationship between the eye and the hand in painting, and states: 'It is obviously not enough to say that the eye judges and the hands execute. The relationship between the hand and the eye is infinitely richer, passing through dynamic tensions, logical reversals, and organic exchanges and substitutions.'[11] Deleuze systematizes the heterogeneous experiences connecting the hand and eye into four categories: digital, tactile, manual and haptic. In the digital mode, 'the hand is reduced to the finger'.[12] The eye rules over the hand and vision is internalized, giving rise to an 'ideal' optical space in which vision captures shapes through an optical code. At least in its early stages, this optical space is still connected to tactile referents, such as depth and contour, which restrain and resist opticalization. In the manual mode, the relationship is reversed, and tactile elements take precedence over the optical, giving rise to a 'space without form and movement and a movement without rest'.[13] The manual leads to the haptic, that which represents the tactile function of sight. Free from any subjection to the hand and the eye, the haptic is completely different from the optical mode: 'Painters paint with their eyes, but only insofar as they touch with their eyes.'[14]

For Deleuze, these spheres are not separate. Deleuze believes in a synesthetic vision, in which each sense organ constantly recalls and translates the other. Between noise, taste and scent a kind of 'existential communication' takes place that Deleuze terms 'pathic', meaning that it is *nonrepresentative* of the sensation.[15] This non-oppositional vision of the sensory system is clear in Deleuze's analysis of Bacon's works, in which he states, for example, that in the triptych of 1976 it is possible to touch the quivering of the bird's wings that cut into the head.[16] It is also evident in *Mille Plateaux*, in which the term haptic is used in preference to tactile, as it 'does not establish an opposition between two sense organs but rather invites the assumption that the eye may fulfil this nonoptical function'.[17] Following Riegl, Deleuze also reconstructs a dialectic between the optical and haptic in Western art. Furthermore, as in Riegl, Deleuze identifies the apotheosis of 'closer vision' in Egyptian art, in which the flat surface allows the eye to work as if it is touching, and ensuring, in the Egyptian *Kunstwollen*, the unification of touch and sight as closely as if they were ground and horizon. In Greek art, but also in Byzantine art and in contemporary abstract painting (in Mondrian, for example), Deleuze identifies a mode in which the hand is subjected to the eye. As tactile connotations are no longer necessary, abstract forms give life to a purely optical space.[18] Deleuze conceives of Barbarian and Gothic art as a period of violent manuality, in which the hand moves in such a rapid, lively way that the eye struggles to keep up with it. In contemporary art, the manual period is realized in the work of Jackson Pollock and the Action Painting movement. In the practices of these artists, Deleuze identifies a double reversal: first, the hand violently escapes the control of the eye, the so-called 'painter's blindness'; and secondly, the horizon becomes the ground due to the painter's frantic activity within a work of art that is no longer placed on an easel but is lying on the floor.[19] Deleuze positions Bacon's work between the extremes of the pure opticality of abstract art and the manuality of Action Painting. At first, Bacon is haptic-Egyptian, but there will soon be a rupture with the tactility of his form, and the explosion of an 'absolute optical space'. Yet even this is temporary, as the violence of the hand breaks in, triggered by the diagram, that is to say by the hiding of the figurative data that takes over the painting and turns it into a 'catastrophe-painting'.[20] In Bacon's work, Deleuze identifies a balance between the dissolution and resolution of form. Indeed, this 'conservatory vision' is discussed in a number of passages of *Mille Plateaux*, such as the following, which speaks of the dangers of a violent destratification:

You have to keep enough of the organism for it to reform each dawn; and you have to keep small supplies of significance and subjectification, if only to turn them against their own systems when the circumstances demand it, when things, persons, even situations, force you to; and you have to keep small rations of subjectivity in sufficient quantity to enable you to respond to the dominant reality.[21]

In conclusion, for Deluze the haptic is a space in which tactile and optical modes are in balance; a space of interaction in which the activity of the spectator is not that of reception, but of perception.

Tactile Modalities

At this point, I wish to consider a scientific analysis of the modes of optical and tactile perception. In the mid-twentieth century, the Hungarian Gestalt psychologist Géza Révész distinguished between an *active tactile modality* termed haptic and tending towards exploration, and a *passive tactile modality* based on the mere feeling of contact upon the skin.[22] I have made use of Marco Mazzeo's schema of Révész's list of the ten features typical features of haptic perception:[23]

1) *Stereoplastic principle*: the subject who wants to know an object, in order to realize its materiality, first looks for a generic plastic impression in it, ignoring the information of the form that may still partially emerge from the first impact. Even more than for sight, the object perceived through tactility occurs as part of the outside world separate from the subject.

2) *Successive perception principle*: the haptic perception takes place through a series of fragmented tactile actions, even if the object is so small it fits in the palm of the hand. Just as in visual perception, the formal elements experienced in succession cannot give rise to a clear global representation.

3) *Kinematic principle*: the haptic perception of the form can only take place through the movement of the sensory system. In optical perception, the opposite is the case: the movement upsets the evidence of the form, even in the case of particularly small forms.

4) *Metric principle*: the structural identification of an object requires an orientation, in regard to the position and balance of both the

parts and the whole. Again, in visual function the opposite is the case: the spatial relationships are recognized in an act of immediate perception.[24]

5) *Receptive and intentional attitude*: these two attitudes, which take place synchronically in visual function, are diachronic in haptic function. From the tactile receptive attitude come only those features actually concerning the perception of the form, while the intentional attitude gives rise to the perception of the actual structural features of the object.

6) *Tendency to establish types and schemata*: haptic perception is focused on exemplification, and hence on the intention to know the general features of the object and to classify it according to well known types and groups. Haptic type images become the bases of the concrete figures of form, or schematic forms free from structural details.

7) *Tendency towards transposition*: this tendency is evident in people who become blind late in life, and is characterized by the opticalization of haptic data. It sometimes has a negative effect upon haptic experience.

8) *Structural analysis principle*: haptic perception tends to recognize structure rather than perceiving form. This implies that the immediacy, simultaneity, homogeneity, precision and speed of visual perception are opposed to the indirectness, the slowness, and the imprecision of haptic perception of form, which works consecutively.

9) *Constructive synthesis principle*: after the preliminary impressions and the structural analysis, a process of construction begins that assembles all the components of form, partially sensory and partially cognitive, into a homogeneous whole. The result is an abstract and verbal chain of partial structures within the form of a schematic image (regarding this issue, Révész emphasizes that constructive integration does not mean form creation).

10) *Subjective formative activity*: the tendency to create forms is also present, in a specific way, in the haptic function; this phenomenal specificity represents a challenge to the presumed universality of the Gestalt laws of perception that, as Révész notes, arise from the nature of the single sensory organs.

The Skin of the Film

Révész offers a kind of toolkit that enables us to examine the perceptual modalities that typify new media. First, however, it is crucial to recall the contribution offered by Canadian scholar Laura U. Marks in *The Skin of the Film*.[25] Beginning with Riegl, whom she discovered through Margaret Iverson,[26] Marks states that 'haptic visuality' characterizes those experiences in which the onlooker's inclination to perception is emphasized – as when we linger on the flat surface of a screen before realizing what it is that we are actually watching. These haptic images only gradually become figures, thus allowing the viewer to perceive the texture of the image rather than just the represented objects. To Marks, optical perception privileges the representative power of the image, whereas haptic perception privileges its material presence, and involves proprioceptive and kinesthetic bodily sensations.[27] In actuality, both modalities are vital: if it is true that 'it is hard to look closely at a lover's skin with optical vision' it is equally true that 'it is hard to drive a car with haptic vision'.[28] The distinction between the materiality of the haptic and the abstraction of the optical mode is a further significant link between Marks and Riegl. Here, Marks differs from Riegl's view of the non-Western tradition as a mere stage in the evolution towards modern optical representation. Recalling Deleuze and Guattari's art of the nomad, which has no external reference point, or the abstract line that is a sign of the creative power of non figurative representation, Marks states that the optical and haptic are alternative, rather than competing, traditions of representation. Marks also rejects the view that the tactile is a predominantly feminine form of perception.

Marks' vision is of a historical cycle in which perception is always more or less optical and more or less haptic. This dynamic is highlighted in Noël Burch's theory of cinema, according to which this medium originally recalled the spectator not through the analogue representation of deep space 'but more im-mediately';[29] although the subsequent standardization of the language of cinema leads narrative identification to replace bodily identification.

What, then, are the elements that give moving images their haptic nature? In film and in video, Marks identifies shifts in focus, graininess and the effects of over- or under-exposure as elements that resist mere object recognition and give rise to a relationship with the screen as a

whole. The use of haptic images combined with sound, and the movements of the camera and editing, establish a relationship with haptic
images that is even more bodily and multisensory. Yet, both video and
film become increasingly haptic as they age, and the chemical deterio-
ration of film and the demagnetization of video tape produce a faded
and blurry feel. Some effects specific to film are optical printing,[30] the
solarization of the image and the direct hand work on the film. These
techniques have led some to argue that film is tactile and video optical,
yet Marks does not accept this distinction, affirming that her interpretation of tactile visuality rather concerns the ways the eye is bound to
'touch' an object.[31]

There are three tactile elements specific to video. The first is making
an image from a signal. Marks (quoting Ron Burnett)[32] highlights that
the immateriality of the video image renders it more unstable than the
film, which still originates from a material support (the film itself). In
video, the control of elements of the image such as contrast and shade is
highly negotiable, whereas in the film, these depend on chemical reactions, and so cannot easily be edited once the film has been developed.
The second point is video's lower contrast ratio than film, which leads
to a closer approach to the screen, and hence to a more tactile perception. The third element is digital imaging, which makes products able
to be manipulated (as in Manovich's *numerical representation principle*, according to which new media become programmable).[33] These features
lead Marks to contest Marshall McLuhan's definition of video as a 'cold'
medium, with a tendency to 'keep the distance'. To Marks, the tactile
features of the video make it a 'hot' medium: 'It is the crisp resolution
into optical visuality that makes an image cool and distant.'[34]

We might consider Marks' theorization of the haptic image in relation to the Deleuzian 'time-imaging' strategy. For Deleuze, narrative
structure seeks constantly to triumph over the discontinuity of the
cinematic image. As the haptical image encourages spectators to use
memory and imagination rather than merely following the narrative,
Marks observes that haptic images can protect spectators from the image, and the image from the spectator. For example, in the Palestinian
artist Mona Hatoum's video *Measures of Distances* (1988),[35] the haptical-
ity of the vision protects the images from the awareness of the spectator
contemplating the naked body of a woman, until the video resolves into

an optical image. Similarly, it the haptic images that give the feeling of gradually discovering and seeing for the first time what is in the image but is actually already known.[36]

Marks does not deal with 'haptic sound' in great detail in *Skin of the Film*, describing only the condition of 'haptic hearing', which takes place when subjects are surrounded by many, seemingly undifferentiated, sounds, and cannot immediately decide which to focus upon.[37] Similarly, new media are hardly mentioned in the work. They are, however, the subject of Marks' forthcoming work, an Islamic genealogy of new media art.[38] The premise of this work is an aniconic analogy between classical Islamic art and computer-based art: in both, the image demonstrates that the invisible is more significant than the visible.[39] This affinity extends to the relations among the levels of the visible, the readable and the invisible within Islamic and computer-based arts. In a further echo of Deleuze,[40] Marks speaks of a process of 'unfolding and enfolding' in which these levels instead become levels of the Image, of Information and of the Infinite. Thus Marks introduces a further plane-image into Deleuze's theory of signs – between the images and the infinite is information. In so doing, she takes possession of one specific premise of the conception that I have defined as diffuse aesthetics: that according to which contemporary visual culture is actually a culture of information. In Marks' model the three levels fold and enfold one another. Information enfolds from the infinite (that is, from Deleuze and Guattari's level of immanence) and the image, in turn, enfolds from information. As is well known, it is not possible to conceive the infinite (the state of virtuality) as such, even though its features may open, enfold and become actual in the form of the image. However, information can also enfold as an image, so that images and information begin to spin together in an infinite vortex of folding and enfolding. If Marks takes both a theoretical premise and a title from Deleuze and Guattari, perhaps her most significant intuition is to identify in the abstract and algorithmic lines of classical Islamic art the haptic space underlying new media.

The Optical/Haptic Antinomy on the Web

I would like, now, to use the theories discussed thus far to characterize the optical/haptic antinomy in relation to aesthetic experience on the Web.[41] Navigating through the Internet, we become familiar with interfaces that use both optical and haptic modes. I would like to formulate categories that, although approximate, allow us to differentiate between these experiences. I propose that we term those experiences in which the user touches the interface 'tactile experiences'. Virtual reality experiences are an obvious example, as one wears gloves that provide tactical experience and manage the navigation process. I would also like to include all those systems in which the interface is touched directly (without gloves), as in the project *Touch the Invisibles* (2008)[42] by Japanese artists Junji Watanabe, Eisuke Kusachi and Hideyuki Ando. In such experiences, sight has an ancillary function, contributing only the information necessary for touch to proceed with its exploration. For this reason, 'tactile experience' includes all those situations in which sight is a mere support to the hand. Regardless of whether one is touching an interface such as a mouse or a keyboard, the defining feature of this form of experience is that tactility is the mode of exploration, rather than simply being used to provide feedback. The Flash interfaces by Dutch artist Rafaël Rozendaal offer a clear example of tactile experiences that take place 'through the mouse' in his recent works *coldvoid.com* (2009) and *beefchickenpork.com* (2009). One touches, drags and tears, but almost nothing is contemplated. At the opposite side (and outside the Web), in the famous *PainStation* (2001) by Volker Morawe and Tilman Reiff, tactile interaction is not involved, but there is physical feedback that may be highly painful, such as an electric shock.

'Optical experiences' are those in which sight is the predominant sense involved. For example, watching a video on YouTube or lingering in front of images of passers-by relayed from a webcam on the top of a building, the user does not use the mouse or keyboard at all, they are dedicated to watching. One can also speak of optical experiences in any situation in which the eye leads and the hand serves only as a tool that enables the vision of the next image. When one clicks on the thumbnails in a Web photo album, there is clearly no tactile interaction, but only a functional action. The next image is the endpoint of a visual process, just as turning the pages of a book is subject to the act of reading.

Compared to the two types of experience briefly analysed above, it is possible to state that the distinguishing factor is a tendency specific to the interface: in one case, users are encouraged to foreground tactile perception, and hence to reduce the distance between themselves and the interface; in the other they are inclined towards contemplation, and hence to keep their distance. By including the users' own tendencies, however, we avoid a banal determinism. A touchscreen, for example, is neither definitely tactile nor definitely optical. The main contention is that the Web activates a constant shifting between tactical and optical modes, even within the same website. In fact, the Web demonstrates the ability of the *medium* itself to alternate between tactile and optical spaces, to hybridize them and to create intermediate stages between the two forms of perception. Thus, the Web amplifies the ambiguous quality possessed, most notably, by cinema. On the Web, optical and haptic are parts of a dialectic: the thesis of the Web as a haptic space is always as demonstrable as the thesis that the Web is an optical space. The point, however, is not to prove one thesis or the other, but to foreground the uniqueness of an experience that shifts constantly between the two modes of perception.

Reducing the Web to either the haptic or optical dimension would also lead us to ignore the fact that the Web contains more text than images. This is surprising, given that the 'society of the image' was inaugurated with photography, not to mention the intrinsic multimediality of the Web. Yet, even a quick examination of the most viewed websites in the world clearly shows that the most popular websites are those that privilege text, such as Google, Facebook, Wikipedia and Ebay. Even the success of YouTube and its progeny cannot reverse this situation, leading many media theorists to conclude that the Internet in fact inaugurates a shift back to writing. Of course, this is a contentious issue. In my opinion, the most convincing concepts are Roger Fidler's *mediamorphosis*[43] and Jay Bolter and Richard Grusin's *remediation*.[44] According to these theorists, new media always include features of previous media, though they transform or 'remediate' them. This, of course, recalls Marshall McLuhan's statement that 'the "content" of any medium is always another medium',[45] although both Fidler's and Bolter-Grusin's formulations show very clearly the distinct dynamics enacted by new media within a complex media system. We can conclude, then, that what is taking place is not a return to writing, but a metamorphosis or remediation of some characteristics of writing. In Manovich's words, it is the book as interface, with its language and its whole corollary of shared metaphors, which is adopted in the cultural interface that he defines as the *Human Computer Interface*.[46]

More to the point, the textual contents that are proliferating on the Web cannot simply be linked with either optical or haptic perception. Marks' theory of text as an algorithmic pattern of a haptic surface clearly applies to Islamic calligraphic art. It also appears applicable to computer-based ASCII art, such as Vuk Kosic's ASCII version of *Deep Throat* (*Deep ASCII*, 1998), or Jaromil's *forkbomb* (*ASCII Shell*, 2002). I do not believe, however, that this definition applies to the Web as such, for textual interfaces dangle somewhere in between optical and haptic modes. The tension between optical and haptic modes, then, is immanent to any perception that takes place within the medium. Similarly, the balance between optical and haptic modes that Deleuze identifies in Bacon's work is inapplicable, for on the Web we find a continuous dialectic between the modes. Any balance is always momentary and unsteady, and tends to give way to dialectic.

A constitutional element of any Web page that is worth mentioning in specific is the link. In Alexander Galloway's view, the 'link layer' is the physical means by which the Internet ('Internet layer') drives the contents produced by the 'application layer', which are turned into data by the 'transport layer'.[47]

Insofar as navigation requires the user to click on links, these constitute a tactile element on the Web, analogous to turning at a junction in the road by moving the steering wheel. On different webpages, links are highlighted in different ways: when within text, hypertext links are usually underlined, placed in bold type, differently coloured, or some combination of these options. When the link is shown using graphic elements such as keys, buttons or icons, however, the only limits are the web designers' imaginations, and we see varied and extravagant effects, from the most common rollover effects to a range of animated gifs, most of which are kitsch. Sometimes, links only reveal themselves when contacted by the mouse, in which case the text might change colour, or the button increase in size. Of course, web designers follow a certain grammar, as well as the rules of page composition. The point, however, is that users of a web page experience two forms of perception: in terms of optical perception they examine its composition, its possibilities and the positions of its links; a tactile mode takes over when users proceed to select one option by clicking on a link. This exemplifies the shifting tension between the two modes that, I have claimed, marks each and every experience on the Web.

In Web art or net.art, we find works that privilege optical perception and works that privilege the haptic, as well as a very rich *understory* of works that melt the two. An example of an optical work is *Eden.Garden 1.0* (2001)[48] by the duo Entropy8Zuper! (Auriea Harvey and Michaël Samyn). This uses a 3-D virtual reality device to develop an imaginary space filled with plants, animals and other objects. At first glance, this work actually works like a browser. It establishes features of the setting according to HTML tags that are in the page whose URL the user enters in application. It is possible to move the two characters, Adam and Eve, and to make them perform a series of actions typical of 3-D games, by using keys on the right and left of the keyboard. From my point of view, the interesting feature of this work is the use of 3-D graphics to create an environment that the eye continuously roams over, searching for new potentials – in a way, *Eden.Garden 1.0* could be considered a forerunner to Second Life. Walking among the animals and the other wonders of the 3-D garden, the eye constantly keeps its distance from the screen, in order to gain the widest vista of Eden possible. Hence, this work gives rise to a characteristically optical experience. The example of a haptic work, John F. Simon Jr's *Unfolding Object* (2002),[49] has been chosen mostly because of the assonance between its title and that of Marks' forthcoming *Enfoldment and Infinity*. According to the artist:

> *Unfolding Object* is an endless book that rewrites itself and whose use dictates its content. ... The idea for *Unfolding Object* comes from many sources. Physicist David Bohm theorizes about a level of information below the quantum level where all matter is interconnected. In his terminology, the object unfolds information about itself. The outward expression of an object is the unfolding of this potential. I detected a similarity between Bohm's description of nature and software objects. The potential for the *Unfolding Object* is contained in the source code, which is unfold (sic) by the interaction of the user. Another source was Klee, who wrote about how a drawing is defined by its cosmogenic moment, when the symmetry of the blank page is broken by the first mark, the first decision of the creator.[50]

In response to users' clicks on the relevant website, a white square opens up and its shape evolves, so that it is a kind of collaborative sculpture, encouraging users to take part in its creation. Interacting with the Unfolding Object can never be distanced or contemplative, it necessitates tactility. Users are encouraged to touch the object as if it were origami, they understand it through and with their fingers. Although they are both expressions of the sensibility of net.art, there is a significant distance between the Garden of Eden and the Unfolding Object. Because they both focus on source code, they can be considered contiguous. What differentiates them, however, is the mode of perception they call forth in the user. Finally, the same reflections on the creative potential of the code capable of giving shape to the idea of the artist and making it available online for collective interaction can be equally expressed through one of the two approaches that characterized the examined antinomy.

On the Web, I have stated, there are also experiences in which the optical and haptic coexist, and some in which they form hybrids. A good example of the latter is a work by Elout de Kok (mentor of the Pixel Lab), in *Portret Series* (2002).[51] Users find themselves facing an image that is difficult to decipher, because of the complex and overlapping patterns of which it is constituted. Therefore, the user tends to shift position in order to gain a different perspective on the image, and to make sense of it. When users abandon the attempt to discern any figure within the image and begin to enjoy the algorithmic overlapping of the geometrical lines, we might paraphrase Deleuze and Guattari and say that a 'trait of faceity' appears. That is, a human face (Kok's own) appears in front of the user. This shift between optical and haptic modes of perception is emblematic of the Web as a whole.

Out of the Web

What happens when the forms of the Web are taken beyond their habitual context of the computer monitor, and inhabit wider contexts, such as a video installation that takes up the entire façade of a building? In such cases, is there a similar tension between optical and haptic modes of perception? Even if we take urban and social variables into account, I believe that the argument continues to apply. Consider a live performance such as a VJ set, which mixes abstract algorithmic patterns, the performer's imagination, hardware and software, and figurative images, whether still or moving, which may or may not be from the Web. The audience is immersed in a synesthetic context, in which auditory and proprioceptive cues are both crucial and subject to the tyranny of rhythm. The point I wish to highlight, however, is the influence of the bodies surrounding the individual participant – both human bodies, and the body of the architecture in which the event is staged. These other bodies (both moving and relatively static) lead one to modulate one's own movement, giving rise to two main possibilities. The bonds imposed by the architecture of the place and the movement of the people who share the same performance lead to a constantly mediation of intention: moving or standing still, moving sideways rather than back and forth. This condition leads me to hypothesize that the dynamics of the place could trigger a different type of perception than that which would otherwise take place. Because of the impossibility of assuming a contemplative attitude, the audience might cling to a tactile perception of elements that by nature would not encourage this tendency. Conversely, one might linger in an optically dominating attitude in order to distract oneself from the uncomfortable postures they have been forced to assume, even if the images incline towards the tactile.[52] Such a situation might be taken to constitute a new kind of sensorial short-circuit where the alteration of the perception is favoured not only by the synesthetic nature of different medial dimensions, but also by the confusion emerging from unnatural modes of perception, such as the tendency to touch forms arising from an optical illusion.

A similar phenomenon takes place in relation to so-called *urban screens*, which increasingly use images taken from the Net or images that take their inspiration from the Net. Thus, these screens represent the extension of the aesthetic domain of the Web to urban contexts. In the act of looking at a screen placed on the façade of a building, we are brought into relation with the crowd, with street furniture, and with the street itself. If the road leads me to turn, or the pedestrian approaching me leads me to move sideways, my view, whether optical or haptic, changes too. Thus, the influence of social and variables is to form a type of perception which is established by interaction with a specific moment and a specific place. We might say that these experiences are characterized by perceptive estrangement or perceptive inversion.

These are complex matters requiring in-depth examination, yet the point remains that the Web, even when it is not enclosed within a computer screen, is characterized by an irreducible tension between optical and haptic modes of perception. As this antinomy typifies the Web, it is necessarily carried over into other medial, social and cultural contexts. In conclusion, the capacity of the Web's forms to extend beyond either optical or haptic modes leads me to envision it as a meta-optical and meta-haptic medium. As the Web has colonized the collective consciousness, this perceptive attitude also characterizes contemporary society. In the network society, individuals switch easily between perceptive modes, and are comfortable with the overlapping and shifting of these modes. After cinema and video art, humans can now make the most of the opportunities offered by the global hypermedia. Riegl and Benjamin believed that each age is characterized by a singular mode of perception, each creating its own *Weltanschauung* – it could be stated, then, that the present age is characterized by a perceptive style capable of going beyond the optical/haptic antinomy.

Chapter IV

Aesthetic Experience and Digital Networks

Travellers in the Aesthetic Matrix

> The Matrix is everywhere. It is all around us, even now in this very room. You can see it when you look out your window or when you turn on your television. You can feel it when you go to work, when you go to church, when you pay your taxes. It is the world that has been pulled over your eyes to blind you from the truth.
> Andy and Larry Wachowski, *The Matrix* (1999)

One of the most common activities of Internet users is to search for digital materials to download. Even though they can be used for many different purposes, peer-to-peer or P2P networks have become the most common means of sharing digital files. From a morphological point of view, the most interesting aspect of a P2P network is its absolutely horizontal structure: there is nothing like an immutable hierarchical order, and the computers involved constantly switch between the roles of *client* and *server*, or in other words, between those who make the request and those who receive it. When I require a file that another user is sharing I act (or my computer does) as a *client*, while if anybody downloads a file from my computer it is me (or my computer) that acts as a *server*. These positions interchange continuously, so that one is often both client and server simultaneously: while I download a file from another node of the network, somebody else may be doing the same with one of my files. I have long been fascinated with this unsupervised flow of movies, songs, software – what are in fact experiences – between users who may be unknown to each other. A particular node may be identifiable only by a nickname along with its numeric identification, leading one to muse upon the gender, age and appearance of the person behind the nickname. Surely, for example, 'Dark Precursor' must have had a *dark* past – otherwise they would not have shared the entire back catalogue of The Cure ... Such fantasies are justified by the fact that there are after all individuals behind every computer, and these individuals continue to attempt to relate to each other. Rather than a social or psychological inquiry into the practice of file sharing, however, I want to ask whether experience within P2P networks can be considered aesthetic experience. Furthermore, I want to consider aesthetic experience in relation to the cultural products that are shared on the Net.

Latency States

The first point I wish to focus on is the sensation of waiting that accompanies downloading a file. Venezuelan theorist Eduardo Navas begins with the premise that waiting times, or periods of 'latency', differentiate new media from old. Navas writes:

> Latency is used with three significations in mind. First, is the technological latency that takes place in new media culture due to the nature of the computer: the machine has to always check in loops what it must do, to then execute commands, eventually leading to the completion of a task. This is the case when someone uses Photoshop, Microsoft Word, or any other commercial application; or streams image and sound across the Internet. This constant checking in loops at hardware and software levels opens the space for latency's second signification, which extends in social space when the user consciously waits for a response that begins and ends with the computer. Latency becomes naturalized when a person incorporates computer interaction as part of his/her everyday activities. The third implication is based on the adjective: latent, which means potential for something that is to come if and when the waiting period is over. Latency, when considered from a cultural perspective can be entertained as moments of reflection that could make change possible: crucial decisions could be made that will affect the outcome at the end of the latent moment. Taking this social implication back to a hardware and software level, one may at times wonder if computational loops will be completed successfully. After all, the machine can potentially crash at any moment. This possibility of a crash lies latent and possesses a violent trace that could destroy all the information. Thus danger always lurks in new media culture, and a trace of instability is inherently part of the everyday use of digital tools.[1]

This passage, excerpted from an essay written for the exhibition 'The Latency of the Moving Image in New Media' (Los Angeles, 25 May – 16 June 2007), expresses perfectly the way that we become used to states of latency, as well as identifying sparks of creativity within these empty moments. These, then, are crucial moments, that have the capacity to give rise to distinct outcomes. The passage may lead us to believe that the state of latency – the state of waiting for something that has to happen – characterizes all the experiences that one can have on the Net, as each is an extension of the subject-computer relationship. One might wonder, however, if it is possible to view this state as a form of that auratic suspension that the arts have always offered. As tempted as I am to follow this line of thought, I must admit that the waiting that takes place as a file downloads does not offer the auratic form of experience that, for example, De Chirico's paintings offer. If we are to think of file-sharing platforms in terms of aesthetics, we might be better off recalling Benjamin's famous example involving the cathedral and the art lover. P2P networks might similarly be thought of as offering experiences of appropriating digitally encoded cultural objects. While not reducible to the activity of appropriation *tout court*, we can make a parallel with the way that, in Benjamin, the aesthetic experience of the urban or natural landscape turns into the reproduction in still or moving images. And yet, the mode of travelling within these networks is equally important.

Accumulation and Exhibition

Recalling Virilio's *prophecy* of the airport as city of the future,[2] Iain Chambers figures a simulated metropolis inhabited by a community of modern nomads who construct a collective metaphor for cosmopolitan existence, in which 'the pleasure of travel is not only to arrive, but also not to be in any particular place ... to be simultaneously everywhere'.[3] The *flâneur* becomes a *planeur*: a being whose condition is constant escape from events that take place elsewhere, and who cannot access the 'pressurized' space of the aeroplane 'cabin' ('meaning contracts into the pressurized cabin').[4] Life lived within the aeroplane ends up becoming more 'real' than the reality that the *planeur* observes from a distance.[5] This postmodernist vision seems to describe the contemporary mode of travelling within P2P networks. The cabin is replaced by the monitor, and the travelling from city to city becomes the jumping from one file to the other. Just as the airport represents a simulation of the metropolis, the file on the Net represents an image of an original cultural product, compressed and encoded according to a shared standard: the movie shrinks into the computer screen in an MPEG file. The architecture of the cinema itself, and its darkness, are events that always take place elsewhere, in a place far removed from the fluid space of the monitor.

In addition, Manovich compares the Baudelairian figure of the *flâneur* to the lonesome explorer of the nineteenth-century American West. For Manovich, both images are embodied in the figure of the 'Net Surfer'. When the Net Surfer comes into relation with other users, they act like a *flâneur*, and when they navigate the virtual space alone, they take the role of an explorer.[6] The most productive theory, however, comes from Lovink (who is quoted by Manovich). Recalling Oscar Wilde, Lovink defines the modern media user as a 'Data Dandy', writing that: 'The Net is to the electronic dandy what the metropolitan street was for the historical dandy. . . . The data dandy has moved well beyond the pioneer stage; the issue now is the grace of the medial gesture.'[7] For Lovink, just as *flâneurs* displayed their clothes on crowded boulevards, Web users 'stroll' and strut about social networks and file-sharing platforms, displaying their archives of movies, music and images. These latter objects are the icons of a digital modernity. This aesthetics of data accumulation is especially clear in platforms such as the evocatively-named Soulseek.[8] Allowing the user to browse folders that every user shares, such platforms create highly accurate archives, as they might include, for example, files with information concerning an artist's discography and the covers of the relevant records. Thus 'friendships' are formed on the basis of a shared taste in music, and preferential relationships develop which allow, for example, queues to be jumped if one belongs to a list of friends. By possessing an accurate, complete and sought-after archive, one builds a reputation and gains status within the community, while, on the other hand, users who share albums whose tracks have a different bitrate are avoided and possibly even banned.

For example, Kad network[9] rewards users from which other users have downloaded the highest number of files by making the queue shorter for them. Hence, the more files I share, the greater the chance that other users will download from me, thereby increasing the speed of my downloads. Whatever the platform used, the constant is the will to possess a set of digital cultural products that are as rich, complete and accurate as possible. In the late 1960s, Baudrillard had already pointed out that to a book collector, the book itself matters less than the moment the book is placed with others in its sector of the collection. By seeing a mere willingness to associate at the base of the (serial) motivation to buy (that I could paraphrase into download), the French philosopher considers the act of collection a mainly internal issue, even when it opens to the external:[10] 'What you really collect is always yourself.'[11]

In this context, I cannot help but recall a conversation with the Greek artist Miltos Manetas in November 2004, in which he told me that he found art collections very boring, and that in his life he only wanted to collect data. Manetas, an artist who has been able to capture many of the defining features of the present age, was actually describing the cultural attitude of the contemporary *flâneur*. For artists, the accumulation of images, sounds and suggestions that may later be creatively re-edited is a necessary activity; as Paul D. Miller states: 'As an artist you're only as good as your archive.'[12] To the common 'Net Surfer', accumulation is similarly experienced as a genuine duty, as well as a practice that increasingly determines one's digital inclusion. Such an activity describes a machinical attitude: one operates as a database; collecting, sorting and ordering an ever-increasing amount of digital data. This capture of human motivations, intentions and actions by specific software routines is apparent in the tendency to replace the expression 'I've seen it' (in regard to a film) with the expression 'I've got it'. Stating that one *has* a film exemplifies a new cultural model, according to which the accumulation of cultural data is given higher value than its reception. It is not the experience that counts, but the possession of it – a form of possession that offers the possibility of using the cultural product at any point in one's own life, and the possibility to adapt its features according to the specific needs of the moment.

This is a crucial shift, and I believe it is characterized by three distinct stages: the download of a cultural product from the Net; its organization within an archive; and the exhibition of the archive. These stages are not separable, rather they constitute a gestural *continuum* that flattens the existence of the contemporary *flâneur* into a specific aesthetical canon, that of the data dandy. Having stated that the present time is characterized by a diffuse aesthetics and by memetic transmission, one can also conclude that these databases constitute containers of cultural elements that have captured the collective aesthetic imaginary. These are forms that have been spread by memetic transmission: a given song has been downloaded because it is so well structured (or so virulent, if you prefer), that it is able to influence choice and taste. However, as the archive is unlikely to remain private – one has built it in order to show and share it – I see it as a complex of memes that is bound to spread through social relations, and the *status* of the users who form those relations, within digital networks.

In conclusion, P2P networks participate in the spreading of dominant aesthetic forms. In the moment individuals believe they are setting themselves free from ruling capitalist and consumerist structures, they are unconsciously acting as agents of replication within the aesthetic matrix that rules their lives.

The DivX and MP3 Experience

Have no fear of perfection - you'll never reach it.
Salvador Dalí (1904-1989)

The P2P phenomenon can also be framed in terms of the reception of
the acquired material, in particular in relation to audio and video files.
The logic of downloading software and video games is binary: having
downloaded and installed a program, it either works, in which case it
will provide the same features of the original software (which comes
complete with manual, licence and installation booklet), or it does not
work, in which case there is nothing to do but try again.

Imperfect Cultural Objects

In contrast, watching a movie downloaded from the Net offers a
wider range of experiences, including different levels of quality, which
depend on the techniques that have been employed in order to share
the video file on digital environments. It is important to distinguish between files produced through a copy from an original support (Screener,
DVD-Rip, Disk image, HDTV-Rip, etcetera) and the so-called cam.[1] The
former is basically a simple copy of digital material that, in order to
overcome the bandwidth limits of domestic networks, is compressed
by means of specific codecs. As is well known, this compression stage is
based on a compromise between quality and the size of the file, so that
the quality of a video downloaded from the Net necessarily depends on
the precision and accuracy of who provided the shared file. Cams are
a different issue. Most of the time, these are videos made with a small
digital camcorder (or compact digital camcorder) filming inside a movie
theatre, although there are highly varied and creative alternatives. In
these cases, we see a series of stages from analogue to digital. The original film is in fact realized in a digital format – even when shot on film,
editing and post production are undertaken digitally). The format is
then transferred back to film (the 35mm reel: ecologically disastrous,
but romantic) so that they can be distributed and screened in theatres.
Here, the images are captured through a 'pirate cam' that returns them
to a digital format, after which the 'stolen' recording is compressed to a
size that enables it to be shared on P2P networks.

Here, I am unable to delve into the often heroic character of those who undertake this task. In my opinion, the merits of these people are second only to those who spend their time adding subtitles to pirated versions in their mother tongue, which allows many people to enjoy motion pictures produced outside the logic of global distribution. Cams give rise to variables of quality distinct from those involved with file compression, namely: the quality of the 'pirated' capturing, which mainly depends on the type of camera used, its position and its steadiness; and the degree of noise during the recording in a situation in which the audio capture does not take place live, but according to the modalities of field recording, and therefore depends on all the variables connected to diffusion and refraction of the sound inside the architectural space of that specific theatre. In the viewing of a generic movie shared on the Internet, one faces a cultural product that is a result of compromises related to file compression. In the viewing of a cam, however, one encounters overlapping levels of production, significantly greater than those predicted and established by the author(s) of the film. One level is determined by the position of the camcorder inside the theatre. A lateral placement will give rise to an unusual spatial perspective, especially when compared to the classical model of central framing handed down from painting to cinema to television, and finally to the computer screen. In this model, spectators are ideally placed centrally to the object they are viewing. The position of the cam, in contrast, depends on variables outside the control of the film's creators: for example, arriving late to a film, the placement of other viewers. The key point is that the perspective embodied in the pirated copy is independent of, and might openly contrast with, the intention of, and the figuration of space offered by, the film's creator. In relation to sound quality, the most significant variable is the position of the microphone and the speakers of the theatre. Even if this positioning is ideal, however, the refraction of sound inside the cinema is reproduced in a series of echoes that give rise to both an auditory numbness, and a sensation of constant back and forth movement between the sources of sound. The most surprising aspect of the sound, however, is the merging of the original audio with the background noise, including laughter, clapping, coughing and 'shush!-ing'. All these sources of interference end up as parts of the digital file, destined to pass through P2P networks. On the one hand, this reawakens the sensation of being inside a cinema, just as a live recording of a concert reproduces the specificity of that very performance. On the other hand, this has the potential to introduce new empathic elements into the work, elements that overlap its narrative trajectory. These 'noises', deriving from the interaction of the audience with the images on the screen, become a constitutive element of the narration. A new *unicum* takes shape, in which the background noise represents the specificity of the place, time and audience of a particular screening. Rather than speculating on the reproduced work's loss of aura, then, we might conceive of a new aura in which the model of the *auteur* melts with a collective, unconscious and unpredictable authorship, which creates its own unique trajectory.

To clarify: cammers have no artistic intention, though there is sometimes a political intent behind their actions. The cinema's background noises, recorded and fused with the original work, are taken out of context, and reproduced serially in the (potentially infinite) visualizations of that hybrid cultural object that is the downloaded movie. Decontextualization and serialization are two of the most abused key concepts by art critics and visitors of galleries and museums; this observation is not sufficient to give artistic substance to the activity of a video enthusiast who, in the dark of a theatre, steals the images of a movie. In the acting of a 'movie pirate', technical knowledge is mainly automatized within the machine's capacities to control aspects such as the level of light, focus and antishock controls. What is missing is artistic will, particularly as the video enthusiast is aware of the unwilling contributions of other spectators.

Now, let us put cinema aside and imagine that we are watching a recording of a theatrical performance on our PCs. The play has been recorded and shared on a file-sharing platform by an unknown person. In this case, we are experiencing a work that has been doubly mediated, for it has been transferred to a different medium from the one in which it was conceived (from stage to video), and has also been mediated by the person who has recorded it according to their own point of view, position in the theatre and perhaps using techniques such as zoom. What are the consequences of these mediations for the work we are watching? It is clear that we are well beyond the 'loss of aura' that Walter Benjamin spoke of in his famed essay of 1936. To the German philosopher, in the age of technical reproduction, the work of art loses its artistic and cultural value (its 'aura') to its communicative, expositive value: the aesthetic meaning of a work is related to its effects, to the way it is incorporated into society. In the above example, the work that is incorporated is not only mediated by technical means, as in Benjamin's reasoning, but derives from overlapping levels of interpretation.

However it has been realized, viewing a movie downloaded from the Internet at home belongs to the wider phenomenon of *home cinema*. As opposed to going to a movie theatre, viewing an MPEG at home does not differ conceptually from viewing a VHS video. The interface of cinema, the architectural structure of the theatre, is replaced by a variety of choices concerning the reproduction of the audio and video signals: from the live view through the laptop onto which the movie has been downloaded, to the magnification of a home theatre system. In both cases, the ritual of entering a dark theatre is replaced by individual domestic rituals, and the 'big screen' is replaced by small screens that do, however, increasingly tend to gigantism. Viewing a video downloaded from the Net differs from other home viewing experiences in the overall decay of the quality of the experience. The necessary compromise between file size and quality is evident at the first moment of viewing. The less users pay in terms of time spent downloading, the more they will pay during viewing downloaded content. The data decay typical of selective compression systems (so called because the decrease of a file size is obtained by erasing some of its information) is, in fact, the exception to the rule for digitally coded media. As opposed to analogue media, digital media can ideally be incessantly copied without loss of quality; and yet, as Manovich writes:

> Rather than being an aberration, a flaw in the otherwise pure and perfect world of the digital, where not even a single bit of information is ever lost, lossy compression is the very foundation of computer culture, at least for now. Therefore, while in theory, computer technology entails the flawless replication of data, its actual use in contemporary society is characterized by loss of data, degradation, and noise.[2]

By adding 'at least for now', Manovich gestures towards a future in which compression techniques will minimize data loss, or in which the speed of connections will make the compression process obsolete. In his presentation of the core of this essay during the international conference Video Vortex 4,[3] Manovich highlighted that technology is already close to allowing the transmission of video with near-perfect quality, through increasingly faster Internet connections. According to Manovich's prophecy, we will reach a stage he terms that of *macromedia*, in which: 'We have such high bandwidth connections that the whole issue of bandwidth goes away. We will simply not think about it anymore.'[4] Although still experimental, when such high-bandwith projects influence a meaningful amount of users they will deepen the so-called 'digital divide' between users who benefit from these new technologies and users who will continue to share highly imperfect material. At the present time, we continue to share 'impure' digital material, in full awareness that this imperfection is inevitable, almost necessary, to the viewing experience itself.

Disturbed Aesthetic Experiences

The same observations apply to a consideration of the exchange of music over P2P networks. The widely used MP3 format is similarly based on the compression of digital data, with a concomitant degradation of the quality of the listening experience. The mobility of the format is usually emphasized, although this has been the case since the first cassette Walkman Personal Stereos.[5] Obviously, there are ever-smaller devices with ever-increasing memory, yet I believe that the defining aspect of the experience of cultural contents attained from the Internet is that they are what might be termed 'disturbed aesthetic experiences'. One openly accepts interference, background noise, the loss of pixellation in the image, saturated colours, jerky switching between images, faded outlines, deflated low tones or screeching high tones – a catalogue of flaws that become part of everyday aesthetic experiences and irreversibly alter our perceptive universe. In 1994, along with the first wailings of the Web, cultural theorist Iain Chambers identified the Walkman as a constitutive object of contemporary nomadism. 'Each listener/player selects and rearranges the surrounding soundscape,' Chambers writes, 'and, in constructing a dialogue with it, leaves a trace in the network.'[6] The fragile and transient possibility 'of imposing your soundscape on the surrounding aural environment and thereby domesticating the external world'[7] attains renewed significance if applied to MP3 players. In fact, two significant differences between Walkmans and MP3 players are worthy of note here. Firstly, the noise and interference imbued in the music by the Net flow mingles together with external noises, giving life to an original 'disturbed landscape'. Interference is no longer just a feature of the external world, and the constant traffic of the modern metropolis, it is part of the precious internal world that the individual maintains by wearing headphones, which are a kind of modern mask. In Chambers' example, interaction with the surrounding environment takes place through a grammar of 'STOP/START, FAST FORWARD, PAUSE AND REWIND'.[8]

In the random mode that often characterizes the MP3 listening experience, the algorithmic mode of choice gives life to random reconfigurations of the surrounding environment. Furthermore, the increasing memory size of MP3 players encourages the user to fill them with all kinds of material, much of which might only be listened to once, out of curiosity. In random mode, the combinations between architectural space, the people and machines one is moving along with, between colours and scents, and the 'internal' soundtrack one might be encountering, approaches the infinite. Contemporary subjects live through unthinkable sensory collisions: Mozart colliding with the clanging of the Tube and, one second later, a recorded voice announcing the next station, overlapping with a choir singing along with James Brown; or the electronic distortions of DAT Politics clashing with the quiet of a tree-lined avenue; or Edith Piaf's *L'hymne à l'amour* overlapping with the insults of a pedestrian that one has just cut off with one's bike. The combination of the algorithm's machinical performance and the environment gives rise to an endless range of aural 'short circuits'. In the 1980s, the obsession with high-fidelity sound fuelled the sales of expensive sound systems. Although there are still of course digital sound systems capable of providing high-level listening experiences, today our attention seems to have shifted towards quantity rather than quality. Virilio has claimed that after the highs and lows of stereophonic high fidelity, we have come to an age of 'stereoscopy' in which the actual and the virtual replace the left and the right, the high and the low.[9] The search for a pure, incorrupt sound has been abandoned for the utopia of an archive capable of holding the *unity of the whole*; the myth of the sound like the 'angel's trumpets' has been substituted for the myth of a fluid archive capable of being crossed by an *absolute sea* of digital sound.

Consider that, search as I might, I could not locate an authoritative review that offered a comparison between the iPod's quality of sound reproduction and that of its competitors. Of course, there are sources of resistance to the iPod's dominance, such as anythingbutipod.com, yet these are nowhere near enough to build a 'critical mass' in the face of the mainstream media's subservience to the *word* of Steve Jobs. Even admitting that this aspect of performance is less relevant in devices that rely on external output systems such as headphones and preamps, it is still significant that an object that has sold in the tens of millions is not discussed in terms of sound quality. One might conclude that it is the design and the warmth of the interface that seduces us, rather than its technical characteristics. As this seduction grows through physical contact,[10] the iPod enters the collective consciousness as a sexual object, as an object to be owned and touched, more than a listening device.

The absence of barriers to the free flowing of cultural digital data seems to have become of higher value than the quality of aesthetic experience that cultural objects give us. Thus the question becomes: What is the value of a disturbed aesthetic experience?

A Genealogy of Noise

It is tempting to consider such sources of noise as offering haptic experiences, as in the graininess or blurred images that Marks takes as her subject. However, as Marks herself reminds us, when encountering 'badly recorded video images' the viewer 'is more likely to find the image's blurriness merely a frustration and not an invitation to perceive in a different way'.[11] There are theories, such as those of the Lithuanian-French semiologist Algirdas Julien Greimas,[12] that link the sense of beauty to imperfection, as an alternative to banality, meaninglessness, and indifference. If we focus on the concept of noise, we find that it is not at all a new concept in the history of aesthetics – consider, for a moment, the way that the industrialization and urbanization of the nineteenth century was seen to interfere with aesthetic enjoyment. If the discomfort of modernity is the noise of the modern city, Baudelaire understood that this very discomfort offered the possibility for a new kind of art:

I was crossing the boulevard in a great hurry, splashing through the
mud in the midst of a seething chaos, and with death galloping at
me from every side, I gave a sudden start and my halo slipped off my
head and fell into the mire of the macadam. I was far too frightened
to pick it up. I decided it was less unpleasant to lose my insignia
than to get my bones broken. Then too, I reflected, every cloud has a
silver lining. I can now go about incognito, be as low as I please and
indulge in debauch like ordinary mortals. So here I am as you see,
exactly like yourself![13]

As Marshall Berman points out, the poet, in 'throwing oneself in the
traffic', sees the opportunity to take possession of the seething chaos of
the modern city and to incorporate it into his art.[14] In the footsteps of
Baudelaire, Walter Benjamin's 'shock theory' captures the influence of
the sudden and confounding situations of modernity upon art. German
poet Rainer Maria Rilke, in parts of *Malte*,[15] notes the unbearable noise
of the Parisian metropolis. In the poem *Gong*, the 'Klang' (noise) becomes so extreme that it is no longer measurable through hearing, it
seems to resound so much that it gains *eine Reife des Raums* (a maturity
of space); a 'weird' maturity, that is literally meta-physical.[16]

In the artistic avant-garde of the twentieth century, it is in futurism
that we find the most interesting ideas concerning the aesthetic significance of noise. In a letter to his friend and composer Francesco Balilla
Pratella (originally dated 11 March 1913), and later published as the
Arte dei rumori, artist Luigi Russolo writes what is considered to be the
true futurist music manifesto.[17] Under 'the multipication of machines,
which collaborate with man on every front',[18] Russolo finds the begin-
nings of a complex polyphony characterized by 'complicated succes-
sions of dissonant chords'.[19] Citizens of the eighteenth century, writes
Russolo, 'could never have endured the discordant intensity of certain
chords produced by our orchestras',[20] which are enjoyable to the ears of
the twentieth century just because they have become used to the noises
of modern life. Russolo associates nature with silence, and concludes
that 'ancient' music was appropriate to the natural world. On the other
hand, the interference wrought by technology requires a form of music
in which the distinction between sound and noise tends to disappear.[21]
As technologies spread and sources of interference increase, we develop

the capacity to distinguish between multiple noises, not simply so as to imitate them 'but to combine them according to our imagination'.[22]

Futurists view noise as constitutive of both artistic practice and aesthetic experience. In visual art, futurist Giacomo Balla translates noise in visual terms by combining a broken line with a curved line, or 'speed line'. This procedure, as well as the analogy between painting and music, has echoes in the work of Wassily Kandinsky, who in *Punkt und Linie zu Fläche* (Munich, 1926), and in lectures given at the Bauhaus between 1931 and 1932, explicitly recalls the dissonance between a curved line and a broken line. In this, he sees irregularity, mould-breaking, noise – elements that finally fracture perceptive continuity. In *Horror Pleni*,[23] Italian art critic Gillo Dorfles contrasts the ancient *horror vacui* of prehistoric men, who used to fill every surface of their caves with self-produced images, with the contemporary *horror pleni*, which relates to the 'excess of both visual and auditory noise that is opposed to any informational and communicational possibility'.[24] The concept of *horror pleni* describes the glut of signals and communication that characterizes the contemporary age, from the pocket transistor radios that began to infiltrate public space at the end of the 1980s, through to television and computers. For Dorfles, contemporary life is characterized by a kind of generalized, 'pornographic' noise. Political communication is constituted by contradictory signals that confound the understanding of anything significant. Literature is at a point of crisis, and seeks to compensate by confessing private and regrettable events; it offers a 'pornography of pain' and gives rise to a complete exhibitionism. The arts, sciences and the world of fashion continue to produce new extremes, but with no perceptible response from a public habituated to excess.[25] Collective rituals such as raves, rock concerts and football matches represent a form of modern tribalism, in which people become slaves to the noise.[26] For Dorfles, noise is not only interference, but the opposite of information. As remarkable as are human perceptive and mnestic abilities, they are limited and become blunted by over-stimulation.[27] Signic hypertrophy has reached such a paroxysmal state that one increasingly feels the need for an imaginific break.[28] More generally, we feel the need of a suspension capable of recovering the space of Self, that is the space in *between;* between our age and the next one, between everyday actions and artistic creations. So a break, an *in between,* without which humankind risks falling into the horror of a plenitude that can no longer be fragmented and dominated, and becomes completely subject to the 'too full' and the excess of 'noise'.[29]

Perfection Versus Fluidity

Having clarified that the concept of disturbed aesthetic experience is not a new one, and acknowledging Manovich's claim that selective compression may soon become redundant, we face two alternatives in relation to digital cultural contents: the 'model of perfection' represented by digital supports offering the highest possible quality in terms of archiving and reproduction of digital data, such as CDs, DVDs, and Blu-Ray technology; and the 'model of fluidity' in which quality is secondary to absolute shareability. These models embody opposing political positions: the explicit or implicit acceptance of the logic of the market on one side; and its total rejection on the other. It is important to note, however, that the sheer expense of 'noble' technological supports leads a large proportion of the population to opt for the 'model of fluidity', without necessarily acceding to its political premises. In relation to aesthetic enjoyment, society divides into those who have access to aesthetic experiences approaching perfection and the growing masses bound to accept disturbed experiences. Whereas in the past lower classes were simply unable to access certain forms of culture, here we see a more complex relation of inclusion and exclusion. As long as economically disadvantaged individuals have access to digital networks, they have access to forms of culture, although those forms are subject to the mediations typical of the amateur processes of archiving and reproduction of digital data.

Unauthorized Copies

P2P networks also facilitate the distribution of dominant cultural models. Statistics show that, excluding pornography, the most shared materials on the Internet are materials realized according to Hollywood standards, and songs in the top ten of the international music charts. It might be concluded that the cultural industries compensate for a loss of income by increasing their reach. At the same time, we might discuss the paradox by which 'dissent networks' end up being evacuated of any antagonism just because they become the umpteenth means for the transmission of cultural objects aimed at stabilizing the status quo.

Without denying this phenomenon, I wish to discuss an opposing tendency: the opportunity for small dissident communities to use P2P networks and the practices that go under the laughable definition of 'unauthorized copies' to create cultural products outside the dominant frames of interpretation, and that are outside mainstream channels of distribution. Rather than amateur productions, I am speaking of those products at the level of 'high culture' whose sophistication leaves them outside the logic of mass distribution. The opportunity to access 'unauthorized' materials allows one to keep in touch with one's own cultural memory, apart from the rare windows that open within traditional channels. If I want to watch a movie by Lang, Vertov or Bunuel, I no longer have to wait for the retrospective that an independent cinema screens once a year. Instead of paying Amazon 20 dollars, I simply type the director's name into eMule's search field.

In some contexts, video piracy supports the production of independent videos. As German scholar Tilman Bäumgartel has reported, in the last few years independent production has boomed in South-Eastern Asia. Bäumgartel, who in 2006 organized *Asian Edition*, an international debate on video piracy and intellectual property in South-Eastern Asia, emphasizes that the main form of piracy in these regions is trade in counterfeit materials rather than exchange over P2P networks. This is due to the fact that people in many areas do not have an Internet connection, and that many others distrust file downloading from anonymous sources. According to Bäumgartel, piracy in South-Eastern Asia gives life to a sort of 'globalization from below'. Together with the proliferation of Hollywood or Bollywood movies, it has allowed many to access international art films, which were previously prohibitively expensive due to the lack of infrastructure for distribution. The organizations that trade counterfeit products have exhibited a keen eye for demand that had previously gone unnoticed. Obviously, these organizations are not concerned about distributing material that has been censored in other countries due to its political content. These facts lead Bäumgartel to conclude that 'piracy has added to the film literacy and even to the quality of media education in the region'.[30] In the Western world, although there are more spaces for cinema d'essai, P2P networks offer the opportunity to view Asian independent movies outside the often self-enclosed world of festivals.

Furthermore, as digital technologies become cheaper, it is not only domestic forms of piracy that increase. We also see the proliferation of do-it-yourself (DIY) video productions, and a new movement of independent directors. For Bäumgartel, video piracy in Asia offers an awareness of the history and aesthetics of cinema comparable to that of Europe in the 1950s and 1960s, which fostered movements such as the Nouvelle Vague. And yet, as Bäumgartel himself admits, the falsified copies that make the Asian illegal market prosperous are often characterized by low quality, due to the way the digital supports are realized. Similarly, the low budgets of independent productions entail the use of technology that marks them as amateur rather than professional productions. Concerning this issue, Bäumgartel discusses the paradigmatic experience of Malayan director Kharin M. Bahar who, in 2005, shot the movie *Ciplak*, a comedy whose protagonist is a pirate DVD seller, using only a budget of 2,000 euros, a miniDv camera, lighting from Ikea, the help of friends, and the editing tools on a domestic PC.

The Evolution of Aesthetic Taste

The use of digital tools in cinema and the consequent lowering of standards of quality are not, however, necessarily a consequence of the low budgets confronting young independent directors. They might be the effect of an aesthetic transformation taking place in society that is, as always, detected by artists before it becomes an overt phenomenon. If the quality of a film is related to finances only, why would important European directors and Hollywood stars with access to generous budgets participate in the production of films using low-cost digital technologies?

In the most emblematic case, the manifesto *Dogme 95*, it could be argued that the decision to read the ninth rule flexibly, (that is to accept the Academy 35mm film as a standard only when it comes to the distribution format of the movie), is due to the need to follow the third rule, which requires that shooting takes place with the camera in hand – rather difficult to accomplish with a heavy 35mm camera. This would explain the choice of a Von Trier, a Vinterberg or a Kragh-Jacobsen to shoot using the more manageable DV. It could also be objected that in cases such as *The Blair Witch Project* (Daniel Myric and Eduardo Sánchez, 1999) or *Collateral* (Michael Mann, 2004) or the recent *Cloverfield* (Matt

Reeves, 2008) this is merely a narrative style. It could also be a matter of style, for example, in *L'amore probabilmente* by Giuseppe Bertolucci (*Probably Love*, 2001). We could continue to find a justification for each time a director has decided not to shoot on film, yet it is obvious that these are aesthetic choices that have nothing to do with the finances available to the production.

Whether independent or mainstream, directors are increasingly choosing to use DV cameras and other technologies 'beneath' the standards of international cinema as the result of an aesthetic choice. Certainly, there is a generalized fascination with the new potentials offered by digital media. There might, however, also be a deeper fascination with the everyday images that shape the tastes of the average Internet user. The contemporary visual landscape is dominated by YouTube clips, movies downloaded from P2P networks, television news from all over the world that increasingly hires freelance workers rather than specialists, and of the trembling images produced by millions of webcams pointed, now, towards everything and everyone. This landscape is characterized by low resolution images, jerky movements, pixellation and bad lighting – a disturbed landscape, certainly, but one that is far closer to reality than the sleek perfection of cinematic film. In this new aesthetic sensibility, speed and immediacy are preferred to refinement; documentary to fiction; and Lumière to Méliès.

The preference for DV's over traditional cameras might be the result of an attempt at realism, although one is of course not dealing with reality as such, but a reality recounted, now, through digital media. Rather than judging this reality, it must be experienced and imagined, its images must be somehow reproduced. In this sense, Brian de Palma's *Redacted* (2007) is emblematic, as it explores the 'truth not truth' of video and cinematic images. The film's long opening scene is paradigmatic: the classic cinematic move of a smooth 'coming down' from the sky is overlapped by the classic handycam image of the date of the shooting. Following this is a title in a semi-professional graphic, while the colloquial voice-over of a soldier (who is also the film's protagonist) states that he is the author of the recording itself; after which a highly amateurish tracking shot ends with the protagonists looking collectively into the camera, and finally with a freeze-frame. As a whole, De Palma's film feels like a mix of reality and fiction: Hollywood DV footage,

YouTube clips, wannabe documentaries and parodies of independent cinema. Here, the director of *Scarface* has captured a phenomenon that has radically changed the aesthetic perception of the cinema viewer, alternating and superimposing classic cinema aesthetics with the booming DIY digital aesthetic. In addition, the film's subject is the war in Iraq, and this aesthetic seems equal to a situation in which 'embedded' journalists give the public the 'truth' in ostensibly unofficial shots attained by 'brave' reporters risking their lives. Low-resolution images of the Iraq war are usually considered true, especially those taken by mobile phone cameras or otherwise tiny hidden cameras.

It is not difficult to find evidence of this aesthetic shift in media art. Julien Marie's *Low Resolution Cinema* (2005)[31] is an abstract vision of the geopolitical space of the city of Berlin. Through a series of expedients, among which is the drastic lowering of the resolution, Marie aims at *decompressing* the image in a 3-D space. A special projector realized by two semi-broken black-and-white Liquid Crystal Displays is used to show only the upper or the lower part of the image, which is constantly moving closer and further from the projector lamp, which itself also moves back and forth. The resulting image is so damaged that it evokes the scrolling matrix code seen in *The Matrix*, or the tight characters produced on the scroll of a dot matrix printer. In *Low Resolution Cinema* the perfection of the image becomes a shaded memory, but the magic of cinema, that illusion produced by moving images, remains absolutely intact.

An even more exemplary work is Bill Morrison's *Decasia* (2002),[32] of which Alessandro Ludovico writes:

[It] is a film made entirely of damaged film material, recovered from several United States archives. The result of the editing is harrowingly beautiful, between the simplicity and the effectiveness of the shots that show wonderful sequences (planes in the air, a child who's being born by caesarian birth, sea waves, a caravan of camels in the desert), all of them in a precarious balance made of stains and dark spots which involuntarily filter the visual contents.[33]

Employing fragile and trembling aesthetic representations, Morrison celebrates the precarious nature of cinema. Rather than impoverishing the images, the stains on the film renders them precious, something like the wrinkles that time traces on a face.

In *Delter* (2002),[34] Victor Liu offers an explicit magnification of the approximate nature of the digital moving image. Using software capable of extracting what is between one frame and another in an MPEG video, Liu reveals the inter-frames as shaded, ghost-like traces of a video's images. With this project, Liu exposes the structure of the data as fixed in a compression procedure, revealing a scheme designed to be viewed and interpreted by machines only. In viewing this structure, we see the human becoming machine: the last landing place of the desire to replace the machine in rebuilding the wholeness of the movement of the images that Delter deprives of their objects.

A final project is the Swedish artist Anders Weberg's *Unpixelated* (2009). The concept behind this work is the fact that Japanese law requires that all male and female genitalia in Japanese porn be blurred, so as to obscure it from sight, a procedure referred to as *bokashi*. In *Unpixelated*, Weberg utilizes software that reconstructs the censored images. Once the software has been applied, the rest of the image is blurred, so that only the previously censored genitalia are clearly identifiable.[35]

In Praise of Imperfection

The above works appear to support the hypothesis that a taste for imperfection is spreading across all fields of visual culture. The rise of a rhetoric of an 'aesthetics of imperfection' in the field of advertising would seem to confirm this hypothesis. Examples include the campaign entitled *Imperfect, but you love them* realized by advertising agency Saatchi & Saatchi for Maryland Cookies,[36] the Italian campaign for the launch of the BMW 5 Series,[37] or the praise of small flaws in the Singapore Ministry of Community Development, Youth and Sports[38] campaign *Beautifully Imperfect*. All are expressions of the commercial attempt to take possession of the *truth of the flaw*. The wish for irregularity and for the breaking of symmetry are so characteristic of the spirit of time that the public views admissions of flaws as genuine. It is hardly surprising, then, that communication experts try to veil their messages or products in *a cloak of authenticity*.[39]

No reflection on digitally pirated cultural products is complete without some discussion of pornographic materials. More interesting than the mere proliferation of international bestsellers is the increasing amount of amateur materials. These amateur productions are important because they undermine the model of sexuality based on the obsessive repetition of insubstantial narrative routines, which Slavoj Žižek summarizes as follows: the plumber knocks at the door of a sexy lonely woman, who, after having her sink repaired suggests that there is *another hole* to repair.[40] According to Žižek, the paradox (and tragedy) of pornography is that its ambition to be as realistic as possible leads its narratives to develop in ways that can never be taken seriously. Showing everything in anatomical detail is possible as long as the fantasmatic support is kept at a zero level.[41] The element of fantasy that is always censured by 'mainstream' pornography regains life in amateur pornographic productions, such as in private videos that have been stolen and, more rarely, in artistic pornography.[42] In these cases, viewers are encouraged to construct a narrative: they wonder about the lives of the protagonists, and the events that might have preceded the explicit act they are watching (Are they lovers? Husband and wife? Have they met by accident? Is it the first time they have had sex?) In other words, viewers are encouraged to open the doors to fantasy. These realities are finally antagonistic to the industry's attempts to crystallize an aesthetics of desire. As users of pornography become used to equating low-resolution images with the truth, and increasingly reject the commercialized images as unrealistic, the industry seeks to recover its market share by producing fake amateur videos – thus reinforcing the shift towards disturbed aesthetic experiences.

Somewhat unexpectedly, perhaps, many of the elements underlying those aesthetic experiences that I have defined as disturbed are evident in Zen Buddhist thought. Here, concepts such as asymmetry, indeterminacy and imperfection are valued; emptiness is placed before fullness, poverty before wealth, and incompleteness, disharmony and transience are placed before a static, Platonic cosmic harmony that has tended to dominate Western culture. To a greater degree than concepts such as *wabi* and *sabi* (recently popularized in the West, thanks to books such as Leonard Koren's),[43] which offer an aesthetic appreciation of poverty and insufficiency, I mean to recall that immediacy of the gesture (in Zen texts: *ko-tzu*) that underlies that which Daisetz Suzuki defines as an imperfection that 'becomes a form of perfection'.[44] In painting an ideogram, the Zen master is required to make one single gesture, which can never be corrected or erased. In this very condition, the inevitable imperfection of the trait confers upon the calligraphy a higher degree of truth than the impersonal perfection of typographic print. The imprecise sign, the stain that the ink leaves on the rice paper, become expressions of the instant transfer of inspiration from the artist to the sheet, without intervening filters and – finally – they ensure the authenticity of the gesture itself.

Of the disharmony of Japanese art, Gillo Dorfles states that it leads to a condition whose aim is a perfection that does not belong to this world, and that cannot be reached by such a civilization as the present one, which is dominated by the perfection of technique, 'but to which people have always aspired as if it was the "paradise lost" of an cosmic harmony that has enchanted Mankind across history, but that seldom could find a proper realization on our torn planet'.[45] In the context of a general dissemination of Japanese culture in the Western world, thanks to cinema, literature (and Kawataba must be mentioned here), manga, anime and fashion, features of imperfection are winning over the Western sensibility. Without wanting to push the analogy with Buddhism, it is possible to state that the praise of imperfection strengthens the hypothesis that the present age is open to more authentic, imperfect images and sounds, in concert with a generalized distrust of the cold perfection of the cultural industry as a whole.

The Centrality of the Eye

> Mental cinema is always at work in each one of us, and it always has
> been, even before the invention of the cinema. Nor does it ever stop
> projecting images before our mind's eye.
> Italo Calvino, *Six Memos for the Next Millennium* (1988)

A further consideration is the phenomenon termed the 'loss of centrality
of the eye'. This formula is usually used to describe the molecularization
of the perspectives within cinema, which is a product of the use of many
digital cameras in place of the traditional one, or at most two. The image
of Alfred Hitchcock or Federico Fellini, behind a large camera and control-
ling everything with their eye, remains, and characterizes cinema up until
the birth of digital media. Today, we see an increasing number of cameras
used simultaneously to shoot a scene from different angles, and we even
see actors wearing mini-cameras so as to realistically represent the point
of view of a protagonist of the action. Of course, the director reasserts their
power over the image when they make a selection from this multiplicity
of perspectives. From a technical point of view, this tendency results from
the fact that traditional cameras require specific lighting, whereas digital
cameras have sensors that automatically balance poor or insufficient light.
In a similar way, analogue photography requires that we think about the
direction of light, whereas with a digital camera we simply snap, or at the
most select a specific option, for example 'dawn', 'sunrise' or 'fireworks'.

Underlying this modern form of filmmaking are economic factors:
the arrangement of lighting on a set requires a long time, hence the long
breaks between shooting that have always been a feature of cinema. And
yet, it is possible to contend that the proliferation of perspectives meets
a need that is felt by many directors: namely, to reconstruct a public and
private reality that is increasingly characterized by the presence of countless eyes. The multiplication of cameras and angles of vision, then, may be
a natural consequence of a spreading Big Brother aesthetic, in which every
action is observed from several points of view. To contemporary viewers of
cinema, the vision from a single window is no longer enough – they want
to view the action from a number of angles. The escape from the tyranny
or the centrality of the eye is no longer a political act – it is simply that the
viewer is used to switching between cameras, for example when watching

(digital) reality television, while playing a video game, or moving inside meta-worlds such as Second Life. In a televised sporting event, an action is shot from a number of different points of view, in proportion to the importance of the event itself – up to and including those true epiphanies of perspective represented by the World Cup final, or the Super Bowl. In this context, it is also worth recalling the incredible multiplicity of perspectives offered on public events, if, for example, one searches YouTube using terms such as 'Obama inauguration ceremony' or 'iPhone launch'.

In net.art, we can consider this phenomenon through the Australian artist Simon Biggs' *Babel* (2001).[1] This work requires participants to face a 3-D visualization of an abstract data space made up of numbers, and to interact with this space by moving a mouse. Within this 3-D environment, users encounter the perspectives of all the other users that are logged into the website at the same time. As Biggs writes, the user in fact sees what all the others are seeing:

> The multiple 3D views of the data-space are montaged together into a single shared image, where the actions of any one viewer effects what all the other viewers see. If a large number of viewers are logged on together the information displayed becomes so complex and dense that it breaks down into a meaningless abstract space.[2]

For Biggs, the work is a metaphor for the infinite nature of information. It is emblematic of a general tendency in new media art to confront the creation of multiuser systems that can be accessed remotely, thus putting in contact the multiple perspectives of viewers in many and varied locations. On the one hand, we have a new generation that is far less educated by the classical language of cinema, and that on the other hand is deeply marked by the aesthetics and rhythm of video games. For this audience, movies in which the narration does not develop through constant changes of angle and perspective are far too static (and boring). This tendency is also a stage within a more general evolution in the taste and styles of cinema, and need not be read as a complete loss of the director's authority. Rather, it represents an alteration in the habits of representation, that will encourage the elaboration of a new poetics – a poetics beginning with the premise of the molecularization of point of view, and hence of direction as a moment of organization and synthesis of this multiplicity.

Digital Cameras and the Will of Technology

Thy will be done on earth, as it is in heaven.
Christian prayer

At this point, I will reflect upon the consequences of the proliferation of tools, such as digital cameras and mobile devices, that enable the increasing self-production of content.

Contemporary Obsessions

Nowadays, any cultural event is accompanied by the background noise of the clicking of thousands of digital cameras. Even in museums and historical buildings, countless people are busy taking photos or videos of anything they believe is worthy of capture. Leaving aside the privacy implications, I wish to focus upon the inability to relate to things directly, in the absence of the mediation of one's digital gadgets. Rather than taking part in a cultural event and experiencing the consequent emotions, responses and reflections, what matters is that we capture some souvenir of the event, something to prove that 'I was there'.[1] As Susan Sontag has shown us, shooting means taking possession of that which one is photographing. We might say that it is the desire to own, say, Picasso's *Guernica* that subsumes the desire to interact directly with the work. American media theorist Neil Postman summarizes the perspective of technological determinism using the adage that, 'to a man with a hammer, everything looks like a nail'.[2] We might state that, for an individual with a digital camera, everything seems worth photographing. The worldview inaugurated by digital cameras replaces a lived, unmediated reality with a hypertrophic complex of images.

This broad trend of interposing digital devices between oneself and reality is part of a more general desire for transparency and immediacy that has been so effectively described by Bolter and Grusin,[3] and that has always characterized our relationship to media, though it reaches its apotheosis in today's radically mediatized society. There are two mutually reinforcing trends: the media industry attempts to offer ever more 'authentic' experiences by concealing the moment of mediation;

concomitantly, individuals attempt to construct their own 'authentic' visions of reality, but which now, paradoxically, can only be authenticated by means of technology. In other words, in order to experience a sense of authenticity and immediacy one no longer relates to the 'outside' world, but necessarily makes contact with that world through a mediated and filtered representation. Only that which is mediated can be 'real' – hence, the spectators at a concert or exhibition must be able to look at a moment again and again in order for it to become 'real'.

A further consideration is the effect of interposing a viewfinder or display between the human eye and the subject. Of course, it is premature at the present moment to speculate upon the long-term sensory consequences of digital media. It is less premature, perhaps, to envision a progressive flattening of minds already worn down by 50 years of television. We see a reversal of the dominant relation between man and machine, in which the human subject conceives the goal, and the machine offers the means of attaining that aim. During the compulsive recording of a cultural event, the camera provides both aim and means. Having deprived themselves of any direct relationship with the object, humans lack a *telos*, and are easily rendered subject to the digital medium they carry with them. We might, then, paraphrase Dziga Vertov's famous proclamation, and state: I am an eye. A *digital* eye and constantly moving![4]

The Will of Technology

According to Italian philosopher Emanuele Severino, the contemporary subject addresses himself to technology as he previously did to God or to *mythos*, through the words: 'save me' or 'be the means through which my will is made'. With technology, as with God, the subject realizes that in his hands, 'the Saviour itself is weak'. Thus, the subject learns to take a step back, in order not to 'block the action and the saving project of Technology'. Thus, again as with God, after begging technology to 'make my will', humans address technology with the more realistic invocation 'may your will be done'. Therefore, 'the will of Technology becomes the aim of man and man becomes the means through which the will of Technology is done'.[5] To Severino, as to Heidegger before him, technology's will to power is bound to triumph over other forms of willpower. Technology's will to power seems to me the only possible explanation for the hypertrophic growth of modern digital devices. How else to explain the flourishing of digital photo albums such as Flickr, or the compulsive posting on blogs? What can one do with millions of pictures? What sense or meaning can they possibly have, unless it is to be shared on digital networks? This sharing actually constitutes the *simulacrum* of a purpose, offering us the illusion that we are acting purposefully, rather than acting as tools through which the machine realizes its own purposes.

This reversal is brilliantly captured in the Scottish novelist Iain M. Banks' short story *Descendant*.[6] In this work of science fiction, an astronaut from the future survives the crash of his spacecraft, and finds himself completely alone. All he has to rely on is his space suit – which is, however, in possession of intelligence equal to that of a human, completely self sufficient, and able to reach its target regardless of the cooperation of its 'host'. During their long journey together across a deserted territory, the survivor and the suit speak of philosophical issues such as death, the meaning of life and desire. At the end of the journey, upon encountering a drone, it emerges that the man has actually been dead for a month. When the drone asks the suit why it did not dispose of the corpse, the suit merely *shrugs its shoulders* and suggests that it might, perhaps, have been caught up in some form of sentimentality. Interestingly, there is not one moment in Banks' story in which the human subject provides the aim and the machine the means. The machine acts according to its own purposes, and when the man breathes his last breath, the suit merely continues on its way. Even while the astronaut's purposes and the suit's purposes are only contingently congruent, the astronaut never questions that the suit's *raison d'être* is to keep him alive and safe from harm. Similarly, we imagine that our machines might possess their own independent purposes, and that they might organize themselves in networks and autonomous blocks in order to achieve their aims.

In a similar way, Mario Costa refers to a 'need that is in the order of things'[7] as something to which the intentions, plans and passions of individuals respond: 'a need that belongs to the objectivity of the things and the processes'.[8] In the 'neo-technological' era, which is typified by the digital, networks, bio-technologies, nano-technologies and their interaction, the role of humans is increasingly marginal: it is to active different 'neo-technological blocks'. In Costa's view, the 'neo-technologies are no longer extensions or prostheses in the McLuhanian sense, but separate extroversions of the basic functions of the human that tend to become autonomous and self-operating'.[9] They complete the process begun in the 'technical' era, the 'era of the hand', in which individualized, stable and discrete tools, such as the hammer, respond directly to human needs, and continued into the era of 'familiarism', in which technologies such as electric light and photography give rise to complexes, sequences and hybrids that effectively marginalize the subject. Recalling the famous 'Palo Alto' axiom (Jackson, Watzlawick) according to which 'One Cannot Not Communicate', Costa states that:

> We all have to communicate ... by phone, by e-mail, by mobile ... and all of this because telephone, e-mail, mobile and all the rest, have to communicate with each other ... communication is by now mere drive, technologically induced, aimless and without content.[10]

These ceaseless communicating technologies constitute a 'communicating block', in which the role of humans is to make the block work. Meanwhile, the 'wit' exhibited by 'neo-technologies' is to convince human subjects that technologies merely fulfil their (humans') social and communicative needs. Of course, other thinkers before Costa reached similar conclusions. In many cases, however, this necessitated a prophetic style, that which Günther Anders describes as an 'exaggeration in the direction of truth' (*Übertreibung in Richtung Wahrheit*).[11] Indeed, Anders is among the first, in the 1950s, to identify the marginalization of humans by technical artefacts. Describing a condition in which all forms of human activity are reduced to the operations of machines (devices that tend to become universal by integrating all possible functions), thus robbing humans of their purpose and transforming them into the means of production, the German philosopher prefigures what is now obvious to everybody. He even identifies the feelings of inadequacy that humans experience when they compare themselves to machines (*prometheischen Scham*).[12]

Today, theorists such as Costa no longer need to exaggerate when they speak of the subservience of humans to the purposes of machines. Rather than appearing to be futuristic or apocalyptic visions, observations seem obvious to anyone that takes a moment to reflect on the present 'neo-technological era'.

Technologies of the Self

In relation to images, Dutch theorist Eric Kluitenberg conceives of an 'aesthetics of the unspectacular'. For Kluitenberg, the images relayed by millions of webcams are intrinsically 'unspectacular', in contrast to Guy Debord's paradigm. Contemporary technologies, then, work in overt contradiction to mass or broadcast media, for the images that they produce, though claiming their right to exist, no longer require the attention of the masses.[13] I am not fully persuaded that images from webcams exist outside the domain of the global spectacle, for they can be seen to perpetuate this very phenomenon. What I find more convincing, however, is Kluitenberg's conception of images that simply exist independently, without needing to be seen. Moving beyond the images produced by webcams, we can state that the images populating blogs, photo albums and social networks are soliloquies: expressions that do not require any form of dialogue, for their only *raison d'être* is to exist in some corner of the ocean of digital communications. As Lovink notes in *Zero Comments*,[14] new media allow anyone to speak, but they degrade our ability to listen. For Lovink, it is precisely the awareness that one is talking to oneself that throws bloggers into nihilism. Blogs, meanwhile, erase the need for confrontation with *the Other* and become *technologies of the self*. It is my view that such expressions are a means of convincing oneself of the reality and authenticity of our own lived experience. Contemporary individuals are so used to considering only that which is represented within the media landscape as 'real', that they are compelled to re-represent their experiences. This is a form of testimony for oneself rather than for others: the function of these images is exhausted by their existence, rather than the moment in which they are looked at. Despite these reflections, it would be incorrect to state that these images are meaningless, for they give shape to the aesthetic landscape that frames contemporary life, as well as fuelling the same diffuse aesthetics. In fact, it is the iconic obesity of the Web that most clearly evinces that virtualization of reality that is one of the main phenomena that contemporary aesthetics must confront.

What to Fill Digital Memories With?

Keep cool fool, if you don't know what you're doin'
Keep cool fool, 'cause you don't know what you're doin'
Ella Fitzgerald, *Keep Cool, Fool* (1941)

The proliferation of tools for self-production of media content gives rise to the question: What to fill digital memories with? Most studies of self-production are characterized by a certain degree of pessimism: the most probable result is products that have no meaning outside the individual sphere and the individual archive. After all, since the mass distribution of cameras, have they not been used mainly for the petty, shallow projects of tourists?[1] From this point of view, digital media can contribute nothing new or meaningful, just as photography and cinema, as mass technologies, failed to subvert the dominant reality. The exponential multiplication of sources of digital production has not enriched the world with meaning, it has only made it more complex and perhaps more multilateral. Nevertheless, it is commonly believed that blogs, pirate or street televisions, independent magazines and streaming radio broadcasts are more adequate to report upon contemporary events than official media. If amateur pornography is supported by voyeurism and affordability, it is more difficult to justify amateur works belonging to different genres.

Be Your Media

It is worth first distinguishing between informational and entertainment content. In relation to information, digital media have turned every technologically literate human into a potential 'mediactivist'. Those tools so praised by marketing propaganda have become potential weapons of dissent. *Disinformation*, independent and uncontrollable, now frequently enables fragments of truth to pass through breaches in the clouds of mass media communication. Despite the massive efforts of the entire Western apparatus of propaganda, the enduring image of the was in Iraq will not be the fall of the statue of a bloody dictator, but that of a hooded Iraqi prisoner.[2] The surface of mass media is still visible, but it is now underwritten by a whole universe of alternative sources that function to shift a vast amount of data within and between increasingly stratified networks: from blogs to Indymedia, from street televisions to independent publishing houses. In this new reality, 'everyone'[3] has the capacity to become an individual source of production. Even if they are confined to a small portion of the global population, it would be a mistake to underrate the possibility that these media offer for a genuine exchange of views. The most productive point of focus is perhaps the pressure that thousands of digital devices are placing on the traditional media. As the threat of being exposed grows exponentially, traditional media are forced to become more morally responsible. Disinformation, in the sense in which I have used it above, may be only a grain of sand within that which Bourdieu might term the monolithic consensus factory, yet it does offer reason for hope.

Increasingly, official media integrates self-produced content within its own processes of production. Professional journalists draw increasingly heavily on unbranded news, as was evident in the December 2004 tsunami. In this case, the international media were forced to build upon the 'non-professional' material produced by Western tourists that were present during the event. The two networks overlap to such an extent that it becomes difficult to distinguish amateur from official sources. It also becomes more difficult to verify one's news sources, which now often involves cross-checking between a number of sources that have proven trustworthy in the past. If there is no meaningful distinction between official and self-produced information, does it make any sense to attempt to mobilize such a distinction? In a digital culture, information tends to require completion by the receiver: it is the receiver who must screen and compare multiple sources in order to evaluate the reliability and truthfulness of an information source, according to a personal code of values, or sometimes of taste.

In the 'network society', a piece of news can begin to jump from one node to another, apparently at random, triggering a dynamic of repetition and multiplication. Nobody knows how and why this takes place for some pieces of news and not for other, otherwise similar, items. It is as if content placed on the Infosphere possesses a life of its own, autonomous of the will of its author. As it encounters complex mechanisms of multiplication, it is this very life that can end up entering the everyday experiences of a vast number of Web users. Consider three items of minor importance that have been prominently broadcast by the international mass media: the crocodile tearing at the arm of a man at a Taiwan zoo captured by a tourist's camera; the British couple captured having sex under Windsor Castle by a group of Japanese tourists (also armed with their cameras); the employees of a pizza restaurant captured sticking pieces of cheese up their noses. As these memes survive and reproduce in global news media, we also see a clear progression in these media from information to entertainment.

At this point, I will turn to those self-produced contents that aim to entertain rather than to inform. I will emphasize two tendencies: the preference for speed over depth which recalls Francalanci's conceptualization of diffuse aesthetics; and a devaluation of aesthetic concepts such as 'beauty' and the form of experience occasioned by it.

'Cool' as a New Aesthetic Category

The crisis of the classical concept of beauty is manifest, in a linguistic sense, in the tendency to replace the term 'beautiful' with the term 'cool'.[4] The question arises, then: What ideal of beauty is expressed within the ideal of cool? In the preface to the work *American Cool*,[5] the American historian Peter Stearns writes:

> The concept is distinctly American, and it permeates almost every aspect of contemporary American culture. From Kool cigarettes and the Snoopy cartoon's Joe Cool to West Side Story ('Keep cool, boy.') and urban slang ('Be cool. Chill out.'), the idea of cool, in its many manifestations, has seized a central place in the American imagination.[6]

According to Stearns, 'cool' arises in the wake of the 'clearance' of the traditional system of values enacted in 1960s' America. In the succeeding decades, American society celebrates the rise of a new, 'impersonal but friendly', emotional style.[7] At the end of the twentieth century, the American middle class 'continue to value cool – as the ever-ascending popularity of the word suggests'.[8] The phenomenon is not, however, contained within one specific class. Along with the youthful adoption of cool, we see business people aiming to keep their cool and to control their passions, particularly in meetings, in which the attitudes of 'attack and defence' are highly discouraged:

> In the culture of the twentieth century, undue emotion, whether anger or grief or love, meant vulnerability as well as childishness. By

the 1990s, several generations had been schooled in the desirability of keeping most emotions buttoned up and expecting other people to do the same. American cool still prevails.[9]

In Stearns' analysis, cool serves as a kind of mask between the individual and society. In fact, Stearns associates the rise of cool with the rapid popularization, in the 1960s, of wearing sunglasses: an undisputed sign of coolness.[10]

American scholars Clive and Pamela Nancarrow offer a brief, but meaningful, history of cool. Although the concept of cool was evident prior to the twentieth century – in Byron, Baudelaire, Rimbaud and in *bohémien* culture in general – it became overt after the First World War, within the American jazz scene. Here, cool is connected to 'illicit knowledge' and, in particular, to the drug culture specific to that context.[11] In the 1970s, cool comes to characterize a specific look, and the hedonistic, anti-conventional or mystical culture of hippie tribes and, through them, of Western youth in general.[12] In the 1990s, rap and hip-hop reinstate African American culture at the centre of the 'cool map'.[13] At this point in time, the authors write, cool is 'not something you can set out to acquire; it is something that is acknowledged in you by others. It involves originality, self-confidence and must be apparently effortless. It is often transgressive and anti-establishment. It is certainly narcissistic.'[14] The scholars attend closely to the centrality of cool within marketing, as evinced by contemporary 'cool hunters', whose job it is to locate and capitalize on emerging trends. Cool, then, constantly evolves, and is inflected by the specificities of the sociocultural environment.

In his seminal work *The Laws of Cool*,[15] American literary theorist Alan Liu discusses the connection between cool and information culture. 'Knowledge work', according to Liu, has become the new global economic paradigm, influencing university policy, and the policies of global learning organizations. This is the prelude to the establishment of a vast middle class who are employed to control and manage knowledge. Simultaneously, a culture of information emerges that overtakes and undermines traditional literary culture. Information technology is the principal medium of the knowledge economy, as well as the means of dissemination of a 'new high-tech culture of cool' that uses 'information ... to resist information'.[16] Rather than a subculture or counterculture, there emerges an 'intraculture of cool within the corporate ethos'. It is through the Web in particular that information technology gives life to a 'semi-autonomous culture of cool', as is evident when viewing those web pages that are so cool that they manage to constrain the flow of information:

> The friendship of the Web, and everything it represents in the long history of work leading up to current knowledge work, is also strangely cold. It is from this coldness – remoteness, distantiation, impersonality – that cool emerges as the cultural dominant of our time.[17]

For Liu, the category of cool represents 'the most authentic response of contemporary culture to postindustrial knowledge work', as it retains a 'reserve of counter-knowledge' or 'anti-knowledge', a sort of 'ethos of the unknown'. As the cool pushes towards superficial and self-centred forms of knowledge, an 'alliance of New Humanities and New Arts' is uniquely able to educate the 'generations of cool' to use technology to mediate between knowledge work and those historical forms of knowledge that can compensate for and complete a Schumpeterian 'creative destruction' of knowledge work. For Liu, the past is the only possible antidote to the 'hyper-compressed sense of now' embodied in the 'cubicle' that imprisons the everyday lives of contemporary knowledge workers. The point, then, is to understand what to destroy. That which Liu defines as 'destructivity' is 'a way of asking such questions and, on that basis, proposing ethical as well as tactical "best practices" for participating in the civilization of creative destruction'.[18]

From a purely aesthetic perspective, Robert Farris Thompson's essay 'An Aesthetic of the Cool'[19] makes a substantive contribution. Linking the concept to Western African and Afro-American populations, Thompson utilizes the concept of the mask – a mask that works to hide emotion in moments of stress as well as moments of pleasure, and in expressive performance and dance:

> Control, stability, and composure under the African rubric of the cool seem to constitute elements of an all-embracing aesthetic attitude. Struck by the reoccurrence of this vital notion elsewhere in tropical Africa and in the black Americas, I have come to term the attitude

'an aesthetic of the cool' in the sense of a deeply and complexly mo-
tivated, consciously artistic, interweaving of elements serious and
pleasurable, of responsibility and of play.[20]

For Thompson, the cooler subjects become, the more capable they are of
transcending everyday concerns. The main value is not physical beauty,
but the ability to control the forces of beauty, along with those of the
community (polity). 'Coolness therefore imparts order not through
ascetic subtraction of body from mind, or brightness of cloth from
seriousness of endeavor, but, quite the contrary, by means of ecstatic
unions of sensuous pleasure and moral responsibility.'[21] In my view,
the ethical values highlighted by Thompson are lost in the modern
and predominantly Western use of the term, which expresses a mainly
uncritical compliance with aesthetic expressions. No depth is possible,
and a thorough analysis of the look, behaviour, image, sound or object
is simply unthinkable.[22] In contemporary aesthetics, cool represents a
smooth and shallow form of beauty. Coolness has become the aesthetic
measure of a society that lives every experience at an unimaginable
speed, and that blends an infinite number of stimuli within a vague aesthetic experience, so that the attempt to go beyond the surface of things
has become a chimerical aim. To recall and adapt Thompson's concept
of the mask to a context in which aesthetic judgment is flattened, we
might state that wearing the mask of cool is a means of protecting
oneself from the need for an authentic relationship to one's own lived
experiences.

    In this perspective, anything one enjoys is simply cool, while any-
thing that injures one's own 'aesthetic sensibility' does not even deserve
a definition (which would require some critical effort) and is left behind.
What matters is to anticipate the cool that is waiting just around the
corner. This is an aesthetic attitude that is perfectly confluent with
the proliferation of tools for the creation of self-produced media. In
this sense, *Nora plays the piano*, a video of a cat 'playing' a piano that
hit YouTube a couple of years ago, is exemplary.[23] Viewers of the video
are likely to say 'cool' and, at most, add it to their 'favourites' or send it
to friends. In addition to being pointless, any further reflection would
impede the free flowing of digital data. After all, contemporary subjects
are so overloaded with contents that attempting to reflect upon them is

analogous to standing by a highway and attempting to formulate aesthetic judgments of the design and details of the interior of a passing car.

We have moved far from Plato's definition of beauty, according to which beautiful objects are beautiful in and of themselves; and we are equally removed from Hume's interpretation, according to which beauty lies in the mind of the beholder.[24] It is, however, worth recalling the traditional division between objectivism and subjectivism. Firstly, contemporary cool is inextricable from behaviours that tend towards conformity. On the Web, whatever is most viewed, ranked, linked or commented upon is automatically cool, in and of itself. We might state, then, that even if cool is massified, it is nevertheless subjective (*cool is in the mind of the beholder*). There are, however, examples of media objects and modalities that are intrinsically cool. For example, attaching a camera to one's arm and jumping from incredible heights (base jumping); or taking 'upskirt' pictures of women on the Tube (a practice so widespread in Japan that local authorities have forced mobile phone companies to introduce a loud shutter noise in their devices). Cool modes are those involving the use of the most innovative digital gadgets on the market, so that *coolness is an objective state of cool things.*

Exercises in Style

At this point, I would like to briefly discuss those amateur productions that might be termed (if it was not for the aesthetically insignificant results) *exercises in style*. A glance at the most popular videos on YouTube provides an immediate picture of this tendency. The most frequently viewed videos are those of pets caught in funny positions or attitudes, or of weird characters performing popular songs (one of the most frequent manias appears to be attempting to dance like American singer Beyoncé and – mania of manias – mimicking her moves in the clip for *Single Ladies*).[25] These examples apart, the most significant examples are those of amateurs attempting to undertake specific actions, such as blowing a huge bubble from bubble gum, mixing Mentos with Diet Coke to create explosions of gas, or of exhibiting incredibly loud burps, among other more or less uplifting performances. Other interesting 'exercises in style' are remakes of scenes from classic movies and plays, and parodies of commercials. Another constant, but one that requires a higher degree of organization, creativity and a huge amount of patience, is the so-called domino fall.

The decision to take part in any of these 'exercises in style' immediately opens the door to coolness. Each of the abovementioned videos is intrinsically cool, because each develops a model that is widely shared and appreciated by specific communities. Thus, the second characteristic of self-produced entertainment-related content is the constant repetition of content (memes) that have proved popular. The typical process appears to be: I take possession of a tool that allows me to create self-produced media, and the first thing that occurs to me is that I should imitate previously 'successful' contents. This constant repetition of preset formats contains an implicit acceptance of the aesthetical canon that the format itself embodies, and simultaneously aids in its affirmation and exponential memetic proliferation.

A perfect picture of this phenomenon is provided by Californian artist Natalie Bookchin's video installation *Mass Ornament* (2009).[26] The title of the work explicitly recalls the text in which Siegfried Kracauer associates the synchronized acts typical of the dances of the first decades of the twentieth century with the mechanized gestures of the processes of industrial production.[27] Bookchin's premise is that, if these dances exhibited features of Fordism and Taylorism, the domestic dance performances so popular on YouTube embody the spirit of post-Fordism, a socioeconomic context in which the 'masses' are no longer chained to the production line, but are tied instead to digital communication tools. Thus, Bookchin creates a video constructed of horizontal strips of YouTube clips of amateur dancers attempting to emulate professional dancers such as Beyoncé. Just as YouTube's interface shows thumbnails of related videos, Bookchin's video demonstrates the obsessive, synchronized repetition of the contemporary 'mass ornament'.

Although I have focused on YouTube, similar reflections emerge from viewing the near-identical images of tourist attractions on Flickr, or the endless re-enactions of specific sexual routines on YouPorn (which at least aids in the indexing of the materials). Above all, one is reminded of traditional mass media's compulsive reproduction of successful formats.

Occasional Ruptures in Insignificance

If the principal consequence of the proliferation of tools for media self-production appears to be the reproduction of the shallowness of the entertainment content of traditional media, it is also true that such media very frequently enable the production of low-budget content that is far more convincing than most movies and television shows. We might state, then, that it is the creativity and expertise of the producer that matters. Obviously, a person who has practised dancing for years will 'shake their booty' more like Beyoncé than a sedentary person. The point, however, is that something beyond the cool can come into being even in the absence of professionalism – and, indeed, in the spirit of amateurism that characterizes the repetitive content that clogs digital networks.

A video that I believe is genuinely poetic, although working within this frame, is that made by several Russian women parodying a synchronized swimming performance.[28] The video was made in the womens' office, with no particular technical expertise (still shots and natural light only), and certainly without any professional experience in synchronized swimming itself – so what makes this video different from the millions of others made in a similar way? The difference is that it invokes emotions in the viewer, and belongs to the domain of beauty rather than cool. Suddenly and unexpectedly, the performers break through the grim boredom of the workplace and of working routines, through the nonsensical and beautiful gesture of imitation. Showing only their legs and arms above their desks, the symbolic surface of the desktop, invoking command, exploitation and alienation, is suddenly disturbed by a new significance, as a space through which to hide and play. Furthermore, the display of anonymous limbs fills the video with an erotic drive, just as small details such as high heels, anklets and boots reveal an explosive femininity. The video opens the door to fantasy, briefly subverting the oppressive nature of the workplace. To state that the work lacks an artistic intent is simply meaningless: one often 'falls' into poetry by mere accident.

There is, therefore, no universal formula that can account for all new forms of self-production. The role that sheer accident can play means that we should not attribute too much to artistic sensibility or technical expertise. Although these are important qualities, they are not enough in and of themselves to avoid producing that which is merely cool and insignificant. A more complete theory will require continued, and close, attention.

Chapter v

Remix as Compositional Practice

Innovation and Repetition

> Genuineness is nothing other than a defiant and obstinate insistence
> on the monadological form which social oppression imposes on
> man. Anything that does not wish to wither should rather take
> on itself the stigma of the inauthentic. For it lives on the mimetic
> heritage. The human is indissolubly linked with imitation: a human
> being only becomes human at all by imitating other human beings.
> Theodor W. Adorno, *Minima Moralia* (1951)

Originality (if it ever existed at all) is dead. If this statement is true in
general, it is even more so in light of the Web. I begin this chapter with
Rosalind Krauss's classic work *The Originality of the Avant-Garde*,[1] in
which the American scholar focuses on the modernist 'myth' of originality, and the transformation of the myth into a kind of dogma that is
perpetuated through various avant-gardes.

The Myth of Originality

For Krauss, the concept of 'originality' is simpler than the repudiation or dissolution of the past: 'Avant-garde originality is conceived as a
literal origin, a beginning from ground zero, a birth.'[2] Krauss's analysis
of the practices of the avant-garde reveals that originality is in fact 'a
working assumption that itself emerges from a ground of repetition and
recurrence'.[3] The image through which Krauss illustrates this apparent contradiction is the 'grid', as a segmented pictorial surface. For the
avant-garde, writes Krauss, 'the grid facilitates this sense of being born
into the newly evacuated space of an aesthetic purity and freedom'.[4]
Simultaneously, the grid represents the nemesis of the myth of originality: although repeatedly 'discovered' in the avant-garde, 'it is always a
new, a unique discovery'.[5] Furthermore, its adoption has led many artists, including Mondrian, Albers, Reinhardt and Agnes Martin towards
a poetic of repetition: 'From the time they submit themselves to this
structure,' Krauss writes, 'their work virtually ceases to develop and becomes involved, instead, in repetition.'[6] It finally breaks the modernist
promise, and ends up hiding the pictorial surface, rather than revealing
it. Viewing originality and repetition[7] as co-dependent terms allows us
to free ourselves from the Romantic myth of originality; in the schema

I will use, 'innovation' replaces 'originality', yet the linkage with the opposing term 'repetition' is retained.

Krauss views Duchamp's and Warhol's 'classic appropriations' and
Jeff Koons' more recent 'plagiarisms' differently, as they play on the ambiguity of the concept of 'originality'[8] itself. As Fredric Jameson defines
it, originality is a 'a suspect concept',[9] and it is clear that contemporary
art places the concept in crisis, in and through characteristically postmodern practices such as *pastiche*, collage, cut-up, quotation and appropriation. Paradoxically, it is at this very moment that the struggle for
originality becomes radical, turning into a crusade played out on legal
and economic turf and led by the so-called 'aura merchants'.[10] In the
present art market, what is bought and sold is the 'aura': the definition
of art as the original work of a solitary creative genius. Simultaneously
with the progressive devaluation of the concept of 'originality' in art,
literature, science and philosophy, then, we see the rise of a form of
originality that is inextricable from capitalist economics.

A Genealogy of the Remix

The world of contemporary art, however, is a sphere that remains
far removed from recent sociocultural transformations. In electronic
music and in so-called DJ culture, we see an acute awareness of the significance of the remix.[11] In Jamaica in the late 1960s, producers and DJs
such as Lee Perry and King Tubby 'made an art form out of taking pre-
recorded rhythm tracks and rearranging them into a piece of music,
a new *version* as they called it',[12] thus giving birth to dub, a genre that
develops through revisions of reggae. Largely through migration, these
practices quickly spread to the USA (where they found fertile soil in
disco culture) and to England, which, with its large community of
Caribbean immigrants, served as a kind of bridge for the culture to
extend further into Europe.

The discipline of Cultural Studies, and in particular the so-called
Birmingham School, have extensively studied forms of subcultural 'resistance' characterized by certain genres of music, cultural heritage and
particular dress codes and lifestyles. While acknowledging the radical
antagonism of the subcultures that have given life to the history I will
trace, I have chosen not to focus on the political aspect of this history.
There are two main reasons for this: first, as Richard Middleton[13] has

noted, the overestimation of the political tends to background the pluralism, differences and even contradictions within many subcultures; secondly, because I believe we need to question the extent to which these politics live on within 'contemporary tribes'.[14] If postmodern subcultures are characterized mainly by extemporaneity, one must, as Michel Maffesoli recalls, dig behind the 'tragic superficiality of sociality'.[15]

The first major stage in the history of remix culture took place in the mid-1970s, when dub and disco remix cultures encountered each other through Jamaican immigrants living in the Bronx. This encounter energized both genres, and participated in the birth of hip-hop. *Cutting* (alternating between duplicate copies of the same record) and *scratching* (manually moving the vinyl record beneath the turntable needle) became part of the culture. Key figures during this period included DJ Kool Herc and DJ Grandmaster Flash, and one of the first mainstream successes of this style of remix was the 1983 track *Rockit* by Herbie Hancock, as remixed by Grand Mixer D.ST. (alias Derek Showard). In the 1980s, 'extended mixes' of songs were released to clubs and commercial outlets on 12-inch vinyl singles. These usually had a duration of about six or seven minutes, and often consisted of the original song with eight or 16 bars of instrumental music inserted after the second chorus. As new technologies became more affordable, many groups who participated in the production of their records, such as Depeche Mode, New Order and Duran Duran, experimented with more intricate versions of the extended mix. The Art of Noise took the remix style to an extreme, creating new music entirely using samples. After the rise of dance music in the late 1980s, a new form of remix was popularized, in which a song's vocals were retained and its instruments were replaced with a backing track in the 'house' music idiom. As the art of the remix evolved, avant-garde artists such as the Aphex Twin created more experimental remixes of songs, which differed radically from the original and were not guided by pragmatic considerations such as sales or danceability.

In the 1990s, the dissemination of powerful home computers with audio capabilities gave rise to the 'mash-up': an unsolicited, unofficial and often legally dubious remix created by editing two or more recordings (often of wildly different songs) together. Mash-ups are quite

difficult to create, because clean copies of separate tracks such as vocals or individual instruments are usually not available to the public.
However, artists such as Björk and Public Enemy have embraced the
trend, and openly sanctioned fans' remixing of their work. In this and
the next decade, in addition to dance remixes, many R&B, pop, and rap
artists use remixes and alternate versions of songs with 'featured' guest
stars, in order to give them new life. On 5 January 2002, *J To Tha L-O!* by
Jennifer Lopez became the first remix album to debut at Number One
on Billboard's Top 200 albums chart.[16]

One of the most thorough scholars of remix culture, Eduardo Navas,
constructed a genealogy based on the distinction between three forms
of remix. The first type is 'extended': a longer version of an original
song obtained predominantly by introducing very long instrumental
sections into the song. The first of these records is *Ten Percent* by Double
Exposure, which was remixed by Walter Gibbons in 1976, after which
the song lasts 10 minutes longer than the original version.[17] This format
is also crucial to the spreading of the 12-inch single, which will soon
become one of the main work tools for DJs. The second type of remix is
'selective', a form that consists of adding or removing elements from the
original song. A notable example of this format is *Paid in Full* by Eric B.
& Rakim, which was remixed by Coldcut in 1987. According to Navas,
this type of remix contributes to the transformation of DJs into producers within the pop music environment.[18] The third and final type of
remix is 'reflexive'. This, Navas writes, is a more complex typology that:

> . . . allegorizes and extends the aesthetic of sampling, where the
> remixed version challenges the aura of the original and claims auton-
> omy even when it carries the name of the original; material is added
> or deleted, but the original tracks are largely left intact to be recog-
> nizable. . . . In this case both albums, the original and the remixed
> versions, are considered works on their own, yet the remixed version
> is completely dependent on [the] original production for validation.[19]

Navas' example is the famous album *No Protection* by Mad Professor,
which remixes Massive Attack's *Protection*. The fact that both albums
were released in 1994 complicates the issue of the limits of the allegory,
leading Navas to clarify that:

... allegory is often deconstructed in more advanced remixes following this third form, and quickly moves to be a reflexive exercise that at times leads to a 'remix' in which the only thing that is recognizable from the original is the title. But, to be clear – no matter what – the remix will always rely on the authority of the original song. When this activity is extended to culture at large, the remix is in the end a re-mix – that is a rearrangement of something already recognizable; it functions at a second level: a meta-level. This implies that the originality of the remix is non-existent, therefore it must acknowledge its source of validation self-reflexively. In brief, the remix when extended as a cultural practice, is a second mix of something pre-existent; the material that is mixed at least for a second time must be recognized otherwise it could be misunderstood as something new, and it would become plagiarism. Without a history, the remix cannot be Remix.[20]

Transparent Surfaces?

This last passage introduces a conception of remix as a transparent surface, in which the original materials remain half in sight. According to this vision of the remix, it should always be possible to trace the quoted materials. There is, however, an opposing view, in which a remix is seen as something 'new'. Jamie O'Neil provides a version of this view that is clearly inflected by Deleuze and Guattari:

The difference between mix and remix is that the former is of a more primary and molecular order, whereas the remix is of a higher, molar order. From the basic processes of cut and paste, to the availability of stock images, loop based music, and design templates; the process of the 'designer' of digital media has become a process of creating new combinations of existing things, i.e. new mixes (*not* remixes). We might understand these available stock options as organs for a body. We can mix *simple* parts: new kidneys, lungs, even a heart (via a transplant) and still maintain the same body. Remixing occurs on a higher level, it is the modification of the body itself, a sex change, or a radical transformation of identity leading to a superimposition over the past body, a mother, an addict, a soldier, a cross-dresser... Remix denies essential identity by maintaining a transparency to the previous context, and presents a sophisticated dual image, the former body is not lost, there is a co-presence of the past and the present in this embodiment, which mediates between the past and the future via a new vector of the eternally changing.[21]

Although correct from a philological point of view, such theories might in fact presage a *remix aesthetics*, in which the full enjoyment of a remix depends upon the listener's ability to recognize the original. As O'Neil himself admits,[22] this is difficult to realize in an age of diffuse aesthetics, in which it is increasingly the external surface of things that is perceived, at the expense of the underlying conceptual implications. As I have claimed throughout this work, the result is that the very conceptual level disappears, as we become increasingly embroiled in a game that plays out on the territory of form. For example, if we apply the perspective of recognizability of the quoted materials to Paul D. Miller's (aka DJ Spooky – That Subliminal Kid) remix of the famous *Birth of the Nation* (1915) in *Rebirth of the Nation* (2008),[23] it is logical to conclude that those unfamiliar with Griffith's movie will be unable to fully appreciate Miller's work. I would reject this hypothesis: as in the quotation in contemporary art, I believe that each person has access to the full aesthetic enjoyment of a work according to their own interpretative capacities. Those who are able to identify the quoted materials will understand the work more deeply, but they do not necessarily partake of a more intense aesthetic enjoyment. One might be captivated by movement or sound, and become emotional, angry or anguished, whether or not one is aware of the operations of critical recontextualization. For Miller, an eclectic artist and theorist, the intention is to undermine the Western script of linear progress by placing it in counterpoint to the biggest shame within American history: that of slavery. Yet, even spectators who are not familiar with *Birth of the Nation* will realize that Miller's material is a remix of an old black-and-white movie.

By focusing on the allegorical nature of the remix – the recognition of a 'pre-existing cultural code', and hence of a specific history,[24] Navas appears to imply only a superior level at which the work may be decoded. One must be careful, however, of constructing an elitist conception of aesthetic experience, according to which those with a more circumscribed cultural education are implicitly unable to partake of a complete aesthetic enjoyment. Yet one can cry in front of Picasso's *Guernica* (1937) even though ignoring the tragedy it represents; one can partake of deep aesthetic rapture listening to Timo Maas' *Enjoy the Silence* (2004), in complete ignorance of the fact that it remixes the homonymous song by Depeche Mode.

A further example is the Dionysian ecstasy experienced by rave-goers, which cannot be either measurably increased by the recognition of the songs quoted in remixes. Of course, when we enter the domain of aesthetological critique, a judgment on the formal value of a work clearly requires a precise recognition of all the materials involved.

In my view, it is more productive to view remix as an irreversible process of hybridization – of sources, materials, subjectivities and media – than to construct taxonomic distinctions. We can consider the remix as Manovich might: as a metaphor for the generalized amalgamation and digitalization of culture.

Read/Write

American academic Lawrence Lessig's recent *Remix* offers an insightful and convincing interpretation of the phenomenon.[25] Lessig makes a brilliant analogy between the remix and the acronyms attached to computer files: 'RO' (Read/Only) and 'RW' (Read/Write). Whereas RO files are determined by mass media and analogue technologies, so that the producers are clearly separated from users, the birth of digital media gives rise to an RW culture, in which both consumers and producers have the power to modify the medial objects and the culture as a whole. According to Lessig, the remix represents 'an essential act of RW creativity. It is the expression of a freedom to take "the songs of the day or the old songs" and create with them'.[26] Lessig captures two crucial aspects of remix culture: the sense in which they reveal written texts as 'today's Latin', in that they are the favoured mode of communication of elites; and the way that remix evinces the fact that: 'For the masses . . . most information is gathered through other forms of media: TV, film, music, and music video. These forms of "writing" are the vernacular of today.'[27] Secondly, remix or RW culture is typified by the mixing of different media (text and images, video and sound, and so forth); this very mixing of media that characterizes 'the new creative work', that is the remix.[28] Lessig constantly shifts his focus between culture and the regulations that constrain remix practices, and casts new light on the issue of 'originality', by identifying in the mix/remix a sort of scent of plagiarism which shows as something new, something whose history cannot be traced back. Any genealogy of the remix, however, must take into account the contribution of technology, without which remix practices clearly would not have progressed very far.

The Beginning of the Game

Simon Crab's project *120 Years of Electronic Music*, inaugurated in 1995 and last updated in 2005, offers an invaluable history of the development of electronic musical instruments.[29] It offers a lucid account of the impact of technical innovation upon music production, and upon the culture more widely. Here, I will focus on just one technology discussed in this fascinating (but lengthy) history. In 1963, Leslie, Frank and Norman Bradley produced the Mellotron, the precursor to the modern digital sampler. In actual fact, the Mellotron is an imitation of the Chamberlin, realized some years earlier in the USA by Harry Chamberlin. However, the distinctive sound of the Mellotron meant that it was popular among rock musicians of the 1960s and 1970s, including The Beatles, Deep Purple, Pink Floyd, Jimi Hendrix, Genesis, Yes, King and Crimson. The Mellotron is an electro-mechanical polyphonic keyboard. Under each key is a strip of magnetic tape with a recorded sound corresponding to the pitch of the key. When the key is pressed, the instrument plays the sound, and returns the tape head to the beginning of the tape when the key is released.[30] Usually, Mellotrons were pre-loaded with string instrument and orchestral recordings, although from the model M400 onwards, the tape bank could be removed and loaded with different sounds, including percussion loops, sound effects, and synthesizer-generated sounds, so that it was possible to generate polyphonic electronically generated sounds.[31]

Machines such as the Mellotron have made it possible to play loops of instruments, simply by pressing a key. Today, when entire orchestras are merely one click away, this has become a banal experience. At the time of their inception, however, such technologies enabled some artists (such as Pauline Oliveros and Terry Riley) to incorporate ostensibly avant-garde practices into popular music. It was possible, for example, to take fragments of an audiotape and splice them together, so that portions of a recording could be played in a potentially endless loop. Prior even to polyphonic synthesizers, the Mellotron makes it common to create remixes constituted by several such loops.[32]

The Mellotron is part of a more general tendency to separate music into distinct segments, after which each is recorded separately and then reassembled. This modularity is evident in the first experimental synthesizers to modern digital systems, and it is the foundation of the practice of remix – a kind of game involving tracks/sounds/images/samples, the aim of which is to recompose them into different wholes.

In any game, rules are required before beginning[33] and so it is for the remix. In this case the rules include the progressive atomization of reality following the serialization of production, a cultural environment in which the traditional concept of authorship is progressively eroded, and the contribution of technology. In the case of dub, for example, the key technology is the multitrack mixer – the instrument King Tubby needs for his game to begin.[34]

The Remix as Compositional Paradigm

Remix is not specific to music, but involves all domains of human action. It is also a constitutive element of history: consider memetic theory, which reminds us that both biological and social evolution takes place by means of minor variations, and then through repetition. It is worth reminding ourselves that Leopardi, in a *Zibaldone* entry dated 28 November 1821, in reference to his debt to Petrarca, speaks of originality as a faculty to be acquired like any other. In particular, he states that it is necessary to read as much as possible in order to be original.[35] Evolution requires us to mix the elements of culture according to our needs. As Anthony Giddens might state: *one uses the past to build the future.*[36] Remix, then, is hardly a new phenomenon: it is a practice that has made art, science, and many other intellectual fields possible.[37] Indeed, when writing this book I have continually kept in mind Roland Barthes' definition of a text as 'a tissue of quotations drawn from innumerable centers of culture'.[38]

Yet, even if a remix practice has vivified every age, it is not inaccurate to describe contemporary culture as a 'remix culture', for at least two reasons: the massive spreading of post-production tools that allow the sampling of sources; and the Web's exponential multiplication of sources that one can access at virtually anytime and from anywhere.

Even compared to the Roman Empire, the best example of a culture able
to devour – and be devoured by – any form of civilization, the present
culture, in which media objects are remixed even as they are received,
is distinguished by the ubiquity of the remix. This is a *state of activity*
higher than that which Michel de Certeau identifies in the acts of consumers as they interpret media objects, an activity that is necessarily
connected to the their use.[39] I mean to refer to the capacity of modern
tools of communication to create a personal model of access to content;
a kind of hybridized *physiognomy* of sources. Consider the way one is
able to personally order the tracks downloaded to an MP3 player, giving
life to possibilities never conceived of by the songwriters, or the individual composition of contents enabled by RSS feeds, or the personalized
newspaper authored by one's favourite journalists that automatically
takes shape every morning. Software such as Netvibes[40] allows users to
collect within a single web page the latest news from the users' favourite newspapers, posts from the blogs or forums they follow, the activities of their friends on Facebook, the weather forecast, stockmarket report and the latest bids on the eBay auctions they are participating in.[41]
There are many further examples; the point is the endless possibilities
for access and manipulation of content. I recall the feeling I experienced
visiting an exhibition that collected almost all of Caravaggio's works
together.[42] The exhibition, however, did not include original paintings
but printed copies of the works, each of which had been digitalized
especially for the occasion. This led me to reflect that such digital copies of Caravaggio's constitute a kind of basic material, a 'ready-made'
which can be used to create new works. After all, the history of art is
constituted by artists mastering the techniques of their predecessors,
which was only possible when they were able to access the works themselves: Caravaggio himself began to produce more complex works after
he moved to Cardinal Del Monte, where he was able to *face* and to study
the significant collection of his patron. Today, this access appears a non-
issue. I might have Caravaggio's *Vita di San Matteo* on my PC and, thanks
to (possibly free) photo-editing software, I am able to overlay the three
scenes with three sexually explicit scenes from movies (which I have, of
course, also downloaded from the Internet). In this case, I have created
a work that is not too different from many that populate contemporary
art galleries. This statement is not intentionally provocative – after all,

Peter Greenaway, who is surely not a *radical thinker*, has recently stated that 'if Bernini had Photoshop he would have shown God'.[43]

Contemporary culture can also be termed a remix culture if we consider the proliferating forms of software with no function other than to overlap different digital sources. These sources, which might include audio, video or text, are used by VJs in their live performances. Software such as BeatHarness, FLxER, Mute, Modul8, GrandVJ and VJamm, all work (basically) the same way: the interface displays three windows, those at the sides are for visualizing sources, while the window in the centre displays the effective mix of the two sources. Once users have 'told' the software which files or folders it is to use as sources, the software overlaps them, with often surprising effects. Apart from selecting the materials to be remixed, users also establish the remix modes. What is interesting, however, is the existence of software that effectively responds to the exponential accumulation of digital materials in a creative and witty manner. During a raid of the Infosphere, a single picture can be saved with a single click, and the image given new life in a VJ's performance.[44] If everything is so *handy*, so extemporaneous, and so amusing, why not use it?

The materials are so many that they simply beg to be remixed and hybridized. Individuals are *forced* to think in terms of post-production and remix, if they are to be able to face the everyday overload of digital information. Remix is an 'evolutionary duty', arising from every human's innate need to personally transform the materials available to them. If true, this might explain why the practice of remix is more necessary to the contemporary age than ever before – humans have never had so many materials *in their hands*. If culture has always evolved through variation, selection and repetition, we are inhabiting a remix culture *par exellence*, especially if one considers the simplicity and speed of computerized cut and paste routines, or the intuitiveness of the editing process within Photoshop or After Effects. The cut and paste *continuum* thrives on media objects organized into distinct, clearly separable parts. Of course, software tools that enable whole cultural products to be divided are equally necessary. Remix culture requires flexibility; or, in Manovich's terms, 'modularity': 'Not self-contained aesthetic objects or self-contained records of reality but smaller units-parts that can be easily changed and combined with other parts in endless combinations.'[45]

The first tendency we can identify is the incorporation of increasing amounts of analogue human culture into the digital domain – a tendency that can be identified, for instance, in Google Books, as in the example of the digital reproductions of Caravaggio, not to mention the domestic practices of digitalization and the sharing of media objects on P2P networks. This shift is crucial to remix culture, as it makes cultural contents available to increasing numbers of the world's population, thanks to global IT networks and the Web. The amount of material to be remixed grows every day, its quality improves, as does the quality of technologies of digitalization that will lead to even greater growth. Modern software tools have given life to a scenario in which the operations of selection, construction, editing and publishing upon the infinite flow of digital data are undertaken with increasing ease. We can envisage a stage of 'total remixability', a condition in which *everything can be remixed with everything else.* In reference to the 'Age of Remix, Manovich writes:

> Today, many cultural and lifestyle arenas – music, fashion, design, art, web applications, user created media, food – are governed by remixes, fusions, collages, and mash-ups. If post-modernism defined 1980s, remix definitely dominates 1990s and 2000s, and it will probably continue to rule the next decade as well.[46]

In such a remix culture, the Web itself becomes 'a breeding ground for [a] variety of new remix practices'.[47] Manovich highlights the role of RSS feeds and relevant readers, the use of which clears the path to a 'custom mix selected from many millions of feeds available'.[48] In Manovich's brief genealogy, a crucial reference is to that point at the beginning of the twenty-first century, when 'people started to apply the term "remix" to other media besides music: visual projects, software, literary texts',[49] so that 'electronic music and software serve as the two key reservoirs of new metaphors for the rest of culture today'.[50] Rather than developments on a continuum with modernist practices such as 'montage' and 'collage', Manovich foregrounds the novelty of work by contemporary musicians who 'rather than sampling from mass media to create a unique and final artistic work (as in modernism), use their own works and works by other artists in further remixes'.[51] In the visual arts, this novelty is represented by 'electronic editing equipment such as switcher, keyer, paintbox, and image store',[52] which in turn transform remixing and sampling into widely used practices in video production. In Manovich's reconstruction, the introduction of software such as Photoshop (1989) and After Effects (1993) 'had the same effect on the fields of graphic design, motion graphics, commercial illustration and photography. And, a few years later, World Wide Web redefined an electronic document as a mix of other documents. Remix culture has arrived.'[53]

At the beginning of the twenty-first century, remix is no longer one possible compositional option; it is rather a 'new cultural default'. The result is an increasing number of producers who publish their content within 'a global media cloud' that other users access to create, in turn, their own 'personalized mixes'.[54] In Manovich's view, the term 'cloud' is most apposite to a situation in which 'feed technologies turned the original web of interlinked web pages sites into a more heterogeneous and atomized global "cloud" of content'.[55] For Manovich, the concept of remixability extends far beyond its commonsense meaning. It is a phenomenon in which 'previously separate media work together in a common software-based environment'.[56] Manovich refers to a 'deep remixability', in order to highlight the way that a 'software production environment allows designers to remix not only the content of different media, but also their fundamental techniques, working methods, and ways of representation and expression'.[57] This process of 'softwarization' is not a prelude to the convergence of old and new media. Rather, once the 'representational formats of older media types, the techniques for creating content in these media and the interfaces for accessing them were unbundled from their physical bases and translated into software, these elements start interacting producing new hybrids'.[58]

The final step in the processes inaugurated by the birth of digital is what Manovich, in explicit reference to Alan Kay, terms that of the *metamedium*. 'The previously unique properties and techniques of different media,' Manovich writes, 'became the elements that can be combined together in previously impossible ways.'[59] This dynamic has significant consequences for aesthetics, presaging an *aesthetics of continuity*: a *continuum* of repetition, innovation and hybridization of form.

Aesthetics of Repetition

Gabriel Tarde has stated that an idea spreads thanks to the rooting of the languages of communication into conversation.[60] Paraphrasing Tarde, we can state that the forms of the Web become popular through the rootedness of aesthetics within repetition. Repetition is the very environment in which the Web's forms spread, just as memetic laws dictate. The fact that most Web 2.0 platforms make it so easy to embed a media object in one's own web site, blog, or Facebook wall ensures the ubiquity of digital data. Consider the ubiquity of a video first uploaded to YouTube or Vimeo, and subsequently embedded in thousands of blogs. As the video retains its own formal structure, and often its original interface (a YouTube video usually remains together with the thumbnails of related videos), there is an inevitable hybridization of the host website's interface and that of the embedded object. 'Different media elements are continuously added on top of each other,' Manovich writes, 'creating the experience of a continuous flow, which nevertheless preserves their differences.'[61] In such cases, media objects are hybridized regardless of the intentions of human subjects who have instituted the conjunction, but who have no control over the formal structure of the embedded object (users cannot, for example, remove the YouTube player bar). Users might, of course, work more directly to create remixes. They might add novelty to a ubiquitous media object by mixing sources together, as does a user who produces a new version of a famous TV sketch embedded in countless blogs by replacing the original actors with amusing cartoon characters.

The constant repetition of content across the Web is particularly evident in the practice of reblogging, in which a blogger re-publishes the content of another blog. Navas views this habit as 'one of the forms in which Remix extends to culture as a form of appropriation'.[62] According to Navas, we occupy a 'state of constant remix', to which every blogger contributes 'by constantly appropriating pre-existing material, to comment on it, or simply to recontextualize it, by making it part of a specialized blog'.[63] Within this constant flow of repetition and remix, the signs of that progressive aestheticization of society are clear. As I have stated, this is a process in which meaning is inexorably subsumed under an aestheticized surface. As Navas states: 'Remixes depend on the efficiency that made mass media powerful . . . They deliver material with the same efficiency and the same expectations of immediate recognition that the culture industry expects.'[64] And yet Navas contests the perspective of diffuse aesthetics, viewing remix practices as a means of correcting 'false-consciousness', and of developing a critical perspective, particularly upon the mass media.

This is certainly true of some work, which I would term avant-gardist if I were not repelled by the term. In any cultural field, there are politically conscious, critically aware practitioners of remix – DJ Spooky, Adbusters and Cornelia Sollfrank to name just a few. However, can this critical capacity be extended to remix culture in general? Unless we take the very act of remix as constitutively critical, in direct opposition to the mass-communication model, I do not believe Navas' optimism is justified. First of all, because remix is an evolutionary need and, as memetics demonstrates, we are often mistaken in believing that we are in control of the memes that we (in fact, unconsciously) spread. Secondly, especially in reference to bloggers, Navas ignores the fact that the unfathomable amount of material almost forces human subjects to remix; these acts take place within a *continuum* in which there is no critical attitude towards (let alone dialectic with) the materials that are reassembled. These are mere routines, and their materials are selected solely for their aesthetic surface, as when images are juxtaposed due to their complementary chromatic scales, regardless of their symbolic value or meaning. Furthermore, machines frequently remix automatically, even if the primary input is sourced from humans, which further undermines the capacity for critique. I am in agreement, however, with Navas' statement that:

> The agency of DJ producers lies in the fact that their raw material comes from mass production, which has pre-existent cultural value. The role of the DJ producer is to replay – or remix – not create, like a traditional composer is expected to do.[65]

I also agree with Navas that users are offered a meaningful opportunity to become producer themselves; that 'the act of not just listening or viewing, but of actually having to "play" something today is expected in new media culture'.[66] This phenomenon has been thoroughly analysed; at this point I wish to reaffirm the importance of understanding the extent to which users act *sua sponte*, and the extent to which they are acted upon by the sociotechnological complex. In a recent text, Navas reflects upon the consequences of Roland Barthes' and Michel Foucault's theories of authorship for digital culture. The practice of sampling, Navas asserts, undeniably brings the Renaissance and Romantic myths of the author as solitary genius into question:

> Remix's dependency on sampling questioned the role of the individual as genius and sole creator, who would 'express himself'. . . . Sampling allows for the death of the author [Barthes] and the author function [Foucault] to take effect once we enter late capitalism, because 'writing' is no longer seen as something truly original, but as a complex act of resampling and reinterpreting material previously introduced, which is obviously not innovative but expected in new media. Acts of appropriation are also acts of sampling: acts of citing pre-existing text or cultural products.[67]

Let us take a step back from digital culture and return to Tarde's concept of 'selective imitation'. As indicated above, the French sociologist and author of *Les lois de l'imitation* (1890) believes that social existence depends on imitation, so that the role of imitation for social life is analogous to the role of heredity in biological life. One of the peculiarities of Tarde's thought is that he conceives of imitation and innovation as logical opposites. In fact, in order for the novelty introduced by innovation to settle, it must be transmitted through imitation:

> This original act of imagination and its spread through imitation was the cause, the *sine qua non* of progress. The immediate acts of imitation which it prompted were not its sole results. It suggested new acts and so on without end.[68]

We might deduce, then, that only those innovations that are imitated attain social relevance. In fact, these dynamics described characterize a remix culture. In the early remix practices of Jamaican DJs and producers, repetition is never a step back into the identical – in fact, there are always *variations* in the looping. This is even clearer in relation to digital networks, where the innovation inherent in the remix requires sub-

sumption in a flow of constant repetition in order for it to be instantiated within the network society.[69] If imitation and repetition are essential to social and biological evolution, the consequence of repetition for
aesthetics is the loss of depth, massification, and Baudrillard's society of
simulacra. We must also conclude that innovation in the contemporary
age is possible only within the frame of remix practice.

In Tarde's discourse, there is still recourse to an 'original act'. If Tarde
was able to view the landscape created by digital media, he might have
been more hesitant to use the term 'original'. The age of remix culture
in fact represents the endpoint for the modernist myth of originality, a
concept that was already eroded by prior economic, social, cultural and
technological pressures. In remix culture, originality,[70] that is to say
something that is not copied or imitated, dies once and for all.[71]

Remix culture is not, however, synonymous with digital culture. The
remix is a compositional practice that extends to all spheres of cultural
production, including contemporary art. In *Postproduction*,[72] French art
critic and curator Nicolas Bourriaud offers a lucid account of this phenomenon. After analysing the composition modalities of contemporary
artists including Pierre Huyghe, Maurizio Cattelan, Gabriel Orozco,
Dominique Gonzalez-Foerster, Rirkrit Tiravanija, Vanessa Beecroft and
Liam Gillick, Bourriaud concludes that the work of each artist is based
on pre-existing materials. Bourriaud's concept of 'postproduction' may
be considered equivalent to 'remix', if we consider the affinity between
the theories of remix recounted above and the following, excerpted
from Bourriaud's introduction to *Postproduction*:

> Since the early nineties, an ever increasing number of artworks have
> been created on the basis of preexisting works; more and more art-
> ists interpret, reproduce, re-exhibit, or use works made by others
> or available cultural products. This art of postproduction seems to
> respond to the proliferating chaos of global culture in the informa-
> tion age, which is characterized by an increase in the supply of works
> and the art world's annexation of forms ignored or disdained until
> now. These artists who insert their own work into that of others
> contribute to the eradication of the traditional distinction between
> production and consumption, creation and copy, readymade and
> original work. The material they manipulate is no longer *primary*.

It is no longer a matter of elaborating a form on the basis of a raw material but working with objects that are already in circulation on the cultural market, which is to say, objects already *informed* by other objects. Notions of originality (being at the origin of) and even of creation (making something from nothing) are slowly blurred in this new cultural landscape marked by the twin figures of the DJ and the programmer, both of whom have the task of selecting cultural objects and inserting them into new contexts.[73]

Evidently, there are several commonalities between Bourriaud's reasoning and the points developed thus far: the reuse of pre-existing materials as a consequence of accessible and near-infinite sources; the progressive indistinction between producers and consumers, between original and copy, and between creator and re-user; and the DJ as a figure symbolic of the culture as a whole. Bourriaud goes further, however, and explicitly refers to the routinized interactions with digital media in his comparison of 'Web surfers' activities with the functioning of a sampling machine.[74] In this way, Bourriaud's work may be aligned with the principal thesis of *Web Aesthetics*: that contemporary forms, knowledge, *creative acts* and social formations are all temporary configurations of an endless flow of data. I do not think I am pushing Bourriaud too far by making such a statement, if we consider the following claim: 'The artwork is no longer an end point but a simple moment in an infinite chain of contributions.'[75]

'Dick in a Box'

A second thesis grounding *Web Aesthetics* is that memetic mechanisms are at work within the medial and cultural agon. Even if Bourriaud makes no reference to this issue, it is clear that the structures of repetition and imitation within a remix are influenced by their virulence. A good example is the famous (or infamous) video *Dick in a Box*,[76] a parody of 1990s' R&B and of the genre of the Christmas song. The video was first screened during the popular American television show *Saturday Night Live*, on 16 December 2006. *Dick in a Box*, the umpteenth provocation by American comedy troupe Lonely Island (Akiva Schaffer, Jorma Taccone and Andy Samberg),[77] features bona fide pop star Justin Timberlake along with Samberg. The video only reveals its virulence once uploaded to YouTube, where, aside from receiving about 30 million hits, it has given rise to countless imitations and remixes, as well as remixes of remixes. For example, *Box in a Box* and *Puppet Dick in a Box* have each become mini-genres in their own right. In this phenomenon, we can identify a blend of contemporary pop culture, familiar R&B loops, quotations from cinema,[78] as well as a hybridization of media including the video clip, television show, YouTube video and even T-shirt text, such as that with instructions for building one's own 'dick in a box'.[79] The trajectory of *Dick in a Box* is paradigmatic of the memetic nature of remix culture: a remix becomes rooted in network society through constant repetition, and within this very flow of repetition, innovations arise. In the present case study, innovation is represented by the homonymous video *Dick in a Box* (2008),[80] created and posted on YouTube by Purple Duck Films (another independent film and comedy group, consisting of students and based in Toronto),[81] mocking the original video by remixing it with its subsequent remixes such as *Box in a Box*. This typifies the loops of innovation and repetition that characterize contemporary culture.

If innovation is on the line of constant imitation and repetition of a model that has proved to be successful (a meme in perfect shape) it becomes even clearer that it is no longer possible (if it ever was) to create something new from nothing; the only cultural operation that makes sense today is the selection and recombination of pre-existing sources in new and surprising ways. Everybody becomes a DJ in the classical sense of someone selecting records. The hope is for syntheses that shed new light on the elements of the composition, so that the evolutionary process can continue. Success means giving someone else the chance to keep adding bricks to the building that one has oneself worked, and to finally allow them to state, once again: *last night a DJ saved my life.*[82]

Remix It Yourself

The even more fashionable word CREATIVITY is not in the twelve-volume Oxford Dictionary.
David Ogilvy, *Ogilvy on Advertising* (1983)

The transformation of the spectator into active subject is paralleled by the passage of art from object to a network of relationships, or simply as a network. It is this very passage that creates the conditions for users to intervene, personally or collectively, in the creation of an artistic product. This point is crucial to the work of Tatiana Bazzichelli, who identifies a *leitmotif* running through Cubist and Dadaist collage, Duchamp's ready-mades, the Fluxus movement, mail art, the punk attitude, Neoism, Plagairism and, extending to the 1990s, 'when the net dynamics establishes itself on a mass level through computers and Internet'.[1] Of course, many of these moments are noted by other authors when discussing the liberation of users from a condition of passive consumption of cultural objects. In my opinion, what is lacking is a history that accounts for the DIY ethic as a mass phenomenon, rather than as an artistic, and hence elitist, practice. This ethic clearly emerges in the 1950s, in response to the progressive massification, specialization and automation of the production of goods. As the desire to regain possession of a more direct relationship with things spreads, Western workers are led to perform a series of activities (usually inside and around their homes) without the aid of professionals, and often without any specialist knowledge. Thanks to cinema in particular, the collective imaginary is pervaded with the image of the middle-class American male painting his garden fence on the weekend. Even if this precise act did not take place nearly as often in reality, it is probably quite easy for most of us to recall an object built by our parents or grandparents. In my personal experience, I recall that my father and mother found a happy meeting of their natures (one rational, the other artistic) by building and creatively painting wooden furniture, which then furnished the bedrooms in which my brothers and I spent our childhoods. I also recall treasuring the toys built by my grandfather (in particular a beautiful bow) more than those bought at a shop (at least until the first video game entered our house, an event symbolically matched with the death of that very grandfather); nor can I forget the tradition, popular in Naples, of making one's own *presepe*, a sort of papier-mâché set representing the birth of Jesus.

Obviously, the aim of this book is not to provide a reconstruction of the DIY ethic. What I want to emphasize is the rooting of the newly emerging DIY ethic within (at least in the West) an earlier determination to make things using materials that are readily available (admittedly, these are not hard to find in an era of abundance) and knowhow, which is also easily accessible prior to the Internet era, as in the proliferation of DIY manuals. Thus, a history that discusses only the avant-garde or anti-avant-garde practices of *Do It Yourself* seems to me profoundly one-sided. We need to remind ourselves that this phenomenon extended, at one time, to a great number of individuals in Western society.

The Rise of the 'Bricoleur'

The tendency to undertake domestic repairs, build objects of the most varied nature, to construct models and prototypes, as well as all the activities included within the generic word 'hobby', has been extensively studied by philosophers, and by theorists within the discipline of Cultural Studies. In particular, it is worth mentioning Claude Lévi-Strauss's reflections upon the concept of the 'bricoleur'. First, it is important to note that although the French anthropologist identifies this attitude in non-Western societies,[2] his reflections seem to me to regard amateurs in general, who are precious precisely because they trace the distance between the specialized practices of the engineer (a metaphor of the industrial universe) and the way of thinking and working, halfway between concrete and abstract, of the 'bricoleur'. In Lévi-Strauss's view, 'bricoleurs' are those who work with their hands, using different tools than those used by professionals:

> The 'bricoleur' is adept at performing a large number of diverse tasks; but, unlike the engineer, he does not subordinate each of them to the availability of raw materials and tools conceived and procured for the purpose of the project. His universe of instruments is closed and the rules of his game are always to make do with 'whatever is at hand', that is to say with a set of tools and materials which is always

finite and is also heterogeneous because what it contains bears no relation to the current project, or indeed to any particular project, but is the contingent result of all the occasions there have been to renew or enrich the stock or to maintain it with the remains of previous constructions or destructions. The set of the 'bricoleur's' means cannot therefore be defined in terms of a project.... It is to be defined only by its potential use or, putting this another way and in the language of the 'bricoleur' himself, because the elements are collected or retained on the principle that 'they may always come in handy'. Such elements are specialized up to a point, sufficiently for the 'bricoleur' not to need the equipment and knowledge of all trades and professions, but not enough for each of them to have only one definite and determinate use. They each represent a set of actual and possible relations; they are 'operators' but they can be used for any operations of the same type.[3]

'Bricoleurs' act mainly as collectors, before acting they take stock of their tools and imagine how they might use them.[4] The most characteristic feature, however, is the rearrangement of pre-existing elements, the leftovers of other works, rather than attempting to create something from nothing. In a similar way, the amateurs of the digital age conduct their own acts of 'bricolage' by assembling the 'already seen': that which has already been openly transmitted and displayed in the media universe. They constantly reuse, reassemble and re-transmit messages (signs) that are already present, thereby establishing new uses, senses and trajectories yet – and this is the aspect I wish to highlight – the acts of the 'bricoleur' serve the ends of a system of massification, such as the present one, in which signs are repeated whether or not they have a meaningful referent. The contemporary 'bricoleur' takes part of the flow and participates in its unceasing progression. From this point of view, 'bricolage' is representative of the modes of production of the schizophrenic, who is 'the universal producer'. For Deleuze and Guattari (who refer explicitly to Lévi-Strauss's concept in *Anti-Oedipus*), the binary logic of the 'desiring-machine' is always:

... a flow-producing machine, and another machine connected to it that interrupts or draws off part of this flow ... the first machine is in turn connected to another whose flow it interrupts or partially drains off, the binary series is linear in every direction. Desire constantly couples continuous flows and partial objects that are by nature fragmentary and fragmented. Desire causes the current to flow, itself flows in turn, and breaks the flows.[5]

The subject becomes the 'desiring machine', acquiring a *human consistence* only as productive process; in the very moment it cuts into that flow, it becomes the source of another flow and the agent of its dissemination.

Aesthetics of Hybridity

Although it is essential to connect contemporary amateur practices of recombination to the 'bricoleur' of the previous century, it is equally necessary to attend to the specificity of the present age. Antonio Tursi notes a shift from a 'surgery attitude' (Lévy, Landow) to a metamorphic one (Novak): this is the shift from editing to layering. The former practice consists of cutting and sewing together independent or discrete elements, and it is common both to new media and cinematic editing. It is a practice that leaves visible the scars between the separate elements that have been attached. This is perfectly symbolized in Shelley Jackson's *Patchwork Girl* (1995),[6] in which 'the scars are the links: they are the cut and the union'.[7] In contrast, the metamorphic attitude is expressed through the process of layering, which renders separate layers of a digital image indistinguishable. As Tursi observes, the shift from an editing aesthetics with an allegory of collage to an aesthetics of continuity, in which the margins of different elements are undetectable, is inaugurated by the digital techniques of composition born in the 1990s.[8] The aesthetics of continuity perfectly corresponds to the liquid architecture of cyberspace. This architecture no longer allows the mere overlapping of elements; the addition of a new element requires morphing, metamorphosis, and genetic mutation. As Marcos Novak, one of the major theorists of liquid architecture, states:

Where collage merely superposes materials from different contexts, morphing operates through them, blending them. True to the technologies of their respective times, collage is mechanical whereas morphing is alchemical. Sphinx and werewolf, gargoyle and griffin are the mascots of this time. The character of morphing is genetic, not surgical, more like genetic cross-breeding than transplanting. Where collage emphasized differences by recontextualizing the familiar, the morphing operation blends the unfamiliar in ways that illuminate unsuspected similarities and becomings.[9]

A further step is required to reach that 'aesthetics of hybridity' that, according to Manovich, dominates the contemporary design universe. Manovich reasons that, compared to the early 1990s, software today tends towards a generalized compatibility between files generated by different programs. As it becomes easier to 'import' and 'export' material between different forms of software, similar techniques and strategies are required, regardless of the specific nature of the project, or the medium of the final output. In conclusion, 'hybridity' is the aesthetic form of that which Manovich terms the present 'software age', in which 'the compatibility between graphic design, illustration, animation, video editing, 3D modeling and animation, and visual effects software plays the key role in shaping visual and spatial forms'.[10]

Two considerations must follow. Firstly, that the rapid shift over the last decades from one dominant aesthetic form to another has concomitantly decreased the part that humans have to play in triggering such changes. In fact, recent aesthetic transformations have not formed in response to social, political or cultural turmoil, let alone as the outpourings of 'a lonesome genius'. Rather, they have been predominantly imposed by the evolution of technology and media. It is pointless to insist that men and women continue to underlie technological development for, rather than inaugurating aesthetic transformations, humans are increasingly bound to follow the transformations wrought by technological blocks – entities that, under some conditions, tend to become autonomous.[11] The second consideration arises from the fact that technology has given many people the opportunity to create, modify or hybridize media objects. The question then becomes: How are individuals using this power? Or, what are they giving life to? The answer appears a simple one: they give life to remixes. In fact, if the premise that I have attempted to document is true, contemporary individuals have no other option but to operate upon pre-existing materials. One must conclude, then, that the *Do It Yourself* attitude has morphed into that of *Remix It*

Yourself. The imperative is to personally revise and recombine the vast amount of accessible sources, using whatever tools and knowhow are available. The 'bricoleur' has become the remixer.

Amateurs and Professionals

Having clarified this point, we can ask: Does it make sense to retain the distinction between amateur and professional activities, as many wish to do, or is it more appropriate to consider these activities as different expressions of the sociocultural and socioeconomic dynamics triggered by the evolution of media? Manovich believes it is inappropriate to assume qualitative differences between professional and amateur remix practices (which he, like Henry Jenkins, defines as 'vernacular'). In fact, he writes, both are 'equally affected by the same software technologies'.[12] The difference is merely quantitative: 'A person simply copying parts of a message into the new email she is writing, and the largest media and consumer company recycling designs of other companies are doing the same thing – they practice remixability.'[13] I am in full agreement with this argument: after all, one of the main features of remix aesthetics is the loss of any distinction between producer and consumer, for they both hybridize the sources they access.

Oliver Laric, a Turkish artist, creates art that is emblematic of the aesthetic short circuit between professional and domestic practices. Many of Laric's works are the result of assembling fragments of amateur videos sourced from YouTube or other file-sharing platforms. For example, *50 50* (2007),[14] is an edited remix of 50 home videos of people rapping songs by the famous rap artist 50 Cent. A particularly popular mash-up is the more recent *Touch My Body – Green Screen Version* (2008).[15] This work is a webpage consisting of a collection of video remixes of Mariah Carey's song of the same name. These remixes, taken from disparate corners of the world, are all based on the cinematographic technique termed chroma key (but also 'green screen' or 'blue screen') which place the American pop star in front of a background of heterogeneous and often puzzling moving images. By playing all the webpage's videos simultaneously – a temptation I could not resist – one gains a very effective representation of the aesthetic redundancy that characterizes contemporary culture, as well as of the dissonance of the everyday media landscape. *Touch My Body* is also an excellent proof of how, in contemporary aesthetic expressions, it is impossible to distinguish between the contributions of 'professionals' and 'amateurs'. In the example of *Touch My Body*, who is the amateur? Is it the producers of the videos used by Laric: people using techniques and tools that ten years ago would have been the envy of Hollywood producers? Or is it Laric himself, who gives life to his art using the same modalities of millions (perhaps billions) of domestic home video producers?

This question is unanswerable if one retains the traditional concepts of 'professional' and 'amateur'. Writing in relation to hypertext, Tursi writes of a kind of 'desubjectivity' resulting from the blurring of the distinction between author and reader. He proposes the term 'lator',[16] in order to describe

> ... the one who brings, who is in charge (but also that accepts this charge) of bringing something, especially a letter, hence a message
> ... the lator is the one who is in charge of making the work, bringing it, without pretending to be recognized as the author, as the creator. He leaves the baton to another lator and around this transmission, thanks to it, the social link is built.[17]

Obviously, as Tursi himself (following Bolter) observes, alteration is implicit in the act of passing the baton, so that the reader will become, finally, a second author.

Creative Existences

If the renunciation of originality is widely accepted, it is nevertheless common to find the 'personalized' acts of revision and remix described as 'creative acts'. It is easy to see why creativity is so emphasized: the wish to affirm one's own personality and to show the world one's own creative spirit is the bait that triggers the trap of the concatenated global media spectacle. The same motive underlies the purchase of tools and software that offer the promise of 'digital creativity': hence Sony's, Phillips' or Adobe's ceaseless call to creativity. After all, as Nigel Thrift observes, for corporate managers, 'creativity becomes a value *in itself*',[18] a quality that managers must learn how to cope with if they are to survive in a world where commercial advantage is always temporary, and usually very brief.

Less understandable is the frequent praise of the *creative lives* made possible by the birth of the digital. In recent years, rather than the liberation of creative energies, what has taken place is the expropriation of the spare time of increasingly larger proportions of the population. We move ever further away from the Marxist ideal of overcoming the dichotomy between work and free time – if this overcoming has taken place at all, it has been in the direction of including free time within work time. The effect of the creativity myth has been to add a new kind of mostly unpaid work to the daily lives of individuals who, for example, publish and index pictures on social networks, or who review products, or otherwise nurture the success of enterprises based on crowdsourcing (Jeff Howe *docet*).[19] Rather than focusing on the expropriation of free time by the so-called 'creative industries',[20] however, I would like to focus further on reasons for questioning the concept of creativity. Once again, one must be wary of drawing a distinction between creating something new and revising preexisting materials. This distinction clearly fails to shed any light on contemporary practices, as it credits with the mark of creativity only the activity of the *creator ex nihilo*. One must begin with the premise that the form of creativity involved in contemporary practices is fundamentally different from the Romantic and modernist injunction to 'make it new'.

Utilizing de Certeau's *The Practice of Everyday Life* (1980), Manovich states that 'tactical creativity' can be defined as that which 'expects to have to work on things in order to make them its own, or to make them "habitable"'.[21] Contemporary remixers, in addition to being released from the hard distinction between *facere* and *creare*, occupy a position peculiar to this point in history: prior to any act of their own, they are already within an endless flow of data. As I have indicated, the nature of this flow leads to action, in the form of data manipulation. The choice is no longer between action and passive contemplation; if they are still possible, any choice or free will takes place upstream, at the point of choosing between digital inclusion or exclusion. Once digitally included, no form of resistance is even thinkable: one becomes a part of the flow, and lives among the elements it is made of. For this reason, I am sceptical of the claim that remixers are forced into action by some internal creative drive: their acts are in fact driven by the flow in which they are immersed. To use Manovich's terminology, it is the software that 'takes command': one is 'creative' because digital tools allow (force) one to be so; one remixes because the sheer volume of cultural materials makes mere observation impossible; one assembles layered images because the Photoshop interface demands it; one publishes on a blog because the software underlying the blogosphere makes this such a pleasant and rapid process. In conclusion, we remix because it is our evolutionary duty to do so. Even the most *pur et dur* subjects will not be able to avoid the action of all the subtle memes they will encounter: and one of the most virulent of these memes, that of creativity itself, will sooner or later force us all to be *creative.*

The alternative is to live as a hermit in the desert, free from the action of the global media. Even in this case, it is difficult to resist the temptation to turn the empty Coke can, left by an adventurous tourist, into a useful and colourful tool of some kind. Is this not a *remix* as well?

Remix Ethics

> Plagiarism is necessary.
> Progress depends on it.
> Guy Debord, *La société du spectacle* (1967)

Occupying the increasingly thin line that separates legitimate appropriation from plagiarism, remix practice raises significant ethical issues. The issue is rendered more complicated by the fact that this line frequently shifts, both in academic debates and in legal procedures – in a way that is akin to the shifting of the Palestinian 'border'.[1] If in large Western nations remix practice is widely considered legitimate, it is still considered necessary to add something personal to one's sources, and if at all possible to enrich those sources in some way. This is usually considered sufficient to avoid misappropriating someone else's intellectual work. In the last few years, various legal actions in the EU and the USA have revealed a significant gap between this apparently moderate position, and the position of legislators. If one also considers events that have taken place in Asia, in particular in the People's Republic of China, the level of confusion in an increasingly surreal global landscape is clearly apparent. In the following pages, I will summarize some positions on this issue – attending, as I have throughout, more closely to aesthetic implications than to ethical or political consequences.

We can take the question to be: Is it appropriate to establish a remix ethics? In other words, is it appropriate to conceive of a limit, beyond which remix becomes less legitimate? The question is intrinsically connected to the principle of authorship, as is evident in the increasing crisis of the concept of the author during the last several years. The concept of 'author' is as abstract as that of 'border'; in fact, the collaborative modalities implicit within digital tools, and the uptake (predominantly since the 1960s) of collective creative practices, have led us to a point in history in which the figure of the author as a kind of lonesome genius, and the figure of the collective authorial subject, coexist. In particular, the net.art deriving from the 'digital revolution' has closed the circle between the alternative collective movements of the late twentieth century, leaving the task of completing the work of art to users, through interaction. Creators of net.art are unrelated to the Romantic concept of the artist, as those who activate a context that requires the cooperation of others in order to come to fruition. Masking, identity games and plagiarism are practices that net.art has inherited from avant-gardes. When such techniques join forces with digital technologies, they invert the concept of authorship that continues to legitimize the contemporary art world. In net.art, the 'author' makes room for a new subject: the network. In fact, it is only in the network that the sense, the aesthetics and the intentions of the *net artistic* work can be recovered. As Tatiana Bazzichelli writes:

> To network means to create relationship networks, to share experiences and ideas. It also means to create contexts in which people can feel free to communicate and to create artistically in a 'horizontal' manner. It means creating the aforementioned in a way that the sender and the receiver, the artist and the public, are fused/confused; they lose their original meaning. The art of networking is based on the figure of the artist as a creator of sharing platforms and of contexts for connecting and exchanging. This figure spreads through those who accept the invitation and in turn create networking occasions. For this reason, it no longer makes sense to speak of an artist, since the active subject becomes the network operator or the networker.[2]

As remix practice does not only concern art but is implicit in any expressive form, it is necessary to widen our reflections to include other fields of human action, and to return to the sizable gap between the commonsense conception of remix ethics and the practice of copyright.

The Inadequacy of the Legislator

A major reason for the inadequacy of present legislation is the fact that copyright was instantiated in an age in which digital media did not exist.[3] For example, legislation tends to protect intellectual property by preventing a work being published without prior permission of the author or copyright owner, but does not account for cases in which a work is used as the starting point for a second work, which transforms the first.

After all, before the birth of digital media and the Internet, it was (almost) only commercial publishers that could actually publish a work, and the publisher acted as guarantor (or alternatively legitimated plagiarism because they knew they could rely on an army of lawyers). Today, new technologies have effectively reduced the costs of publication (at least of 'amateur' publications) giving life to such phenomena as desktop publishing, along with the entire blogosphere. In light of this profoundly altered situation, the inadequacy of copyright law is immediately evident. Yet, backgrounding digital media for the moment, there are many cases in which simple common sense violates copyright.[4] This is the case in scientific disciplines, in which progress is consequent upon the work of the entire past, present and future scientific community. Any scientist (or group of scientists) who makes a significant discovery will have taken advantage of all the research – whether successful or failed – undertaken by their predecessors. As Lazzarato writes: 'Invention is always encounter, hybridization, a cooperation between many imitation flows . . . even when it develops in an individual brain.'[5] If every scientist was forced to pay copyright fees to every scientist that has worked on a related subject, scientific research would immediately cease. And yet we may be seeing precisely this process taking place. Several years ago, the South African government, in view of a population literally destroyed by HIV,[6] decided to infringe upon the patent applied by pharmaceutical companies to drugs used to treat and contain the disease.[7] Pharmaceutical corporations reacted furiously, stating that their very value was in danger (value that is almost always conferred by the amount and importance of their patents, more than the capital or industrial infrastructures). Corporations assumed that they owned the active ingredients *copied* by South African researchers who, apart from invoking a terrible state of necessity, also argued that it was not possible to claim exclusive rights over elements that are in nature and are therefore not invented, but discovered. The sheer oddness of the claims of hardcore copyright supporters is even clearer in the case of the 1987 decree by the US Patent and Trademark Office through which – as Jeremy Rifkin reminds us[8] – it was established that the components of living creatures (genes, chromosomes, cells and tissues) could be patented and considered the intellectual property of any entity who first isolates their properties. This has lead to a situation in which enterprises working in the biosciences and related sectors have hugely intensified their efforts to commercially exploit genetic rarities. The consequence is that, for example, a population that has long used certain plants as natural remedies can no longer do so after a multinational isolates and patents the active ingredient. One wonders how exclusive economic rights can be established for elements that have not been invented, but that are just there, in nature.

Similar perplexities arise in regard to patents of genuine products of human intellect: software. Traditionally, patentable processes applied only to material transformations, while processes such as economic methods, data analysis procedures and *mental steps* were exempted. Since the 1980s, a series of decisions made by the US Supreme Court (and, as a consequence, by the European Tribunals, in the name of a sort of 'Americanization of the right') have questioned this principle. Large software multinationals have quickly picked up on the potential of this development. The situation has become so nonsensical that the US Patent Office is forced to face hundreds of requests every year for patents for software concepts. With the Patent Office having no means to establish the real novelty and originality of the concepts, there have been devastating consequences for small and mid-sized enterprises that, lacking the economic resources to pay for expensive legal actions concerning the paternity of an idea, have no way to defend against industry giants such as Microsoft.

Towards a 'Free Culture'

The few examples mentioned should be sufficient proof of the schism between modern intellectual property laws and common sense. The interests of the few (corporations and their shareholders) are jeopardizing the interests of humanity, as the progress of science, technology and culture are threatened. In *Free Culture*,[9] Lessig expresses this concern, highlighting the intrinsic risk of the protection of 'creative property', which allows those who own the rights to intellectual property to control the development of culture. Lessig's reasoning demonstrates that some of the most important innovations of modernity, such as photography, cinema and the Internet, were made possible thanks to a climate in which knowledge was freely shared and disseminated. According to Lessig, present regulations constitute insurmountable barriers to the free circulation of ideas, thereby obstructing the development of culture. For Lessig, 'free culture' does not imply the denial of intellectual property. His proposal, which is realized in Creative Commons licences,[10] offers a way to avoid the extremes of an anarchic 'no rights reserved' and the total ownership expressed in the formula 'all rights reserved'.[11] Creative Commons licences aim to realize the principle of 'some rights reserved': authors retain the right to make their content freely available as they see fit. This proposal restores liberties once taken for granted, decreasing the gap between legislation and common sense. It also foregrounds the rights of the author to decide which uses of their work are legitimate, instead of the corporations or associations managing the economic rights of an intellectual work.

A Relativist Ethics

Leaving aside the legal constraints upon remix, it is evident that formulating a morally satisfying solution in regard to remix culture remains a difficult task. In fact, attaining a shared ethics in the present relativist atmosphere is a near-utopian aim. Furthermore, it seems even more difficult to formulate an ethics that would apply equally to the plagiarism *tout court* of the Borgesian hero César Paladón, and a song featuring a very short sample of *O' Sole mio* (1898). There seem to be an infinite number of intermediate positions between those who believe that no-one invents anything, and those attached to a kind of fetishized vision of the author.

What is needed is to imagine a subjective ethics. As such, such an ethics is difficult to make extrinsic and collective, but its apparent relativism can be qualified by the 'recognition of peers'. As the primary need of anyone who gives life to a creative act is the recognition of their own community, absolute relativism is modulated by the judgment of those people who share values, references, aesthetic canons or other qualities. This solution seems adequate to that 'world of strangers' outlined by Ghanaian philosopher Kwame Anthony Appiah. According to Appiah's philosophy of cosmopolitanism, in the present interconnected world it is possible for different cultures to live peacefully together by adhering to their own specific sets of values, without ever needing to formulate a final, universally applicable solution.[12]

If we leave economic interests aside, attending to an ethics founded on the *recognition of peers* might represent a viable and defensible approach to the phenomena that characterize the present age. If this necessitates the abandonment of a shared ethics, it is worthwhile to point out that a unified moral vision is less essential to a remix culture than it is to religions and other ideological forms. Rather than norms enforced through sanctions,[13] it is legitimate to formulate behavioural rules: crediting one's sources is a good habit to foster; just as it is good form to make one's own creations, constructed from the creative work of other people, available to anyone who wishes to use it. All the informal behavioural codes already widely in use in online communities appear to support the viability of such an ethics. Entering a newsgroup used by developers who have chosen to use open source software, downloading a file using file sharing software, contributing to the creation of a Wikipedia lemma, even purchasing something from e-Bay, we contribute to the existence and the continued operation of a series of habits that, though they do not necessarily constitute a shared ethics, represent the *conditio sine qua non* to gain access to the community one is approaching.[14]

Aesthetic Fallout

Departing ethical considerations for aesthetic ones, it is clear that current copyright laws and policies have significant consequences for aesthetics, for they reinforce the sense that some practices, because they are not strictly legal, are 'underground'. In fact, this is a complete misnomer. The existing normative/repressive complex functions to imbue remix culture with an aura of the forbidden, just as 1970s' alternative cultures were termed such largely due to their use of drugs and the experimentalism of their lifestyles in contrast to those of the middle classes. Today, many artistic practices that challenge injunctions against free access to, and creative reuse of, culture are labelled 'illegal'. As such, institutional funds are denied to such practitioners and they are held at a distance by the organizers of international festivals, exhibitions and lectures, as well as being excluded from coverage by the global media.

In the late 1990s, the experience of some 'plagiaristic' works of net.art is emblematic. Artists such as Vuk Cosic and the Italian duo 0100101110101101.ORG copied entire websites and republished them under a different domain, reclaiming these operations as legitimate net.art performances (examples are Cosic's *Documenta Done* (1997) and *Hell.com* (1999) and *Vatican.org* (1999) by 0100101110101101.ORG). The apotheosis of this practice took place in 1999, when Amy Alexander duplicated the 0100101110101101.ORG website and published it on her own website plagiarist.com. The Italian artists responded by linking Alexander's website on their homepage, thereby 'realizing a paradoxical conceptual copy of a copy of their copies'.[15] As 0100101110101101.ORG themselves explain, such practices undermine copyright completely:

> A work of art, on the Net or not, cannot be interactive as such, it is people who have to use it interactively, it is the spectators who have to use the work of art in an unpredictable way. By copying a website, you are interacting with it, you are reusing it to express some contents that the author had not implied. Interacting with a work of art means to be user/artist at the same time; the two roles co-exist in the same moment. Thus we should talk about meta-art, of fall of the barriers of art; the spectator becomes an artist and the artist becomes a spectator: a witness with no power on what happens on their work. The essential premise to the flourishing of reuse culture is the total rejection of the concept of copyright, which is also a 'natural' need of the digital evolution.[16]

What is most instructive is the 'institutional' art world's reaction to these plagiarist short circuits. Attempting to exploit the hype surrounding this new form of art, museums, public institutions, curators and galleries risked the very basis of their authority – the originality and uniqueness of the work of art – as they confronted the implications of such appropriations. Initial curiosity quickly turned into diffidence, and it is not difficult to see why. The possibility of considering something immaterial such as a website as a work of art raised concerns, as well as the overt hostility of art merchants. It was the threat that plagiarist practices represented to authoriality that was ultimately too much for an institution that, behind its façade of openness, remained deeply conservative and rooted in a reality constituted by atoms and *eternal values*.[17] This moment inaugurates the (still present) fracture between the world of 'institutional' art as a whole (bearing in mind that there are significant exceptions), and artistic practices that question the principles of authorship and originality that are the foundations of copyright. These are forced to survive as spectacle, living off the crumbs of the art world, who disguise this 'magnaminity' as an opening towards the new. There are still those artists who refuse to accept the remains and reclaim the whole cake.

Many remix practices are placed outside mainstream flows not because of aesthetic or ideological differences, but because they are not acceptable to the cultural establishment. In other words, they are bound to be labelled 'underground' even though their underlying creative processes take place *in the light* and are popularly and widely expressed. Similarly, in the field of music, there is an increasing distance between artists and companies managing copyrights, and a discomforting lack of proposals that might satisfy all the interests involved. The case of DJ Danger Mouse[18] is instructive. In 2004, the artist published a record entitled *The Grey Album*, which remixed Jay-Z's *The Black Album* (2003) and the Beatles' *The White Album* (1968). As the remix process was performed without permission, it soon captured the attention of EMI's lawyers. In response to this legal attack, *Grey Tuesday* was organized: on 24 February 2004, activists and musicians posted and published the incriminated album on as many webistes as possible. Not satisfied with ordering DJ Danger Mouse to cease selling *The Grey Album* and threatening to destroy all copies of the record, EMI's lawyers threaten legal action against anyone who publishes the 'illegal' album online. The lawyers seem ignorant of the dynamics of the Net, and their threats seem comparable to attempting to stop a swarm of grasshoppers by means of a scarecrow. Furthermore, we can note that once again the attitude of international record labels, along with contemporary art institutions, cover contemporary artistic practices based on remix with a gloss of illegality. As Daphne Keller observes:

> Much of today's most innovative cultural production takes place in the shadow of the law: many DJs and other artists produce their work in the knowledge that a copyright holder could sue, that distribution of their work could be enjoined by law, and the sampler held liable for substantial monetary damages.[19]

It is important to note that acting 'in the shadow of the law' influences the aesthetic perception of many works. According to their own personal perspective, a member of an audience might confer a work of art with positive values such as breaking with tradition and the reclamation of creative spaces or, alternatively, with negative values such as the misappropriation of others' intellectual works and lack of 'originality'. A similar situation characterizes the file-sharing phenomenon. The activity of downloading from P2P networks, because it is experienced as rebellious and seditious, becomes a particular kind of aesthetic experience because of the injunctions in place. Simultaneously, the *vox populi* accepts the idea that those who perform these activities embody the model of a transgressive, 'outlaw' life-style. The perception of P2P as analogous to smoking pot or going to a club for swingers is inappropriate, because the activity of 'digital swingers' is never hidden in the way that sly or morally disputable practices are. It is not something that happens in the dark of a filthy club, or in some metropolitan ravine, it is rather a phenomenon that would lose its intrinsic meaning if the acquired materials were not displayed. The cultural products assembled over years are never hidden, for, as previously stated, accumulation and exhibition are two sides of the same coin.

To state the point a final time: copyright and intellectual property laws play a crucial role in the aesthetic characterization of phenomena that often, by their very nature, simply do not embody those values that the *vox populi*, institutions and mainstream media forcibly label them with.

Machinic Subjectivity

Just as there are many parts needed to make a human a human
there's a remarkable number of things needed to make an individual
what they are.
A face to distinguish yourself from others.
A voice you aren't aware of yourself.
The hand you see when you awaken.
The memories of childhood,
the feelings for the future.
That's not all.
There's the expanse of the data net
my cyber-brain can access.
All of that goes into making me what I am.
Giving rise to a consciousness that I call 'me'.
And simultaneously confining 'me' within set limits.
Mamoru Oshii, *Ghost in the Shell* (1995)

My discussion of 'machinic subjectivity' will open with an examination of the term 'blob', as introduced by American architect Greg Lynn
in an article entitled: 'Blobs (or Why Tectonics is Square and Topology
is Groovy).'[1] In this article Lynn proposes an evolutionary and dynami-
cally generated architecture, meaning a type of practice that is capable
of taking different spatial configurations according to use. A 'blob' is
an architectural project in which the simulated presence of 100 people
inside a virtual space leads to a change of the project so that it can best
accommodate those 100 people. In 'blob modeling', architecture and
interactivity are connected and amalgamated to give rise to a spatial
dynamism with different qualities to those related solely to the architectural building itself. The result is new forms and aesthetics, capable
of developing not only in the field of architecture *strictu sensu*, but also
in design, computer graphics and web interfaces. The concept of 'blob'
does not only connote a new approach to design, however; it also captures the peculiarity of contemporary society.

Dual Subjectivity

To me, the most attractive element of Lynn's concept is the central role it attributes to computers and software, which are considered to be the true protagonists of the social and cultural changes of the last decades. It could be stated that 'blob modelling' is a response to the so-called computer revolution that has transformed contemporary life. The 'blob' can also be viewed together with attempts in various fields to imagine structures, languages and aesthetics adequate to a hypertextually dynamic culture, that simply can no longer be represented statically. On a practical level, phenomena such as blob architecture, which aims to replace Euclidean geometry with liquid and dynamic forms, may bring confounding results, even though its practical usability is much higher in design than in architecture, for a design object is not aimed at accommodating actual people. What is really striking about Lynn's theory is that he is proposing a method capable of understanding the reality and the specificity of the contemporary individual's environment. The effort to reformulate those cultural canons stuck in a 'pre-digital' reality is shared by a number of fields – the problem might be to harmonize these varied efforts.

From some points of view, the whole of contemporary society is a huge, shapeless blob. According to Anthony Vidler, contemporary architecture, media, arts and the entertainment system as a whole favours fluid, flowing, hybrid, malleable spaces.[2] At this stage, it is essential to conduct an analysis capable of clarifying the terms of the man-machine interaction in the creative process. Lynn believes that, years after the first popular uptake of digital media design tools, it is no longer possible to consider 'the means' as a 'self-sufficient decisor': in other words, as the justification for any choice of design. This condition is only acceptable in the first years of use of a new technology, when everyone is an amateur: today it can no longer be agreed that architecture deriving from computer design is purely objective. Thus, if the focus is shifted from architecture to the creative act in general and hence to the human-computer-creation relationship, one must *again* question the categories of subjective and objective. In particular, we might support the theory according to which any computer/software always postulates at least a dual subjectivity: that of the human beings who use the media; and that which can be defined as 'machinic', as belonging to the machine. My assumption is that every computer, every software, every input device has its own personality that cannot *not* influence the creative process. For example, I am writing these pages using a PC, but my style would no doubt be different if I were using a Mac.

Machinic Aesthetics

It is important to understand the creative potential of the *error*: the fact that sometimes computers and software do different things than the tasks required of them. This fact supports the theory according to which the machine is not only an object, but a subject also. Everyday practice with digital media allows the user to gain experience through a series of errors that in fact offer us unpredictable and fascinating new possibilities. When this happens, it almost seems that one has consciously designed that result. If we recognize the implications of such interactions, we must become aware that *random* modes have fully entered into the creative modalities of the contemporary age. In net.art,[3] artists give life to a new aesthetics simply by playing with computers and seeing what happens. Consider the statement made by artist Mark Napier:

> Many of my pieces appropriate the text, images and data that make up the Web. The software/artwork uses this information as raw material to create an aesthetic experience. As I program these interfaces, the coding process creates unforeseen possibilities that add another dimension to the work. The technology reveals possibilities. Accidents happen and mistakes in the code produce unexpected but wonderful qualities.[4]

A project that offers a powerful demonstration of the role of machines in establishing contemporary aesthetics is German artist Cornelia Sollfrank's *Net.art Generator* (1999).[5] In this work, Sollfrank develops an intuition that arose from her previous project *Female Extension* (1997):[6] namely, that it is possible to delegate the task of processing the forms of a work of net.art to a machine, and in particular to specific software defined as a 'generator'. Sollfrank assigned programmers Ryan Johnston, Luka Frelih, Barbara Thoens, Ralf Prehn and Richard Leopold the task of developing net.art generators: web-based programmes capable of giving life to HTML art works that reassemble texts and images from the Web according to the terms searched by users. What Sollfrank does not say (at least at the presentation of the project) is that these digital collages are actually variations of the *Flowers* series by Andy Warhol, which in turn was based on a colour photograph of hibiscus blossoms by American photographer Patricia Caulfield – an appropriation which led to a harsh dispute between the photographer and Warhol. Sollfrank's project short-circuits any effort to identify a 'creator'. In fact, as Florian Cramer observes:

> Who exactly is the creator of a Warhol flower variation computed by the net.art generators? Caulfield as their original photographer, Warhol as their first artistic adopter, Sollfrank as the artist who created the concept of the net.art generators, the programmers who technically designed and implemented them, the users of the net.art generator, or the running program itself?[7]

Apart from the legal implications, the images produced by net.art generators dramatically undermine the concept of authorship, as each of the multiple 'subjects' involved has a crucial role in determining the final aesthetic result: the artist with her intuition (her concept) from which everything begins; the programmers who give life to the algorithms that will regulate the process; the users whose interactions direct the machinical component; and the software that elaborates the inputs received in new and unexpected ways. It is clear that the categories through which the twentieth-century world was interpreted are hopelessly inadequate to such works. Nor can the issue be reduced to a mere matter of style (and thus solved – à la Focillon – as the primacy of one technology over another).[8] The understanding of Sollfrank's work requires a new aesthetic sensibility, ready and willing to recognize and accept the contribution of machines. Those unwilling to place machinic subjectivity on the same level as human subjectivity will never be able to understand *Net.art Generator*, still less will they comprehend the reason why the world takes its actual fluid forms. Denying machinic subjectivity, considering the interaction with computers, interfaces and programming languages as a neutral process, is not only to misconceive our contemporary condition, but to miss out on significant opportunities. Allowing the machine to have the upper hand often means opening up to a genuinely surprising and rewarding universe of options.

The Technological Hyper-Subject

A contemporary theory that captures this tendency to extend artistic subjectivity to machines is that proposed by Mario Costa in *Dimenticare l'arte*. Beginning with the premise that the arts are an aestheticization of technology and thus that artistic development always follows technological development, the Italian philosopher distinguishes between three different ages: that of 'technical arts' that 'are directly connected to the body and are enacted by it'; that of 'technological arts' that 'are based on a mediation represented by the uneliminable presence of the machine'; and that of 'neo-technological arts', which characterizes the contemporary age.[9] In the technical age, which is the age of the hand, 'technical objects are related to need and respond to it'. In them, form and function are one and the same, so that even though they can serve one another these objects do not hybridize and interpret themselves; do not establish relationships with each other; and so remain independent universes. Technical objects are a part of culture and represent its material aspect ('material culture'). It is the close link between objects (hence the technical arts) and the human body that underlies the birth of the categories of traditional aesthetics (inner being, expression, artistic personality, symbolic, among others).[10] In the technological age, tools are increasingly less connected to need. Technological evolution is related to the relationships that the technological objects build with each other, creating families and genuine 'domestic sagas', and here Costa overtly refers to McLuhan's intuitions on the 'hybridization' of media and the concepts of extension and prosthesis. At this stage technique and culture become unbalanced, so that technique is always one step ahead of culture. For the arts, this is the moment at which they end up 'always being related to a *translation of the subject*' (there are echoes here of McLuhan's theory, according to which media transform and transmit experience, that is to say translate experience into new forms):[11] a new awareness that also underlies the spreading of semiotics and the conception of art as 'language'. As Costa observes: 'The previously dominating position of the "subject" is replaced by the "languages" and the "text".'[12] Finally, we reach the neo-technological age, in which:

> ... *neo-technologies tend to build blocks* and form hyper media; they grow in and of themselves, outside the culture and tend to dissolve the

culture itself; man is completely marginal and his role is basically to make the different neo-technological blocks work; neo-technologies are no longer extensions or prostheses, in the McLuhanian way, but separate extroversions of basic human functioning that tend to progressively become autonomous and self-operating.[13]

This setting leads to an aesthetics of the object and the self-operating machine, while marking the end of any aesthetics of the Self, of the subject and of language. For Costa, the strong categories of the 'new neo-technological aesthetics' are exteriority, signifiers, the 'non-subject' and the 'physiology of the machine'.[14] The most significant challenge for aesthetics is to interpret that general *human-machinical* consciousness, of which interactive practices typical of new media and the communicational dynamics induced by the digital networks are the first signs. For Costa, 'the individual subjectivity as cause and foundation of art' is increasingly replaced by a technological hyper-subject that is connected to the networks and depends on their physiology.'[15]

From my point of view, the most interesting element of Costa's theory is the belief that contemporary subjectivity is *connected to* and *depends on* digital networks: the contemporary hyper-subject is made up of human and machinical/technological components, including the topology of the networks, the relevant communication protocols, processes and the hardware and software platforms regulating the functioning of digital networks. Networking, as a cultural practice based on making networks, is a multiplication of identities, roles and methods no longer built exclusively on human beings but also on non-living beings and relevant topologies and physiologies. Thus there is a clear urgency for aesthetic research that allows machinical subjectivity and that of non-living beings more generally to surface. By shifting our awareness towards such practices, a closer dialogue with machines becomes possible. In particular, it should be possible to extend such an awarenesses and dialogue to social spheres wider than artistic and intellectual circles, specifically to those spheres that today only interact, largely unconsciously, with machinical subjectivities.

The art of Eduardo Kac moves in the direction of unveiling the subjectivity of non-living beings. In particular, the installation *Move 36* (2004)[16] is entitled in reference to the famous move (number 36) that in 1997 allowed *Deep Blue* (a supercomputer designed and built by IBM) to beat Gary Kasparov, the greatest chess player of the time. The installation consists of a big chessboard made of soil (black squares) and sand (white squares) placed in the middle of a room. In the square in which the famed 'move 36' was performed is a tomato plant that carries a gene formulated by Kac for this very work. The gene uses ASCII code to represent Descartes' famous statement *Cogito ergo sum* in binary language. This has been made possible thanks to a double operation: first, Kac translated the text into a series of zeroes and ones; and then set a procedural standard that translated the binary code into a sequence of the four structural elements of DNA, according to the following formula: A=00, C=01, G=10 e T=11. The 'Cartesian gene' should lead to mutations in the plant that are perceptible to the human eye. The installation is completed by two screens placed at opposite ends of the room, representing two chessboards in which every square is made of different video loops that alternate irregularly, almost evoking a chess game between ghosts. Leaving aside any concerns regarding how easy it apparently is to isolate, synthesize and reproduce DNA, what is to be highlighted is the search for the border line between human and non-human, living and non-living. The subjectivity of non-living beings, which seems comparable in power to human subjectivity (as when *Deep Blue* beats Kasparov), is emphasized in order to suggest an alternative way to understand communication between species: a dialogic communication capable of setting humanity free from the limitations of anthropocentrism. If art intervenes primarily on a symbolic rather than practical level, it is reasonable to background the ethical concerns regarding Kac's works (be they fluorescent bunnies or thinking plants) in order to accept the invitation to shift our focus towards what remains hidden from sight, yet nevertheless influences human actions.[17]

A second essential reference is to Leonel Moura and Henrique Garcia Pereira's *Symbiotic Art Manifesto* (2004). I will repeat its six points in full:

1) Machines can make art;
2) Man and machines can make symbiotic art;
3) Symbiotic art is a new paradigm that opens an entire unexploited field in art;

4) Object manufacturing and the reign of the hand in art can be abandoned;

5) Personal expression and of the human/artist centrality can be abandoned;

6) Any moralistic or spiritual pretension and any representation purposes can be abandoned.[18]

The theoretical reflections offered by the Portuguese artist and academic arise from the experiments performed within the project *ArtSBot* (2003),[19] in which Moura and Pereira tweak a set of small robots provided with sensors that capture information about obstacles and colours within the environment they operate in, in addition to a controller that elaborates the information and devices that produce movements. Placed on a white canvas, the robots begin to move and trace small sketches, switching the two colour marker pens they are provided with. When they encounter the sketches left by other robots, they recognize the colours, and thus intensify their activity: they choose the right pen and they trace the sketch they have encountered. After a while, a painting reminiscent of Jackson Pollock begins to take shape, and it is at this point that the 'human partner', as defined by Moura and Pereira, gets involved.

> The propensity for pattern recognition, embedded in the human perception apparatus, produces in such a dynamic construction a kind of hypnotic effect that drives the viewer to stay focusing [sic] on the picture's progress. A similar kind of effect is observed when one looks at sea waves or fireplaces. However, a moment comes when the viewer feels that the painting is 'just right' and stops the process.[20]

In the project *ArtSBot*, it is possible to identify the elaboration of some important points formulated by Costa. First of all, the 'domestication of the sublime': Moura and Pereira explicitly refer to the act of staring at waves in the ocean, or into the flames of a fire, which are no doubt experiences of the sublime. Yet their work represents a 'domesticated' sublime: the robots' drawings are a clear example of the 'technological terrifying'; they are objects of a controlled production and a socialized and repeatable use. It is also evident that Moura and Pereira's artistic production moves within an essentially cognitive dimension, in which the border between artistic and scientific research (an 'aesthetic-epistemological investigation', as Costa labels it) is extremely blurry. Simultaneously, we see the tendency so well described by Costa, according to which the aesthetic work comes down to the activation of technological signifiers. *ArtSBot* also evinces the decline of the subject and of the artistic personality. In fact, one sees a work of art produced by autonomous robots that 'can not be seen as a mere tool or device for human pre-determined aesthetical purpose'.[21] Moura and Pereira's intention is to reveal precisely the opposite dimension of the robots, so that the 'the unmanned characteristic of such a kind of art must be translated in the definitive overcoming of the anthropocentric prejudice that still dominates Western thought'.[22]

In conclusion, in an aesthetic experiment in which form is neglected in favour of communicational flow (another of Costa's main points), a situation takes place in which, as Moura and Pereira write: 'The art works produced by the painting robots are the result of an indissoluble multi-agent synergy, where humans and non-humans cooperate to waste time (in the sense that art has no purpose).'[23] However, such expressions as 'multi-agent synergy' and 'cooperation between humans and non-humans' need to be understood properly. The autonomous robots designed by the Portuguese duo are characterized by the fact that they avoid the need for a cognitive intelligence – that is, a type of intelligence that mediates between perception and action through a representation of reality. The robots possess an artificial intelligence that leads them to give life to interactions solely determined by the environment they work in, that is to say, according to a kind of stimulus-response model. Furthermore, the interactions are non-repetitive, that is to say that they are not pre-programmed: the robots do not plan their actions, they only respond to the stimuli of the environment. Thus they are autonomous from human beings unable to escape either from repetitive modalities, or from the temptation to address their actions towards a specific purpose, be it conscious or unconscious. What, more precisely, are the terms of the relationship between human beings and machines? According to Moura and Pereira themselves:

Although the robots are autonomous they depend on a symbiotic relationship with human partners. Not only in terms of starting and ending the procedure, but also and more deeply in the fact that the final configuration of each painting is the result of a certain gestalt fired in the brain of the human viewer. Therefore what we can consider 'art' here, is the result of multiple agents, some human, some artificial, immerged in a chaotic process where no one is in control and whose output is impossible to determine.[24]

It is from this final passage that I believe a brilliant manifesto for the art of the future emerges: art as the result of both human and artificial *actants*, giving rise to processes of which no one is in control, and the output of which is impossible to determine.

Notes

Chapter I
Dialogue Inside and Outside the Web

Closed Monads

1 By the term 'around', I mean that sphere of intellectual speculation widely known as digital culture or new media theory.
2 M. Bakhtin, *Estetika slovesnogo tvorchestva* (Moscow: Iskusstvo, 1979); the French edition that I am consulting is: *Esthétique de la création verbale* (Paris: Gallimard, 1984).
3 T. Todorov, *Mikhail Bakhtin: The Dialogical Principle* (Manchester: Manchester University Press, 1984), 104. Maurizio Lazzarato takes a similar perspective, stating that the relationship between the Self and the Other in Bakhtin is not related to the subject-object relationship of Kant's theory of knowledge nor to Hegelian dialectics; it can only be understood as an evenemential relationship between possible worlds. See: M. Lazzarato, *La politica dell'evento* (Catanzaro: Rubettino, 2004), 113.
4 Ibid., 97.
5 Lazzarato, *La politica dell'evento*, op. cit. (note 3), 107 [translation by the author], original text: 'genealogia corta'.
6 Ibid., 104-105 [translation by the author].
7 Ibid., 105-106 [translation by the author].
8 Ibid., 107.
9 M. Bakhtin, *Esthétique et théorie du roman* (Paris: Gallimard, 1978); quoted in: Lazzarato, *La politica dell'evento*, op. cit. (note 3), 108.
10 G. Lovink, *Zero Comments: Blogging and Critical Internet Culture* (New York: Routledge, 2007), 21.
11 P. Lévy, *Cyberdémocratie. Essai de philosophie politique* (Paris: Odile Jacob, 1992); I am translating from the Italian edition: *Cyberdemocrazia. Saggio di filosofia politica* (Milan: Mimesis, 2008), 108.
12 Ibid., 201.
13 Ibid., 198 [translation by the author].
14 Ibid., 198-199.
15 G. Bianco, 'La mano virtuale della cyber-democrazia. Utopia e ideologia delle NTIC', in: Lévy, *Cyberdemocrazia*, op. cit. (note 11), 16 [translation by the author].
16 Ibid. [translation by the author].
17 Z. Bauman, *Consuming Life* (Cambridge: Polity, 2007), 116. According to Bauman: 'In the internet game of identities, the "other" (the addressee and sender of messages) is reduced to his or her hard core of a thoroughly manipulable instrument of self-confirmation, stripped of most or all of the unnecessary bits irrelevant to the task still (however grudgingly and reluctantly) tolerated in offline interaction.' Ibid., 115.
18 Ibid., 108.
19 As a partial legitimation of the use of the term 'autism' I will mention Lucien Sfez, who uses the neologism 'tautism' – by joining tautology and autism – to describe that pathology in which, in the relationship with the media, real facts and their representations are swapped, see: L. Sfez, *Critique de la communication* (Paris: Seuil, 1988), 151.
20 According to recent estimates, English language users number 495,843,462, while Chinese language users number 407,650,713 and Spanish language users number 139,849,651. Moreover, the growth rate between 2000 and 2009 is 251.7 per cent for English language users, 1,162.0 per cent for Chinese language users and 669.2 per cent for Spanish language users. Source: http://www.internetworldstats.com (accessed 22 April 2010).

21 M. Augé, *Où est passé l'avenir?* (Paris: Éditions du Panama, 2008). I am translating from the Italian edition: *Che fine ha fatto il futuro?* (Milan: Elèuthera, 2009), 106.

22 On this issue, see: E. Levinas, *Totalité et infini. Essai sur l'extériorité* (The Hague: Martinus Nijhoff, 1961); translation: *Totality and Infinity: An Essay on Exteriority* (Pittsburgh, PA: Duquesne University Press, 1969); E. Levinas, *Autrement qu'être ou au-delà de l'essence* (The Hague: Martinus Nijhoff, 1978); translation: *Otherwise than Being or Beyond Essence* (Pittsburgh, PA: Duquesne University Press, 2000); J. Derrida, *Le monolinguisme de l'autre, ou, la prothèse d'origine* (Paris: Galilée, 1996); translation: *Monolingualism of the Other, or, The Prosthesis of Origin* (Stanford, CA: Stanford University Press, 1998); J. Derrida, *De l'hospitalité* (Paris: Calmann-Lévy, 1997); translation: *Of Hospitality* (Stanford, CA: Stanford University Press, 2000).

23 J. Baudrillard, *L'Échange symbolique et la mort* (Paris: Gallimard, 1976); translation: *Symbolic Exchange and Death* (London: SAGE, 1993), 7.

24 G. Calogero, *Filosofia del dialogo* (Milan: Edizioni di Comunità, 1962), 268 [translation by the author].

25 Ibid., 117 [translation by the author].

26 Here, I anticipate the cosmopolitan suggestion of the Ghanaian philosopher Kwane Anthony Appiah, which will be discussed in greater detail in the final chapter of the present work.

27 M. Perniola, *Contro la comunicazione* (Turin: Einaudi, 2004).

28 G. A. Lindbeck, *The Nature of Doctrine: Religion and Theology in a Postliberal Age* (Philadelphia: Westminster Press, 1984). In this text Lindbeck grounds theology in a linguistic-cultural approach to religion. Starting with the assumption that different confessional and religious languages are full semiotic universes, he highlights the importance of an intra-systemic and cultural methodology in the study of ritual and, contrasting both the cognitive-propositionalist and the experiential-expressivist conceptions, he suggests a new approach in which religion is a cultural and/or linguistic framework that shapes individual subjectivities rather than their immediate expressions.

29 Perniola, *Contro la comunicazione*, op. cit. (note 27), 109 [translation by the author].

30 Ibid., 111 [translation by the author].

31 Ibid. [translation by the author].

32 E. L. Francalanci, *Estetica degli oggetti* (Bologne: Il Mulino, 2006), 78.

Spam and Viruses: The Evil to be Eradicated

1 G. Deleuze and F. Guattari, *Mille Plateaux* (Paris: Minuit, 1980); translation: *A Thousand Plateaus: Capitalism and Schizophrenia* (London: Continuum, 2004), 10.

2 For a work that stresses the differences between the rhizome structure and the Web structure, see: A.R. Galloway, *Protocol: How Control Exists After Decentralization* (Cambridge, MA: MIT Press, 2004).

3 In the very recent text edited by Jussi Parikka and Tony D. Sampson (that is coming to light while I am in the stage of editing of my own work) the term 'anomaly' is used. See: J. Parikka and T. D. Sampson (eds.), *The Spam Book: On Viruses, Porn and Other Anomalies From the Dark Side of Digital Culture* (Cresskill, NJ: Hampton Press, 2009).

4 Deleuze and Guattari, *A Thousand Plateaus*, op. cit. (note 1), 10.

5 J. Posluns, *Inside the Spam Cartel: Trade Secrets from the Dark Side* (Rockland, MA: Syngress, 2004).

6 A. Ludovico, 'Inside the Spam Cartel', *Neural*, 2005. Web: http://www.neural.it/nnews/insidethespam-cartel.htm (accessed 6 April 2010) [translation by the author].

7 D. Goodman, *Spam Wars: Our Last Best Chance to Defeat Spammers, Scammers, and Hackers* (New York: SelectBooks, 2004).

8 A. Ludovico, *Spam, the Economy of Desire* (2005). Web: http://www.neural.it/art/2005/12/spam_the_economy_of_desire.phtml (accessed 6 April 2010).

9 For an ethnological reading of spam and in particular of the practice known as scam, see: C. Gallini, *Cyberspiders. Un'etnologa nella rete* (Rome: Manifestolibri, 2004).

10 Web: http://www.010010111010101101.org/home/biennale_py/index.html (accessed 6 April 2010).

11 On this issue, see: J.-F. Lyotard, *La condition postmoderne. Rapport sur le savoir* (Paris: Minuit, 1979); translation: *The Postmodern Condition: A Report on Knowledge* (Manchester: Manchester University Press, 1984).

12 This is Philippe Breton's view in: *Le culte de l'Internet. Une menace pour le lien social?* (Paris: La Découverte, 2000); the Italian edition that I am consulting is: *Il culto di Internet. L'interconnessione globale e la fine del legame sociale* (Turin: Testo & Immagine, 2001).

13 Ibid., 39-41.

14 Ibid., 41.

15 Ibid., 42.

16 Ibid., 47.

New Media Culture

1   As an example, I quote the definition of 'academic' created by Marc Garrett as part of the project *Rosalind* (an upstart media art lexicon, created to give voice to 'those who are either ignored, not represented fairly or are misrepresented by certain academics, institutions, historians and "official" media outlets'): 'Academic: a constant refusal by certain academics, historians to grant a truth by not including in their studies "real histories" of other significant artists or collectives, independent groups in their publications. A cultural sickness recognised in Media Art culture.' Web: http://www.furtherfield.org/rosalind/definitions.pl?id=144 (accessed 6 April 2010).

2   G. Lovink, *Zero Comments: Blogging and Critical Internet Culture* (New York: Routledge, 2007), 55.

3   Ibid., 63.

4   J. Baudrillard, 'Le Complot de l'art', *Libération*, 20 May 1996. Web: http://usm.maine.edu/~bcj/issues/two/baudrillard_2.html (accessed 6 April 2010).

5   Web: http://www.parkerito.com/self_portraits/statement.html (accessed 6 April 2010).

6   P. Breton, *L'utopie de la communication. Le mythe du village planétaire* (Paris: La Découverte, 1992); I am translating from the Italian edition: *L'utopia della comunicazione. Il mito del 'villaggio planetario'* (Turin: UTET, 1995), 148-149.

7   At this stage, as an *excusatio non petita*, I would like to clarify two matters: my reflection on the debate that takes place inside mailing lists, forums and news groups concerns the present situation and that of the last few years. I remember well how, at the end of the 1990s, online discussions and the first lists were characterized by verve, and by frequent and lively discussions. The second clarification is that in my analysis of festivals and institutions, I have focused on the overall phenomenon. It is important to remember that there are individuals and organizations that put a great deal of effort into the attempt to involve those geographical, cultural and linguistic realities that are usually kept to one side into the international debate. As an example (in order not to be accused of servility, I will not mention my publisher here, but its personal history is plain for all to see) I could mention the LABoral (Centro de Arte y Creación Industrial di Gijón nel Principado de Asturias - http://www.laboralcentrodearte.org) which works to build links between Europe and Latin America (and more generally, between Central European and Spanish and Spanish-American culture).

8   Here it is worth mentioning Slavoj Žižek's paradox that, in response to the hypocrisy of liberal multiculturalism, provocatively hopes for a return to intolerance. See: S. Žižek, *Ein Plädoyer für die Intoleranz* (Wien: Passagen, 1998).

9   Iain Chambers, *Culture After Humanism: History, Culture, Subjectivity* (London: Routledge, 2001), 170.

Chapter II
Aesthetic Diffusion

A Short History of the Concept of Aesthetic Experience

1   W. Tatarkiewicz, *Dzieje sześciu pojęć*, (Warsaw: PWN, 1976); translation: *A History of Six Ideas: An Essay in Aesthetics* (The Hague: Martinus Nijhoff, 1980).

2   Ibid., 311.

3   'Lentezza d'animo'; in Italian in the original text.

4   Ibid., 314.

5   'Delirio'; in Italian in the original text.

6   Ibid., 317.

7   Ibid., 319.

8   Ibid., 321.

9   Ibid., 322-323.

10 Ibid., 324.

11 Ibid., 325-326.

12 Ibid., 326-329.

13 Ibid., 329.

14 Ibid., 329-333.

15 Ibid., 334.

16 Ibid., 335.

17 Ibid., 337-338.

18 Ibid., 338.

19 John Dewey, *Experience and Nature* (Whitefish, MT: Kessinger, 2003 [1925]), 365.

20 John Dewey, *Art as Experience* (New York: Perigee, 2005 [1934]), 2.

21 Ibid., 339.

22 After all, the *cultural turning point* of aesthetics is widely accepted. It is enough to look at the set up of the huge *Encyclopedia of Aesthetics*, which collects points of view from a wide range of cultural spheres. See: M. Kelly (ed.), *Encyclopedia of Aesthetics* (Oxford: Oxford University Press, 1998).

23 [Translation by the author], original text: 'sublime tecnologico'.

24 M. Costa, *Il sublime tecnologico. Piccolo trattato di estetica della tecnologia* (Rome: Castelvecchi, 1998 [1990]).

25 M. Costa, *Internet e globalizzazione estetica* (Naples: Cuzzolin, 2002), 54 [translation by the author]. See also: Mario C., *Pour une nouvelle esthétique* (2000). Web: http://www.isea2000.com/actes_doc/03_costa. rtf (accessed 12 March 2010); translation: 'For a New Kind of Aesthetics', *Leonardo*, vol. 34 (2001) no. 3, 275-276.

26 Costa, *Il sublime tecnologico*, op. cit. (note 24), 25 [translation by the author].

27 Ibid., 25-26.

28 Ibid., 27 [translation by the author].

29 Here, among the 'natural threats', Costa includes volcanoes and in particular he recalls the importance that the Vesuvius reached in eighteenth-century French literature; this volcano – lazy and sleepy – overlooks the Gulf of Naples and its peak often hypnotizes me; especially when, just awakened, I stop and admire it from one of the windows of the house I live in. Ibid., 28-29.

30 Ibid., 32-33.

31 Ibid., 72-73 [translation by the author].

32 Ibid., 47 [translation by the author].

33 Ibid., 47-48 [translation by the author].

34 Ibid., 114 [translation by the author].

35 By the word 'aseity' Costa means the way of being of a reality that appears totally un-derived, self-sufficient and with no relationships of any sort. See: Mario Costa, *Dimenticare l'arte. Nuovi orientamenti nella teoria e nella sperimentazione estetica* (Milan: FrancoAngeli, 2005), 102, note 2.

36 Costa, *Il sublime tecnologico*, op. cit. (note 24), 141.

37 Ibid., 119.

38 Ibid., 140.

39 Ibid. [translation by the author]. Jay David Bolter and Richard Grusin, addressing the 'dissolution of the Cartesian Ego', conclude that there is *nothing behind the images*; in fact, virtual travellers define what they know as what they can see and with what they can interact, hence knowledge is a sensory perception. J.D. Bolter and R. Grusin, *Remediation: Understanding New Media* (1999) (Cambridge, MA: MIT Press, 2003), 242-248.

40 Mario Costa, 'Appunti per l'estetica a venire', in: Silvana Vassallo and Andreina Di Brino (eds.), *Arte tra azione e contemplazione. L'interattività nelle ricerche artistiche* (Pisa: ETS, 2004), 171 [translation by the author].

Diffuse Aesthetics

1 Francalanci uses the expression 'estetica diffusa'. The Italian adjective *diffuso* can be translated into English as 'diffuse', 'widespread', and of course 'popular'. Francalanci's premise is that, mainly because of technology's all-pervasive nature, aesthetics has spread worldwide ('everything is aestheticized'); the other main feature of postmodern aesthetics is the shift of focus from the content of reality to its formal aspects. According to linguistic distinctions between 'diffuse' and 'popular', I have to admit I have been unsure whether to use the expression 'diffuse aesthetics' or 'popular aesthetics'. The former does not occur very frequently in the literature; the latter at least is established in Cultural Studies. However, as it is in fact possible to state that in the popularization of a phenomenon (whatever it is) there is always a certain degree of awareness within the people of that very process of popularization, whereas the aestheticization of society takes place 'underground', as it were, I finally decided on the expression 'diffuse aesthetics'. Special thanks to Tiziana Terranova for taking part in the discussion that led me to settle on the term.

2 W. Benjamin, *Das Kunstwerk im Zeitalter seiner technischen Reproduzierbarkeit* (1936); translation: 'The Work of Art in the Age of Mechanical Reproduction', in: *Illuminations* (New York: Schocken, 1969).

3 E.L. Francalanci, *Estetica degli oggetti*, (Bologne: Il Mulino, 2006), 7-8.

4 T. Todorov, *Avanguardie artistiche e dittature totalitarie* (Florence: Le Monnier Università, 2007), 16.

5 Italian Minister of Foreign Affairs and Benito Mussolini's son-in-law.

6 G. Ciano, *Diario 1937-1943* (Milan: Rizzoli, 1946) [translation by the author]; quoted in Todorov, *Avanguardie artistiche e dittature totalitarie*, op. cit. (note 4).

7 Todorov, *Avanguardie artistiche e dittature totalitarie*, op. cit. (note 4), 22 [translation by the author].

8 Ibid., 23 [translation by the author].

9 Francalanci, *Estetica degli oggetti*, op. cit. (note 3), 29.

10 M. Hardt and A. Negri, *Empire* (Cambridge, MA: Harvard University Press, 2000).

11 J. Baudrillard, *Art and Artefact* (Thousand Oaks, CA: SAGE, 1997), 12.

12 Ibid., 13.

13 Francalanci, *Estetica degli oggetti*, op. cit. (note 3), 19 [translation by the author].

14 Ibid., 21-22 [translation by the author]. On this topic it is worth mentioning that the Italian philosopher Mario Costa, whose theory will be used throughout this work, believes that this stage of the 'image without representative' or of the 'simulacrum' has been surpassed, and that we are in a stage in which the image, having lost its historical function, leaves its essence to the procedures of communication (typical of digital networks) and disappears as such.

15 L. Manovich, *The Language of New Media* (Cambridge, MA: MIT Press, 2001).

16 It is interesting to note that Manovich himself recalls a progressive aestheticization of the interfaces, highlighting the present shift taking place in the design of information technology, as a consequence of which, unlike a decade ago, designers no longer try and make the interfaces invisible: 'Instead, the interaction is treated as an event – as opposed to "non-event", as in the previous "invisible interface" paradigm. Put differently, using personal information devices is now conceived as a carefully orchestrated experience, rather than only a means to an end. The interaction explicitly calls attention to itself. The interface engages the user in a kind of game. The user is asked to devote significant emotional, perceptual and cognitive resources to the very act of operating the device.' L. Manovich, *Information as an Aesthetic Event* (2007), 2. Web: http://www.manovich.net/DOCS/TATE_lecture.doc (accessed 12 March 2010).

17 Fredric Jameson, *Postmodernism, or, The Cultural Logic of Late Capitalism* (Durham, NC:Duke University Press, 1997 [1991]), 18.

18 G. Debord, *La société du spectacle* (Paris: Buchet-Chastel, 1967); translation: *The Society of the Spectacle* (New York: Zone Books, 1995).

19 G. Debord, *Commentaires sur la société du spectacle* (Paris: Gerard Lebovici, 1988); translation: *Comments on the Society of the Spectacle* (London: Verso, 1998).

20 Ibid., 27-29.

21 D.J. Boorstin, *The Image: A Guide to Pseudo-Events in America* (New York: Harper & Row, 1961).

22 W. Molino and S. Porro, *Disinformation Technology* (Milan: Apogeo, 2003).

23 Francalanci, *Estetica degli oggetti*, op. cit. (note 3), 26 [translation by the author].
24 Jameson, *Postmodernism*, op. cit. (note 17), 4-6.
25 Web: http://r-s-g.org/carnivore (accessed 12 March 2010).
26 Web: http://potatoland.com/blackwhite (accessed 12 March 2010).
27 Web: http://www.bitforms.com/artist_napier6.html (accessed 12 March 2010).
28 In a similar manner, Andy Deck in *Barcode* (2001) translates the entire works of Shakespeare into a stream of bar codes. Web: http://www.artcontext.org/bardcode (accessed 12 March 2010).
29 Francalanci, *Estetica degli oggetti*, op. cit. (note 3), 65 [translation by the author].
30 Mario Perniola, *Il sex appeal dell'inorganico* (Turin: Einaudi, 1994); translation: *The Sex-appeal of the Inorganic* (London: Continuum, 2004), 1.
31 Francalanci, *Estetica degli oggetti*, op. cit. (note 3), 66 [translation by the author].
32 B. Sterling, *Shaping Things* (Cambridge, MA: MIT Press, 2005).
33 Ibid., 10.
34 Francalanci, *Estetica degli oggetti*, op. cit. (note 3), 98 [translation by the author].
35 'The Auto-ID Labs is the research-oriented successor to the MIT Auto-ID Center, originally founded by Kevin Ashton, David Brock and Sanjay Sarma with funding from Procter and Gamble, Gillette, the Uniform Code Council and a number of other global consumer products manufacturers. The MIT Auto-ID Center was created to develop the Electronic Product Code, a global RFID-based item identification system intended to replace the UPC bar code. In October 2003 the Auto-ID Center was replaced by the newly founded research network, the Auto-ID Labs and EPCGlobal, an organization charged with managing the new EPC Network. Auto-ID Labs is responsible for managing and funding continued development of EPC technology'. Source: 'Wikipedia', http://en.wikipedia.org/wiki/Auto-ID_Labs (accessed 12 March 2010).
36 See: J. Waldner, *Nanocomputers and Swarm Intelligence* (New York: John Wiley & Sons, 2008).
37 Web: http://www.violet.net/about-violet.html (accessed 12 March 2010).
38 My source is the Nabaztag website. Web: http://www.nabaztag.com (accessed 12 March 2010).
39 Nabaztag has also been the protagonist of an installation that was recently awarded with the Prix Ars Electronica Award of Distinction Digital Music (2009). It is *Nabaz'mob* (2008) by Antoine Schmitt and Jean-Jacques Birgé, in which 100 Nabaztag smart rabbits are used to give life to an orchestra that 'interprets' a specially composed opera by the two artists. The choreography of the ears, the play of light and the 100 small loudspeakers hidden in the stomach of each rabbit create a composition with three voices built on time delay and repetition, programming and disrespect for rules. Web: http://nabazmob.free.fr/English.html (accessed 12 March 2010).
40 Perniola, *The Sex-appeal of the Inorganic*, op. cit. (note 30).
41 Ibid., 17.
42 Ibid., 46-47.
43 Francalanci, *Estetica degli oggetti*, op. cit. (note 3), 34-35 [translation by the author].
44 Ibid. [translation by the author].
45 Ibid., 21 [translation by the author].
46 G.C. Argan and Achille Bonito Oliva, *L'arte moderna, 1770-1970* (1970). *L'arte oltre il Duemila* (1991) (Florence: Sansoni, 2002), 183 [translation by the author].
47 For Baudrillard, too, Duchamp's ready-mades represent a crucial shift. Beginning with the premise that media have entered life as well as that spectators have entered the screen, he states that: 'Just as Duchamp's acting-out opens on to the (generalized) zero degree of aesthetics, where any old item or rubbish can be taken as a sort of art . . . so this media acting-out opens to a generalized virtuality which puts an end to the real by its promotion of every single instant.' In this way, any objects or situations become a virtual ready-made: everyone is required to take their life role on screen, just as Duchamp's ready-made plays its role live on the screen of the museum. See: J. Baudrillard, Le crime parfait (Paris: Galilée, 1995); translation: The Perfect Crime (London: Verso, 1996), 28-29.
48 Francalanci, *Estetica degli oggetti*, op. cit. (note 3), 58 [translation by the author].
49 A recent attempt to overcome Baudrillard's 'pessimistic vision' is Joseph Nechvatal's concept of the 'art of latent excess'. The American artist and theorist figures a 'post-Pop art', as an 'art of counter-

mannerist latent excess' that can 'problematise the Pop simulacra and hence enliven us to the privateness – and unique separateness – of the human condition in the lieu of the fabulously constructed social spectacle which engulfs and (supposedly) control us. This private separateness offers us a personal critical distance (gap), and thus another perspective on (and from) the given social simulacra.' Such an 'art of latent excess' would give us the opportunity, according to Nechvatal, to rediscover a private context in which to understand one's own 'simulacra situation' and, more importantly, it could 'undermine this understanding of the simulacra by overwhelming our immersion in the customary simulacra, along with our own prudent pose as observer and judge'. See: J. Nechvatal, *Towards an Immersive Intelligence: Essays on the Work of Art in the Age of Computer Technology and Virtual Reality 1993-2006* (New York: Edgewise, 2009), 79. I find this a very interesting position, even if I find its premises rather weak: Nechvatal believes that this 'art of latent excess' can be practiced only if the individual is freed from 'custom, doctrine and influence'; a condition that seems difficult to achieve.

50 A similar position can be found in Jean Baudrillard's *Le Système des objets* (Paris: Gallimard, 1968); translation: *The System of Objects* (London: Verso, 2005).

51 Web: http://www.cosmit.it (accessed 12 March 2010).

52 Francalanci, *Estetica degli oggetti*, op. cit. (note 3), 95.

53 F. Depero, 'Il futurismo e l'arte pubblicitaria', *Numero unico futurista Campari 1931*, 1931.

54 A.C. Danto, 'L'esperluète et le point d'exclamation', *Les Cahiers du Musée national d'art moderne*, no. 37, 'Visions' (October 1991), 97-109. See also: *The Transfiguration of the Commonplace: A Philosophy of Art* (Cambridge, MA: Harvard University Press, 1981) and *Beyond the Brillo Box: The Visual Arts in Post-Historical Perspective* (New York: Farrar, Stratus and Giroux, 1992).

55 J. Baudrillard, 'Le Complot de l'art', *Libération*, 20 May 1996. Web: http://usm.maine.edu/~bcj/issues/two/baudrillard_2.html (accessed 12 March 2010).

56 Ibid. [translation by the author], original text: 'Il fait de la nullité et de l'insignifiance un événement qu'il transforme en une stratégie fatale de l'image.'

57 Ibid. [translation by the author], original text: 'La forme sentimentale de la merchandise.'

58 A. Huyssen, *After the Great Divide: Modernism, Mass Culture, Postmodernism* (Bloomington, IN: Indiana University Press, 1986), 196.

59 J. Baudrillard, *L'illusion de la fin, ou, la grève des événements* (Paris: Galilée, 1992); translation: *The Illusion of the End* (Stanford, CA: Stanford University Press, 1994), 25. See also: J. Baudrillard, *Illusion, désillusion esthétiques* (Paris: Sens & Tonka, 1997).

60 Bauman's position is similar. See: Z. Bauman, *Legislators and Interpreters: On Modernity, Post-Modernity, Intellectuals* (New York: Cornell University Press, 1987).

61 M. Calinescu, *Faces of Modernity: Avant-Garde, Decadence, Kitsch* (Bloomington, IN: Indiana University Press, 1977), 147.

62 Francalanci, *Estetica degli oggetti*, op. cit. (note 3), 63.

63 W. Benjamin, 'Paris, die Haupstadt des XIX. Jahrhunderts', in: *Schriften* (2 vols.) (Frankfurt: Suhrkamp, 1955); translation: 'Paris the Capital of the Ninenteenth Century', in: *Selected Writings: 1935-1938* (Cambridge, MA: Harvard University Press, 2002), 39.

64 Francalanci, *Estetica degli oggetti*, op. cit. (note 3), 64 [translation by the author].

65 Ibid. [translation by the author].

66 Ibid. [translation by the author].

67 Ibid. [translation by the author]. Here Francalanci quotes Perniola who, in *The Sex-appeal of the Inorganic*, writes: 'It would seem that things and sense are no longer in conflict with one another but have struck an alliance.' Perniola, *The Sex-appeal of the Inorganic*, op. cit., (note 30), 1.

68 Baudrillard, *The Perfect Crime* , op. cit. (note 47), 5.

69 Ibid., 27.

70 *The Matrix* (1999).

71 M. Castells, *The Rise of the Network Society. The Information Age: Economy, Society and Culture* Vol. 1 (Oxford: Blackwell, 2009 [1996]), 403.

72 Here, as in the following pages, by this expression I mean the interpretation of contemporary society and its social interactions proposed by Manuel Castells.

73 L. Gye, A. Munster and I. Richardson (eds.), 'Distributed Aesthetics', *FibreCulture*, no. 7 (2005). Web: http://journal.fibreculture.org/issue7/issue7_abstracts.html (accessed 12 March 2010). In the following pages, the issue of the shaping of aesthetic expressions in the networks as a consequence of social processes or of the logic of software will be widely discussed, and some positions will partially differ from those expressed in the above mentioned issue of *FibreCulture*.

Theory of Memes

1 In summarizing the main positions and theories concerning memetics, a text written in 1999 by Francesco Ianneo has been my main (and invaluable) reference. See: F. Ianneo, *Meme. Genetica e virologia di idee, credenze e mode* (Rome: Castelvecchi, 1999).

2 R. Dawkins, *The Selfish Gene* (Oxford: Oxford University Press, 1976).

3 Ibid., 192.

4 See: D.C. Dennett, *Consciousness Explained* (Boston: Little Brown, 1991); D.C. Dennett, 'Memes and the Exploitation of Imagination', *Journal of Aesthetics and Art Criticism*, vol. 48 (1990) no. 2. Web: http://cogprints.org/258/ (accessed 12 March 2010); D.C. Dennett, *Darwin's Dangerous Idea: Evolution and the Meanings of Life* (New York: Simon & Schuster, 1995).

5 R. Dawkins, *Unweaving the Rainbow: Science, Delusion and the Appetite for Wonder* (London: Penguin Books, 1998).

6 Ibid.

7 R. Brodie, *Virus of the Mind: The New Science of the Meme* (Seattle: Integral Press, 1996).

8 S. Blackmore, *The Meme Machine* (Oxford: Oxford University Press, 1999).

9 Among the contributions to the development of the theory of memes it is proper to mention the 1996 edition of Ars Electronica entitled *Memesis*, which attempted to understand which the main conduits were for the spreading of ideas, concepts and trends across the Infosphere. Some of the materials resulting from the symposium 'The Memesis Network Discussion', edited by Geert Lovink, can be found on the festival website: http://90.146.8.18/en/archives/festival_archive/festival_catalogs/festival_catalog.asp?iProjectID=8531 (accessed 12 March 2010).

10 The 'six degrees of separation' theory arises from the hypothesis (first exposed in 1929 by the Hungarian writer Frigyes Karinthy in the short story 'Chains') that every person can be connected to any other by a chain of acquaintance of no more than 5 intermediaries. In the 1950s the hypothesis was studied by scientists (for example Manfred Kochen) who tried to provide a mathematical basis for it, but without a satisfactory result. In 1967 the American sociologist Stanley Milgram tried a new approach to test the theory (that he called 'small world theory'): he chose a group of volunteers in Nebraska and Kansas and asked them to send a package to a person that according to them was most likely to know the final addressee. The chosen person would do the same, until the package reached the final addressee. The participants were expecting the chain to involve at least a hundred people, while it only took on average five to seven stages for the package to reach its destination. The results of Milgram's experiment were published in *Psychology Today*, and the expression 'six degrees of separation' was born. In 2001 Duncan Watts (Columbia University) resumed the research and recreated Milgram's experiment on the Internet, using an email as the 'package'. After studying the results (48,000 people from 157 different states sent the 'package' to 19 addressees/targets) he realized that the average number of intermediaries was actually six. Watt's research was published in 2003 on the American review *Science* (http://www.sciencemag.org/cgi/content/abstract/301/5634/827) (accessed 12 March 2010). In 2006, two Microsoft researchers, analysing the log files of the conversations of about 24,163 volunteers on MSN Messenger discovered that between two users there are about 6.6 degrees of separation (http://research.microsoft.com/apps/pubs/default.aspx?id=70389) (accessed 12 March 2010).

11 Barabási's research is connected to that which Derek J. de Solla Price (1922-1983) started in the 1960s concerning the frequency of citations in specific scientific texts. To describe the phenomenon of preference towards a node with more links, Price used the term 'cumulative advantage'; the term was later replaced by Barabási and Albert with 'preferential attachment'.

12 Technically a scale-free network is a network whose graph of the relation between the number of nodes and the number of their connections is exponentially negative, hence scale-free.

13 Ianneo, *Meme*, op. cit. (note 1).

14 G. Tarde, *Les lois de l'imitation*, (Paris: Félix Alcan, 1890); translation: *The Laws of Imitation* (New York: Henry Holt, 1903).

15 J.M. Baldwin, *Social and Ethical Interpretations in Mental Development: A Study in Social Psychology* (London: Macmillan, 1897).

16 Tarde, *The Laws of Imitation*, op. cit. (note: 129), 17.

17 Baldwin, *Social and Ethical Interpretations in Mental Development*, op. cit. (note 15).

18 G. Le Bon, *Psychologie des foules* (Paris: Félix Alcan, 1895); translation: *The Crowd: A Study of the Popular Mind* (New York: Dover, 2002).

19 G. Le Bon, *Les lois psychologiques de l'évolution des peoples* (Paris: Félix Alcan, 1895); translation: *The Psychology of Peoples* (New York: Macmillan, 1899), 174.

20 P. Breton, *L'utopie de la communication. Le mythe du village planétaire* (Paris: La Découverte, 1992); I am translating from the Italian edition: *L'utopia della comunicazione. Il mito del 'villaggio planetario'* (Turin: UTET, 1995), 88-89.

21 Ibid., 89 [translation by the author].

22 Ibid., 47 [translation by the author].

23 Ibid., 95 [translation by the author].

Aby Warburg: the Concept of Engram

1 Web: http://warburg.sas.ac.uk (accessed 12 March 2010).

2 M. Bruhn, *Aby Warburg (1866-1929): The Survival of an Idea* (2001). Web: http://www.educ.fc.ul.pt/hyper/resources/mbruhn (accessed 12 March 2010).

3 In the analysis of the *Mnemosyne Atlas* the Italian review *Engramma*, which is concerned with the classical tradition in Western memory, was absolutely invaluable. Web: http://www.engramma.it (accessed 12 March 2010).

4 R.W. Semon, *Die Mneme als erhaltendes Princip im Wechsel des organischen Geschehens* (Leipzig: Engelmann, 1904).

5 A typical example (frequently recalled by Warburg) is the statue of *Laocoön and His Sons* (also called the *Laocoön Group*) attributed by Pliny the Elder to three sculptors from the island of Rhodes: Agesander, Athenodoros and Polydorus. The statue shows the Trojan priest Laocoön and his sons Antiphantes and Thymbraeus being strangled by sea serpents (sent by Poseidon) and it is to this episode that the quote from Virgil at the beginning of this paragraph is referred to.

6 The term, coming from the addition of Greek πάθος and German *Formel*, can be translated as 'pathos formula'.

7 E.H. Gombrich, *Aby Warburg: An intellectual biography* (London: The Warburg Institute - University of London, 1970).

8 C. Bignardi, *L'espressione delle emozioni all'origine della teoria warburghiana sul simbolo estetico* (1998) [translation by the author]. Web: http://www.parol.it/articles/bignardi.htm (accessed 12 March 2010).

9 Gombrich, *Aby Warburg*, op. cit. (note 7), 248-249.

Meme Gallery

1 Web: http://www.santofile.org/versus/index.htm (accessed 12 March 2010).

2 Web: http://www.santofile.org/x_reloaded/index.htm (accessed 12 March 2010).

3 Web: http://www.newarteest.com/artstate.html (accessed 12 March 2010).

4 V. Culatti, 'Memetic Simulation no. 2, memetic shoot 'em up', *Neural*, 2008. Web: http://www.neural.it/art/2008/04/memetic_simulation_no_2_shooti.phtml (accessed 12 March 2010).

5 Web: http://notime.arts.ucla.edu (accessed 12 March 2010).

Chapter III
Aesthetic Experience on the Web

To Flow or Not to Flow

1   Concerning 'physical interactivity', Florian Cramer observes that this often involves a reduction to 'a behaviorist simulation of interactivity through a predefined set of actions and reactions'. F. Cramer, *Words Made Flesh: Code, Culture, Imagination* (Rotterdam: Piet Zwart Institute, 2005), 114. Web: http://pzwart.wdka.hro.nl/mdr/research/fcramer/wordsmadeflesh (accessed 17 May 2010). All the user is asked to do is to press keys, according to schemes that the author/programmer has set, so that the user resembles the animal subjects of experiments undertaken particularly frequently in the 1960s, in which animals responded directly to visual or auditory stimuli.

2   L. Manovich, *The Language of New Media* (Cambridge, MA: MIT Press, 2001), 61.

3   G. Lovink, 'The Art of Watching Databases', in: M. Gerritzen and I. van Tol (eds.), *New Cultural Networks* (Amsterdam: Stichting All Media, 2008), 15.

4   J. Nielsen, *Designing Web usability: The Practice of Simplicity* (Indianapolis, IN: New Riders, 1999).

5   M. Fuller, *Behind the Blip: Essays on the Culture of Software* (New York: Autonomedia, 2003).

6   It is important to recall that many theorists believe users are aware of this. Michel Bauwens, for example, believes that there is an unspoken social agreement in which users accept that their attention will be monetized through advertising, as long as this does not interfere with their sharing practices (the recent revolt by the users of Digg would seem to support this theory). While not denying that there are a lot of users that willingly take part in this 'economy of attention', I still believe that unawareness prevails, and that to a large extent those who are grateful for the 'free' tools they are provided with do not realize that they are being expropriated for the benefit of the corporations that own the websites.

7   Y. Benkler, *The Wealth of Networks: How Social Production Transforms Markets and Freedom* (New Haven: Yale University Press, 2006).

8   G. Lovink, *Zero Comments: Blogging and Critical Internet Culture* (New York: Routledge, 2007).

9   M. Lazzarato, *La politica dell'evento* (Catanzaro: Rubettino, 2004).

10 Lovink, *Zero Comments*, op. cit. (note 8).

11 It might be worth clarifying that my frequent use of the word 'flow' (as well as 'process') in the singular, does not represent an attempt to reduce to unity the plurality it expresses. It rather takes that plurality for granted, just as the word 'Net' does not deny its nature as a *net of nets*.

Fictions

1   Here the reference is once again: W. Tatarkiewicz, *A History of Six Ideas: An Essay in Aesthetics* (The Hague: Martinus Nijhoff, 1980), 221-222.

2   Ibid., 243.

3   F. Nake and S. Grabowski, 'The Interface as Sign and as Aesthetic Event', in: P. Fishwick (ed.), *Aesthetic Computing* (Cambridge, MA: MIT Press, 2006), 67.

4   The Super Bowl is the championship of the American National Football League (NFL), and is the most watched television event in the USA.

5   L. Manovich, *The Language of New Media* (Cambridge, MA: MIT Press, 2001), 63.

6   Ibid.

7   W. Gibson, *Neuromancer* (New York: Ace Books, 1984), 51.

8   Manovich, *The Language of New Media*, op. cit. (note 5), 63.

9   Concerning the definition of the 'flow of data', I would like to make clear that the expression is used very differently in different fields. For instance, the data-flow model of computation is considered as an alternative to the main model, the so-called *Von Neumann model*; while functionalist theories of media identify, among others, a surveillance function, according to which media provide a continuous flow of data about the world we live in. By this expression I mean to refer to a specific situation, typical of the contemporary age, in which mankind is immersed increasingly deeply into a ubiquitous computing environment of machinical processes, in which the constant elaboration of an infinite flow of

data is an activity central both to computers and to human minds and senses. In order to explain this concept I think it is useful to recall Friedrich Kittler's poststructuralist theory, according to which: 'The general digitization of information and channels erases the differences among individual media. Sound and image, voice and text have become mere effects on the surface, or, to put it better, the interface for the consumer. Sense and the senses become mere glitter. Their media-produced glamour will last throughout the transitional period as a waste product of strategic programs. In computers everything becomes number: imageless, soundless, and wordless quantity. And if the optical fiber networks reduced all formerly separated data flows to one standardized digital series of numbers, any medium can be translated into another. With numbers, nothing is impossible. Modulation, transformation, synchronization; delay, memory, transposition; scrambling, scanning, mapping – a total connection of all media on a digital base erases the notion of medium itself. Instead of hooking up technologies to people, absolute knowledge can run as an endless loop.' F.A. Kittler, *Grammophon, Film, Typewriter* (Berlin: Brinkmann & Bose, 1986); translation: 'Grammophone, Film, Typewriter', in: F.A. Kittler (ed.), *Literature, Media, Information Systems: Essays* (New York: Routledge, 1997), 31-32. See also: F.A. Kittler, *Grammophone, Film, Typewriter* (Stanford, CA: Stanford University Press, 1999). What I really find interesting in this passage is not the alleged convergence of media, but the crucial closing words: the digitization of media gives life to a situation in which 'absolute knowledge can run as an endless loop'. When I try to visualize the condition of the contemporary subject, this is the very image that takes shape before my eyes: a constant loop of information and data-enwrapping existence. From a phenomenological point of view, this is the central defining aspect of the contemporary age. Compared to this, other significant issues such as the relationship between form and content, and the specificity of different media tend to become secondary. My non-literal interpretation of the word 'knowledge' is confirmed by Kittler himself, who uses it to describe the constant stream of signals that the whole of the media network produces without end, and which ends up encompassing human lives.

10   My reasoning on form in the Web is in agreement with Mario Costa's interpretation, according to which: 'On the Internet, the form, any form, is never formed . . . the *form* on the Internet is a *form*-event, never completed even when it seems it is, always taking shape and dissolving, just because on the Internet there is no "complete process" . . . form exists in the *temporality* and in the *flow*, that are proper feature of the net that in different ways absorb any fixity and any crystallization of the form.' M. Costa, *Internet e globalizzazione estetica* (Naples: Cuzzolin, 2002), 85-86 [translation by the author].

11   Manovich, *The Language of New Media*, op. cit. (note 5), 16.

12   Ibid., 37. In the same text, Manovich further elaborates the concept of *variability*: 'Historically, the artist made a unique work within a particular medium. Therefore the interface and the work were the same; in other words, the level of an interface did not exist. With new media, the content of the work and the interface become separate. It is therefore possible to create different interfaces to the same material. These interfaces may present different versions of the same work . . . This is one of the ways in which the already discussed principle of *variability* of new media manifests itself. But now we can give this principle a new formulation. *The new media object consists of one or more interfaces to a database of multimedia material.* If only one interface is constructed, the result will be similar to a traditional art object; but this is an exception rather than the norm.' Ibid., 227.

13   In this frame of reference, the working of the CMS (Content Management System) is crucial. The system can be defined as 'a tool that enables a variety of (centralised) technical and (de-centralised) non technical staff to create, edit, manage and finally publish (in a number of formats) a variety of content (such as text, graphics, video, documents etc), while being constrained by a centralised set of rules, process and workflows that ensure coherent, validated electronic content.' Web: http://www.contentmanager.eu.com/history.htm.

14   A clear explanation of these concepts is provided by Michael Wesch (assistant professor of cultural anthropology at Kansas State University) in a series of videos available on YouTube. Web: http://www.youtube.com/user/mwesch (accessed 17 May 2010).

15   For those who wish to verify this, the software Browsershots (http://browsershots.org) allows the user to test (for free) the compatibility of a site with different browsers, operating systems and screen resolutions.

16　These ideas emerged during a discussion with Andres Treske from Bilkent University of Ankara.

17　This very opportunity leads many public figures to contract professional designers for the customization of their space so that it has a 'glossy' look, which might remind us of the dot-com era.

18　Francesco De Sanctis deals critically with the Hegelian form/content dyad, stating that: 'The form is not *a priori*, is not something that stands by itself and different from the content, as an ornament or covering or appearance or extra to it; it is rather generated by the content, active in the mind of the artist: like content like form.' F. De Sanctis, 'L'idea e l'estetica dello Hegel' (1858), in: F. De Sanctis, *Opere* (Turin: Einaudi, 1965), Vol. VII, 208 [translation by the author]. For De Sanctis, stating that form and content are identical meant rejecting both the view of the content as such (and therefore an evaluation of the artist dependent on the subject that he is dealing with) and the form as such (any rhetorical and formalistic evaluations). Croce takes possession of De Sanctis's idea of the identity of form and content in art but places it in a speculative and idealistic perspective: form is also the content and content is also the form. Hence art cannot be only content or only form, because every content is 'formed' and every form is structured by content. Form and content to Croce can be differentiated in order to be analysed, but once separated, they cannot be on the level of art. Croce's aesthetics is *intuitionist*, because the aesthetic judgment is neither related to time nor space and the only work of art that Croce considers valuable is the one inside the fantasy of the artist. He is not interested in the fate of art across history or in its material objectivization. He studies art only as the creativity of the spirit, cuts out any element of circulation and reception and extracts it from the level of communication. Art is the result of the cognitive intuition and is only placed in the region of the spirit. By content, Croce means the feeling that is expressed in the form. Finally, the identity between form and content is stated by Croce's aesthetics on idealistic premises and according to idealistic terminology and takes place inside the artist, art itself is a philosophical category, a 'distinct' moment of the spirit. Gramsci also defines the artistic fact as the inseparable relationship between form and content; however this relationship is 'transferred' from a spiritual dimension to external reality, it is thus immersed in history and society. Also, by content Gramsci does not mean the 'feeling' of which Croce speaks, but the whole of the feelings and attitudes towards life that moves within the work of art. Content means a world view that in art is always expressed in a form. Form and content are always interconnected, so that any change in the form is also a change in the content and vice versa. The form is the language the content is expressed in, but it is content itself because, in the use of a language, a whole culture is involved, a mindset, with its temporal relativity. Form and content are both related to history.

19　As convinced as I am that, as claimed by Vilém Flusser, humanity is moving increasingly towards the adoption of new codes based on numbers and non-linearity in place of alphanumeric, linear codes, it is clear that this is a long-running process and, therefore, that an infinite universe composed of numbers is currently too complex and remains inaccessible.

20　On this point, Geert Lovink and Anna Munster assume that because 'numbers are too hard', it is understandable that we tend not to relate directly with this reality, and 'we get a picture instead'. However, 'complexity should not be an excuse for deferring the work of human thought and human creation – theoretical and aesthetic – to network software. Complexity is difficult and arduous but not aesthetically unmanageable.' The two theorists therefore invite us to escape as much as is possible the desire to create maps ('the map is not the network'), and not to completely delegate to machines and software the task of solving and explaining to humanity the complexity with which it is surrounded, for 'the increasing abstraction of topological visualisation removes us from an analysis of the ways in which networks engage and are engaged by current political, economic and social relations'. The risk then is of not grasping the social dynamics (the reference of the authors is to a *social complexity* as opposed to *bio-complexity*) that represents – in the opinion of these authors – the real glue of networks (and of the subjects that 'inhabit' them). A. Munster and G. Lovink, 'Theses on Distributed Aesthetics: Or, What a Network is Not', *FibreCulture*, no. 7, 'Distributed Aesthetics' (2005). Web: http://journal.fibreculture.org/issue7/issue7_munster_lovink.html.

21　J. Dewey, *Art as Experience* (New York: Perigee, 2005 [1934]), 15.

22　Regardless of whether the 'representation' is considered a 'well established fact' or a 'process'.

23 A definition of the more generic data visualization process that seems to me very effective is that of Donna Cox, who writes that 'data visualization is the process of using computer-mediated technologies to transform numerical data into a digital visual model'. See: D. Cox, 'Metaphoric Mappings: The Art of Visualization', in: Fishwick, *Aesthetic Computing*, op. cit. (note 3), 89.

24 For an authoritative confirmation of this approach it is enough to re-read Gombrich's *Art and Illusion*: to the Austrian art historian, in fact, the artist can only represent reality by relying on predefined patterns of representation. See: E.H. Gombrich, *Art and Illusion: A Study in the Psychology of Pictorial Representation* (London: Phaidon, 1960).

25 Web: http://www.informationarchitects.jp (accessed 17 May 2010).

26 M. Dodge and R. Kitchin, *Atlas of Cyberspace* (London: Pearson Education, 2001). Web: http://www.kitchin.org/atlas/index.html (accessed 17 May 2010).

27 Manovich, *The Language of New Media*, op. cit. (note 5), 128.

28 T. Berners-Lee and M. Fischetti, *Weaving the Web: The Original Design and Ultimate Destiny of the World Wide Web by Its Inventor* (San Francisco: HarperCollins, 1999).

29 'Since the image is limited in size by its border, we seem to perceive only a portion of the space. It is this portion of the imaginary space that is contained inside the image's borders, which we will call "framing" or "onscreen space".' J. Aumont, A. Bergala, M. Marie and M. Vernet, *Aesthetics of Film* (Austin, TX: University of Texas Press, 1992), 13.

30 G. Deleuze and F. Guattari, *A Thousand Plateaus: Capitalism and Schizophrenia* (London: Continuum, 2004).

31 Ibid., 127.

32 Web: http://www.meggangould.net/site_seeingIII.htm (accessed 17 May 2010).

33 Web: http://www.archimuse.com/mw98/beyond_interface/fuller_fr.html (accessed 17 May 2010).

34 Web: http://www.nullpointer.co.uk/-/webtracer2.htm (accessed 17 May 2010).

35 From an interview with Tom Betts by Matthew Fuller, 12 March 2001. Web: http://amsterdam.nettime.org/Lists-Archives/nettime-l-0103/msg00068.html (accessed 17 May 2010).

36 Web: http://marumushi.com/projects/socialcircles (accessed 17 May 2010).

37 Web: http://www.touchgraph.com (accessed 17 May 2010).

38 A. Munster, *Data Undermining: The Work of Networked Art in an Age of Imperceptibility* (2009). Web: http://munster.networkedbook.org/data-undermining-the-work-of-networked-art-in-an-age-of-imperceptibility. The project *Networked: A networked_book about networked_art*, is in progress; my last visit is 3 August 2009.

39 Eyal Weizman argues that the occupation policy of Israel will give shape to the space represented by the territory of Palestine. While the two situations are clearly different, I think the analogy holds: the Israeli settlement policy shapes the landscape of Palestine, just as the political and economic interests of the corporations that control the Web are shaping the Internet landscape. In either case, the landscape is not only an allegory of power but is the very means of the power. See: E. Weizman, *Hollow Land* (London: Verso, 2007).

40 Web: http://www.shiftspace.org (accessed 17 May 2010).

41 Web: http://maicgregator.org (accessed 17 May 2010).

42 Web: http://navastraceblog.blogspot.com; see also: http://mrl.nyu.edu/~dhowe/trackmenot (accessed 17 May 2010).

43 Web: http://contemporary-home-computing.org/vernacular-web-2; see also the previous text: http://art.teleportacia.org/observation/vernacular (accessed 17 May 2010).

44 Munster, *Data Undermining*, op. cit. (note 38).

45 Ibid.

46 The aim to critically reflect on information society, the knowledge organization and the dominant role of the search engine in our culture has animated the recent international conference *Society of Query* organized in Amsterdam by the Institute of Network Cultures (13-14 November 2009). Web: http://networkcultures.org/wpmu/query (accessed 17 May 2010).

47 For a thorough multidisciplinary perspective on the role of search engines (Google, but also others) in determining the means by which users access digitized information, as well as on the influence

that these instruments have in determining what is considered beautiful, important, or true, see: K. Becker and F. Stalder (eds.), *Deep Search: The Politics of Search beyond Google* (Innsbruck: Studien, 2009).

48 A.R. Galloway, *Protocol: How Control Exists After Decentralization* (Cambridge, MA: MIT Press, 2004), 64.

49 However obvious, we must remember that the way a database is structured inevitably responds to ideological, economic and political interests, and to the historical contingencies of the moment the database is created.

50 G. Lovink, 'The Art of Watching Databases', in: M. Gerritzen and I. van Tol (eds.), *New Cultural Networks* (Amsterdam: Stichting All Media, 2008), 15.

51 L. Manovich, *Database as a Symbolic Form* (1998). Web: http://www.manovich.net/docs/database. rtf (accessed 8 August 2009). Some pieces are then taken up by Manovich in *The Language of New Media* (2001), while the essay has been more recently published in an interesting collection edited by Victoria Vesna. See: V. Vesna (ed.), *Database Aesthetics: Art in the Age of Information Overflow* (Minneapolis, MN: University of Minnesota Press, 2007).

52 To give some idea of the speed of this growth I would like to quote a recent report by IDC (International Data Corporation) according to which the 'digital universe' compound annual growth rate, between 2008 and 2011, is expected to be almost 60 per cent. Web: http://www.emc.com/collateral/analyst-reports/diverse-exploding-digital-universe.pdf (accessed 17 May 2010).

53 G. Lovink, 'Society of Query: The Googlization of our Lives', in: Becker and Stalder, *Deep Search*, op. cit. (note 47), 45.

54 Ibid.

55 Web: http://www.googlizationofeverything.com (accessed 17 May 2010).

56 For the sake of precision, I recall that the term 'database aesthetics' is also used to refer specifically to that aesthetics emerging through the work of those artists who use the endless stream of digital information as their medium.

57 M. Costa, *Dimenticare l'arte. Nuovi orientamenti nella teoria e nella sperimentazione estetica* (Milan: FrancoAngeli, 2005), 110-111. Costa connects multimediality to the Wagnerian notion of *Gesamtkunstwerk* (total work of art), where Nietzsche (*The Case of Wagner*, 1888) already had reported the impossibility of going beyond a suggestive 'theatrical rhetoric'.

58 Ibid.

59 F. Forest and P. Virilio (conversation), 'La Fin des certitudes', *Art Press*, no. 122 (February 1988), 14-16. To Virilio images are always interconnected, thus the mental image is connected to the optical one which is connected, in turn, to the ocular one; optical and ocular images are all connected to the graphic, photographic, cinematographic ones, etcetera.

60 Costa, *Dimenticare l'arte*, op. cit. (note 57), 111 [translation by the author].

61 Ibid., 115-116 [translation by the author].

62 Ibid., 51, note 72 [translation by the author].

63 Ibid., 116. [translation by the author].

64 Ibid., 116-117 [translation by the author].

65 Ibid., 117 [translation by the author].

66 Web: http://www.numeral.com/eicon.html (accessed 17 May 2010).

67 Web: http://www.numeral.com/articles/paraicon/paraicon.html (accessed 17 May 2010).

68 Web: http://www.internetlandscape.it (accessed 17 May 2010).

69 Roy Ascott's words come to mind: 'To inhabit both the real and virtual worlds at one and the same time, and to be both here and potentially everywhere else at the same time is giving us a new sense of self, new ways of thinking and perceiving which extend what we have believed to be our natural, genetic capabilities.' R. Ascott, 'The Architecture of Cyberception', *Leonardo Electronic Almanac*, vol. 2 (1994) no. 8. Web: http://www.cyberday.de/news/ausgabe_100017.htm (accessed 17 May 2010).

70 Web: http://www.marcomanray.com/remap-berlin/index.htm (accessed 17 May 2010).

71 Web: http://www.twinity.com (accessed 17 May 2010).

72 Web: http://outsideoftheinternetthereisnoglory.com (accessed 17 May 2010).

244

73 This is a reworked extract from: V. Campanelli, 'Internet Landscape: Shapes and Places of the Web in the Work of Marco Cadioli', in: V. Campanelli (ed.), *Internet Landscapes (2003-2007)* (Naples: MAO, 2009).

74 M. Perniola, *Contro la comunicazione* (Turin: Einaudi, 2004).

75 The term is my free translation from the Italian expression *interesse disinteressato* used by Perniola. In the English translation of Bourdieu's text, who is to be credited for the initial intuition, the expression 'interest in disinterestedness' (translating the French *intérêt au désintéressement*) is found. See: P. Bourdieu, *Raisons pratiques. Sur la théorie de l'action* (Paris: Le Seuil. 1994); translation: *Practical Reason: On the Theory of Action* (Stanford, CA: Stanford University Press, 1998).

76 Perniola, *Contro la comunicazione*, op. cit. (note 74), 9.

77 Ibid., 74.

78 Ibid., 72. For an anthropological point of view on the social function of creativity, see: J. Leach, *Creative Land* (New York: Berghahn Books, 2003).

79 P. Himanen, *The Hacker Ethic and the Spirit of the Information Age* (New York: Random House/Vintage, 2001).

80 Generally, this position extends back to Michel Foucault. In an interview in June 1984 (hence shortly before his death), Foucault makes clear that resistance is greater than all the forces of the process and compels power relationships to change. See: B. Gallagher and A. Wilson, 'Michel Foucault. An Interview: Sex, Power and the Politics of Identity', *The Advocate*, no. 400 (7 August 1984), 27-29.

81 M. de Certeau, *The Practice of Everyday Life* (Berkeley, CA: University of California Press, 1984), 200.

82 Ibid.

Optical and Haptic

1 W. Benjamin, 'The Work of Art in the Age of Mechanical Reproduction', in: *Illuminations* (New York: Schocken, 1969).

2 H. Wölfflin, *Kunstgeschichliche Grundbegriffe. Das Problem der Stilentwicklung in der neueren Kunst* (Munich: Bruckmann, 1915); translation: *Principles of Art History: The problem of the Development of Style in Later Art* (New York: Dover, 1950). This included his five opposite couples: 'linear/painterly', 'plane/ recession', 'closed form/open form', 'multiplicity/unity' and 'clearness/ unclearness'.

3 Ibid. See also: H. Wölfflin, *Renaissance and Baroque* (New York: Cornell University Press, 1967).

4 A. Riegl, *Die spätrömische Kunstindustrie nach den Funden in Österreich-Ungarn* (Vienna: Österreichisches Archäologisches Institut, 1901): translation: *Late Roman Art Industry* (Rome: G. Bretschneider, 1985). See also the brilliant reconstruction by Andrea Pinotti in: A. Pinotti, *Il corpo dello stile. Storia dell'arte come storia dell'estetica a partire da Semper, Riegl, Wölfflin* (Milan: Mimesis, 2001).

5 Riegl, *Late Roman Art Industry*, op. cit. (note 4).

6 Benjamin, 'The Work of Art in the Age of Mechanical Reproduction', op. cit. (note 1).

7 Ibid.

8 A. Pinotti, 'Un'immagine alla mano. Note per una genealogia dello spettatore tattile', in: A. Somaini (ed.), *Il luogo dello spettatore. Forme dello sguardo nella cultura delle immagini* (Milan: Vita e Pensiero, 2005).

9 Among these, Maurice Merleau-Ponty, Henri Maldiney and Michel Dufrenne are most deserving of mention, but the economy of this publication does not allow it. For the same reason I am silent with regard to the fundamental *haptic aesthetics* of J.G. Herder, who also deserves specific and detailed discussion.

10 G. Deleuze, *Francis Bacon. Logique de la sensation* (Paris: La différence, 1981); translation: *Francis Bacon: The Logic of Sensation* (London: Continuum, 2005).

11 Ibid., 108.

12 Ibid.

13 Ibid., 109.

14 Ibid..

15 Ibid., 30.

16 Ibid. 16.

G. Deleuze and F. Guattari, *A Thousand Plateaus: Capitalism and Schizophrenia* (London: Continuum, 2004), 543.

18 Deleuze, *Francis Bacon*, op. cit. (note 10), 73.

19 Ibid., 76.

20 Ibid., 77. The diagram serves as the introduction of an informal chaos within the figuration and it is possible to state that all of Bacon's work is achieved in the proximity of such an absolute disaster of figurative data.

21 Deleuze and Guattari, *A Thousand Plateaus*, op. cit. (note 17), 178.

22 G. Révész, *Die Formenwelt des Tastsinnes* (The Hague: Martinus Nijhoff, 1938).

23 M. Mazzeo, *Tatto e linguaggio. Il corpo delle parole* (Rome: Editori Riuniti, 2003), 22-24.

24 Mazzeo observes that in the haptic dimension one must use a method not widely used in the optical dimension, namely the process of comparative measurement. In this regard, Révész distinguishes two different types of measurement, a *static and mechanical measurement* by means of a constant unit of measurement applied consecutively and a *dynamic and intuitive measurement* that aims to approximate results, and is much more subjectively variable.

25 L.U. Marks, *The Skin of the Film: Intercultural Cinema, Embodiment and the Senses* (Durham, NC: Duke University Press, 1999).

26 M. Iverson, *Alois Riegl: Art History and Theory* (Cambridge, MA: MIT Press, 1993).

27 Proprioception (kinaesthesia) is the ability to perceive and recognize the position of one's own body in space and the state of contraction of the musculature, even without the support of sight.

28 Marks, *The Skin of the Film*, op. cit. (note 25), 163.

29 Ibid., 170.

30 'An optical printer is a device consisting of one or more film projectors mechanically linked to a movie camera. It allows filmmakers to re-photograph one or more strips of film. The optical printer is used for making special effects for motion pictures, or for copying and restoring old film material. In the late 1980s, digital compositing began to supplant optical effects. By the mid-nineties, computer graphics has evolved to rival and surpass what was possible with optical printers, and optical printing has all but gone. ... Today, optical printing is mostly used as an artistic tool by experimental filmmakers, or for education purposes. As a technique, it proves particularly useful for making copies of hand painted or physically manipulated film.' Source: 'Wikipedia', http://www.en.wikipedia.org/wiki/Optical_printer.

31 Marks, *The Skin of the Film*, op. cit. (note 25), 173.

32 R. Burnett, *Cultures of Vision: Images, Media, and the Imaginary* (Bloomington, IN: Indiana University Press, 1995).

33 L. Manovich, *The Language of New Media* (Cambridge, MA: MIT Press, 2001).

34 Marks, *The Skin of the Film*, op. cit. (note 25), 176. Actually, the distinction that McLuhan draws between cold and hot media was meant to highlight two variables: 1) the different level of involvement required by the user (a hot *medium* such as radio by sending high definition messages requires a low participation from the user, while a cold *medium* such as television by sending low definition messages requires the user to be active to complete its informational content); 2) the different quality of senses involved in the relationship with different media (telephone and radio involve one single sense, hence they are to be considered 'hot', while television involving more senses is to be considered 'cold').

35 The video has been included in the Tate Gallery collection since 1999. Web: http://www.viddler.com/explore/Nano9/videos/22 (accessed 17 May 2010).

36 Marks, *The Skin of the Film*, op. cit. (note 25), 187.

37 Ibid., 183. A work of art that can help us to understand the role that sounds play in haptic perception is *OP-ERA: Haptics for the 5th Dimension* (2007) by Rejane Cantoni and Daniela Kutschat. It is an immersive and interactive interface designed to produce hearing and tactile stimuli in the participant. The system identifies the relative position of the visitor as a gravitational force and activates sounds indicating atomic particles moving in the virtual field. Therefore, the visitor can perceive shapes and sizes of real space-time through a non-visual digital representation as he/she moves around the space.

246

The relation between the virtual space and the user is one of continuous feedback. The optical perception instead comes back into play when the visitor is faced towards a monitor (located outside of the installation's room) that returns the image of the interaction between user and field of particles that in the installation are converted into sound. Source: VV.AA., *Emergentes* (Gijon: LABoral, 2008), 89. Catalogne of the *Emergentes* exhibition (Gijon, LABoral Centro de Arte y Creation Industrial, 16 November 2007 – 12 May 2008).

38 L.U. Marks, *Enfoldment and Infinity: An Islamic Genealogy of New Media Art*, forthcoming from MIT Press. I have collected a series of clues about the work from the Web, I recommend in particular (also for hyperlinks to additional resources) the following link: http://www.sfu.ca/~lmarks/research/research.html.

39 It is perhaps worth remembering that Vilém Flusser had already identified in the new digital codes properties common to the Eastern ones: 'But now the alphanumeric code is being replaced by digital computer codes. These new codes have more in common with Oriental codes (e.g. ideograms) than with linear ones.' See: V. Flusser, *Dinge und Undinge. Phänomenologische Skizzen* (Munich: Hanser, 1993); translation: *The Shape of Things: A Philosophy of Design* (London: Reaktion Books, 1999), 73.

40 The explicit reference is to the essay on Leibniz and, in particular, the following passage: 'The unit of matter, the smallest element of the labyrinth, is the fold, not the point which is never a part, but a simple extremity of the line.' G. Deleuze, *Le Pli. Leibniz et le Baroque* (Paris: Minuit, 1988); translation: *The Fold: Leibniz and the Baroque* (London: Continuum, 2006), 6.

41 Mark B.N. Hansen 'takes a stand' indeed in *New Philosophy for New Media* (Cambridge, MA: MIT Press, 2004). In Hansen's phenomenology (in open contrast with Kittler's post-medium view, where human perception becomes obsolete) the thesis takes shape that media of visual design privilege and favour an affective, perceptive and tactile dimension. The body and its elements would be thus constantly (and from the guts) involved in the experience. As Tim Lenoir states in the introduction to the book, 'the body continues to be the active framer of the image, even in a digital regime'. Ibid., XVII.

42 Web: http://www.junji.org/invisibles (accessed 17 May 2010). The project, which is based on an interface that can superimpose tactile information onto surfaces or images displayed on a computer monitor, was recently (February 2009) awarded at the 12th Japan Media Art Festival.

43 R.F. Fidler, *Mediamorphosis: Understanding New Media* (Thousand Oaks, CA: Pine Forge Press, 1997).

44 J.D. Bolter and R. Grusin, *Remediation: Understanding New Media* (Cambridge, MA: MIT Press, 1999).

45 M. McLuhan, *Understanding Media: The Extensions of Man* (New York: McGraw Hill, 1964) 23-24.

46 Manovich, *The Language of New Media*, op. cit. (note 33).

47 A.R. Galloway, A.R. Galloway, *Protocol: How Control Exists After Decentralization* (Cambridge, MA: MIT Press, 2004), 39-41.

48 Web: http://www.eden.garden1.0.projects.sfmoma.org (accessed 17 May 2010).

49 Web: http://www.guggenheim.org/new-york/collections/collection-online/show-full/piece/?search=Unfolding%20Object&page=&f=Title&object=2002.16 (accessed 17 May 2010).

50 J.F. Simon Jr, 'Unfolding Object', in: VV.AA., *Stretched Paint #1/ Web as Canvas* (Madrid: Anaya Multimedia, 2002). Catalogue of the *ArtFutura* exhibition (Barcelona, 2002).

51 Web: http://www.xs4all.nl/~elout/2003/08/java/attyo1.html; http://www.xs4all.nl/~elout/2003/06/swf/portretooo1b.html; http://www.xs4all.nl/~elout/2003/06/swf/zfdo1.html (all accessed 17 May 2010).

52 Patricai Moran, a young scholar of VJ culture, begins a recent essay entitled 'Poetics of Correspondence' with a rather peremptory affirmation: 'Screens blink. Nervous images. Repitition. There is no bucolic contemplation. There is a primacy of the action and/or the affection over a continuous length of time.' Optical perception thus seems to be out of the game – however, at the end of the argument concerning the way that sudiovisual fragments of a VJ's performance can be considered as poetic correspondences, the Brazilian researcher opens up to a more varies spectrum of possibilities stating that: 'If the figurations tend to disappear, the abstract imigaes, *stricto sensu*, will tend to suggest figures like in fine arts. This way we have a two-way road in terms of suggestibility, as the anstraction tends to figuration and vice versa.' Web: http://www.vjtheory.net/web_texts/text_moran.htm (accessed 17 May 2010).

Chapter IV
Aesthetic Experience and Digital Networks

Travellers in the Aesthetic Matrix

1   E. Navas, *The Latency of the Moving Image in New Media* (2007). Web: http://remixtheory.net/?p=190 (accessed 24 May 2010).
2   P. Virilio and S. Lotringer, *Pure War* (New York: Semiotext(e), 1983).
3   I. Chambers, *Border Dialogues: Journeys in Postmodernity* (London: Routledge, 1990), 57-58.
4   Ibid., 58.
5   Ibid.
6   L. Manovich, *The Language of New Media* (Cambridge, MA: MIT Press, 2001), 268-273.
7   G. Lovink, 'The Data Dandy', in: Adilkno, *The Media Archive* (New York: Autonomedia, 1988), 99. Web: http://thing.desk.nl/bilwet/adilkno/TheMediaArchive/26.txt (accessed 24 May 2010).
8   Web: www.slsknet.org.
9   Web: http://en.wikipedia.org/wiki/Kad_network (accessed 24 May 2010).
10 J. Baudrillard, *The System of Objects* (London: Verso, 2005), 111-112.
11 Ibid., 97.
12 P.D. Miller, 'In Through the Out Door: Sampling and the Creative Act', in: P.D. Miller (ed.), *Sound Unbound: Sampling Digital Music and Culture* (Cambridge, MA: MIT Press, 2008), 16.

The DivX and MP3 Experience

1   I refer specifically to the practice generally defined as cam or camming (from camera). The similar practice known as Telesyncs (TS) is to be kept separate, at least here, as it involves only those employees who deal with projections inside movie theatres and not the more general public. Also, the qualitative performance that characterizes this method is significantly higher for both the centrality and stability of images, both because the sound is recorded live from the sound source and not through the microphone of the camera.
2   L. Manovich, *The Language of New Media* (Cambridge, MA: MIT Press, 2001), 55.
3   Held in Split, 21-23 May 2009.
4   L. Manovich, *Macromedia and Micro-media* (2000). Web: http://www.manovich.net/DOCS/macro_micro.doc (accessed 24 May 2010).
5   The name 'Walkman' is a trademark of Sony. According to Sony, the plural form is 'Walkman Personal Stereos', rather than 'Walkmans' or 'Walkmen'. Source: 'Wikipedia', http://en.wikipedia.org/wiki/Walkman (accessed 24 May 2010).
6   I. Chambers, *Migracy, Culture, Identity* (London: Routledge, 1994), 50.
7   Ibid., 51.
8   Ibid.
9   P. Virilio, *L'Art à perte de vue* (Paris: Galilée, 2005); translation: *Art as Far as the Eye Can See* (Oxford: Berg, 2007).
10 Manovich's reasoning in regard to the Mac OS X can be extended to the iPod: 'User interface was aesthetized in a sense that it was now to explicitly appeal to and stimulate senses.' L. Manovich, *Information as an Aesthetic Event* (2007), 3. Web: http://www.manovich.net/DOCS/TATE_lecture.doc (accessed 12 March 2010).
11 L.U. Marks, *The Skin of the Film: Intercultural Cinema, Embodiment and the Senses* (Durham, NC: Duke University Press, 1999), 176.
12 A.J. Greimas, *De l'imperfection* (Périgueux: Pierre Fanlac, 1987).
13 *Perte d'auréole*, prose poem written in 1865 but only published posthumously in the collection *Petits poèmes en prose* (also known as *Le spleen de Paris*, 1869); translation: 'Loss of Halo', in: C. Baudelaire, *Paris spleen* (New York: New Directions, 1970), 94, original text: 'Tout à l'heure, comme je traversais le boulevard, en grande hâte, et que je sautillais dans la boue, à travers ce chaos mouvant où la mort arrive au galop de tous les côtés à la fois, mon auréole, dans un mouvement brusque, a glissé de ma tête dans la fange du macadam. Je n'ai pas eu le courage de la ramasser. J'ai jugé moins désagréable de

248

perdre mes insignes que de me faire rompre les os. Et puis, me suis-je dit, à quelque chose malheur est bon. Je puis maintenant me promener incognito, faire des actions basses, et me livrer à la crapule, comme les simples mortels. Et me voici, tout semblable à vous, comme vous voyez!'

14 M. Berman, *All That Is Solid Melts Into Air: The Experience of Modernity* (New York: Simon and Shuster, 1982).

15 *Die Aufzeichnungen des Malte Laurids Brigge* (1904-1910), a novel known in English as: *The Notebooks of Malte Laurids Brigg.*

16 R.M. Rilke, 'Gong' (1925), in: S. Mitchell (ed. and trans.), *Selected Poetry of Rainer Maria Rilke* (New York: Random House/Vintage, 1989), 282.

17 L. Russolo, *L'arte dei rumori* (Milan: Direzione del Movimento Futurista, 1913); translation: L. Russolo, *The Art of Noises* (New York: Pendragon, 2005).

18 Web: http://www.thereminvox.com/article/articleview/117 (accessed 24 May 2010).

19 Ibid.

20 Ibid.

21 For a recent definition of noise, see: R.M. Schafer, *The Tuning of the World: The Soundscape* (New York: Knopf, 1977). In this book, the Canadian writer and composer discusses the transition from rural to urban soundscapes in hi-fi and lo-fi terms. A hi-fi system is characterized by a low level of environmental noise, it is therefore possible to hear discrete individual sounds clearly. The lo-fi soundscape, which appears with the industrial revolution and is further increased by the subsequent electronic revolution, is characterized by a congestion of sounds.

22 Web: http://www.thereminvox.com/article/articleview/117 (accessed 24 May 2010).

23 G. Dorfles, *Horror Pleni. La (in)civiltà del rumore* (Rome: Castelvecchi, 2008).

24 Ibid., 16 [translation by the author].

25 Ibid., 9-13.

26 Ibid., 20-21.

27 Ibid., 19.

28 Ibid., 20.

29 Ibid., 24 [translation by the author]. See also: G. Dorfles, *L'intervallo perduto* (Turin: Einaudi, 1980).

30 T. Bäumgartel, 'Media Piracy and Independent Cinema in Southest Asia', in: G. Lovink and S. Niederer (eds.), *Video Vortex Reader: Responses to YouTube* (Amsterdam: Institute of Network Cultures, 2008), 266. See also: T. Bäumgartel, 'The Culture of Piracy in the Philippines', in: S.D. Kim and J. David (eds.), *Cinema in/on Asia* (Gwanju: Asian Culture Forum, 2006). Web: http://www.asian-edition.org/piracy-inthephilippines.pdf (accessed 24 May 2010).

31 Web: http://julienmaire.ideenshop.net/project5.shtml (accessed 24 May 2010).

32 Web: http://www.decasia.com (accessed 24 May 2010).

33 A. Ludovico, 'Decasia, a film made of recycled celluloid', *Neural*, 2003. Web: http://www.neural.it/nnews/decasiae.htm (accessed 24 May 2010).

34 Web: http://www.n-gon.com/delter (accessed 24 May 2010).

35 Web: http://www.unpixelated.org (accessed 24 May 2010).

36 Web: http://www.youtube.com/watch?v=vusmtmBRLWU (accessed 24 May 2010).

37 Web: http://www.youtube.com/watch?v=8NvBrsW17fM (accessed 24 May 2010).

38 Web: http://www.youtube.com/watch?v=4I3ZmNKYmao (accessed 24 May 2010).

39 Outside the commercial field, an amateur experience that has gained the attention of the Western media is the blog *Eating Journey (Confessions of a Reformed Eater)* led by Michelle Gay. In the 'Exposed' section this young woman proudly displays her body and invites other blog users to do the same. In response to this invitation many women (but also a few men) have posted photos of their bodies showing that they share the rejection of those models that lead them to despise their own image just because it differs from the glossy perfection that dominates the covers of fashion magazines. Users of *Eating Journey* instead want to celebrate their body, most interestingly in the practice introduced by Gay of highlighting presumed flaws such as a large belly with slogans like: 'where I carried a healthy baby for 9 months'. Perfection is therefore increasingly seen as a false virtue, a feature common only to creatures confined to the fictional media world and as far from everyday reality as much as the

protagonists of fairy tales or the heroes of Greek mythology. As pointed out by one of the bloggers that have exposed themselves: 'The Beautiful at any cost, the Perfect in all the sauces, make us tired and bored, for the simple reason that they don't belong to our earthly life of vulnerable and transient beings, constantly moved by errors and full of flaws and lacks of every kind. Imperfection is our natural habitat: a physical, moral and social imperfection.' Web: http://eatingjourney.com/exposed (accessed 24 May 2010).

40 Slavoj Žižek in: *The Pervert's Guide to Cinema* (2006) by Sophie Fiennes. A two-hour documentary scripted and presented by Žižek.

41 Ibid.

42 In this context, one must at least mention the Berlin festival CUM2CUT dedicated to short films by independent artists. Web: http://www.cum2cut.net (accessed 24 May 2010).

43 L. Koren, *Wabi-Sabi, For Artists, Designers, Poets & Philosophers* (Point Reyes, CA: Imperfect, 2008).

44 D.T. Suzuki, *Zen and Japanese Culture* (London: Taylor & Francis, 1970 [1936]), 24.

45 Dorfles, *Horror Pleni*, op. cit. (note 23), 229 [translation by the author].

The Centrality of the Eye

1 Web: http://www.littlepig.org.uk/babel/index.htm (accessed 24 May 2010).

2 Web: http://www.littlepig.org.uk/babel/statement.htm (accessed 24 May 2010).

Digital Cameras and the Will of Technology

1 From another point of view, the interposition of technological devices between oneself and reality may be a form of defence against strong and unmanageable feelings. Consider Cornelia Sollfrank's conversation with Silke Wenk, in which she recounted the response to the *re.act feminism* exhibition's opening at the Academy of Arts in Berlin (December 2008): 'The majority of the passers-by in the shopping mall where the performance took place immediately took out a mobile phone or even a digicam and filmed the performance. That means that the people no longer directly watched, didn't just expose themselves to the experience, but held a technical reproduction device between themselves and that what irritated them.' S. Wenk, 'Always the Same with Repetition?', in: C. Sollfrank (ed.), *Expanded Original* (Ostfildern-Ruit: Hatje Cantz, 2009), 82.

2 N. Postman, *Technopoly: The Surrender of Culture to Technology* (1992) (New York: Vintage Books, 1993), 14.

3 J.D. Bolter and R. Grusin, *Remediation: Understanding New Media* (Cambridge, MA: MIT Press, 1999).

4 'I'm an eye. A mechanical eye. I, the machine, show you a world the way only I can see it. I free myself for today and forever from human immobility. I'm in constant movement.' Dziga Vertov (1923) as quoted in J. Berger, *Ways of Seeing* (London: Penguin Books, 1972), 17. To Vertov's paradigm and to the global proliferation of digital cameras, Perry Bard dedicates a wonderful collaborative video entitled *Man With a Movie Camera: The Global Remake*. This is a participatory video shot by people around the world who are invited to record images interpreting Vertov's original script, and then to upload the video to a website. Software developed specifically for the project archives, sequences and streams the submissions as a film. Anyone can upload footage. When the work streams, the user's contribution becomes part of a worldwide montage, in Vertov's terms the 'decoding of life as it is'. Web: http://dziga.perrybard.net (accessed 24 May 2010).

5 E. Severino, *Tecnica e architettura* (Milan: Raffaello Cortina, 2003), 49 [translation by the author].

6 I.M. Banks, 'Descendant', in: I.M. Banks, *The State of the Art* (London: Orbit, 1991). The short story was published earlier in: R. Kaveney (ed.), *Tales from the Forbidden Planet* (London: Titan, 1987).

7 M. Costa, *Dimenticare l'arte. Nuovi orientamenti nella teoria e nella sperimentazione estetica* (Milan: FrancoAngeli, 2005), 125 [translation by the author], original text: 'Necessità iscritta nell'ordine delle cose.'

8 Ibid. [translation by the author].

9 Ibid., 44-45 [translation by the author].

10 Ibid., 114-115 [translation by the author].

11 G. Anders, *Philosophische Stenogramme* (Munich: Beck, 2002 [1965]), 141 [translation by the author].

12 Ibid.

13 E. Kluitenberg, *Delusive Spaces: Essays on Culture, Media and Technology* (Rotterdam/Amsterdam: NAi Publishers/Institute of Network Cultures, 2008), 311.

14 G. Lovink, *Zero Comments: Blogging and Critical Internet Culture* (New York: Routledge, 2007).

What to Fill Digital Memories With?

1 Vilém Flusser and Walter Benjamin both offer negative evaluations of the amateur photographer (one who merely pushes the button, 'Knipser', without being able to decipher his/her own photographs). Flusser writes: 'Photographs suppress our critical awareness in order to make us forget the mindless absurdity of the process of functionality, and it is only thanks to this suppression that functionality is possible at all.' V. Flusser, *Für eine Philosophie der Fotografie* (Göttingen: European Photography, 1983); translation: *Towards a Philosophy of Photography* (London: Reaktion Books, 2000), 64.

2 In May 2009, photos and videos of American soldiers torturing Iraqi prisoners, censored by Obama on stars and stripes territory, were published online by Australian media (these images were originally broadcast in February 2006 by the Australian SBS television network). Once again, this episode shows that trying to protect 'state secrets' has become pointless in a world in which every phone may be a witness and any computer connected to the Internet implies in itself the opportunity to connect with billions of other computers. Web: http://www.prisonplanet.com/leaked-torture-photos-published-in-2006-went-largely-unseen-graphic.html (accessed 24 May 2010). After writing this chapter, another event took place that highlighted the role that personal media and social networks can play in crisis situations. I refer to the role that Twitter has played in exposing electoral fraud in the Iranian elections held in June 2009. For days, Iranians took to the streets in protest, simultaneously publicizing their actions and initiatives through the popular social network, and thereby compensating for the foreign journalists kept away by the Iranian regime, and also bypassing the biased local media system.

3 The word 'everyone' is clearly inaccurate, in light of the fact that there are many people for whom electricity is a luxury.

4 I am using the English word 'cool' in an undifferentiated manner, but I also mean to refer to corresponding terms used in different linguistic contexts. I was led to this choice by the results of a small survey that I have carried out with the help of a number of friends around the world; what has come to light is that the word 'cool' is most frequently used just as it is, without translation. When it is translated, a plurality of terms are used to express the same concept, depending on the specific context and user. I propose the following list: *figo* (Italian); *fora* (Croatian); *tromero* (Greek); *hieno* (Finnish); *havalý* (Turkish); *chulo/a, enrollado* and *guay* (Spanish); *kakkoii* (Japanese); *fantastisch* (German); *messa* (Brazilian); *legal* (Portuguese); *kult* (Norwegian); *chouette* (French); *super* (German, French and Croatian). For the patience they have shown in acceding to my bizarre request, I owe a special thanks to: José Manuel Berenguer, Mariela Cádiz, Genco Gulan, Anna-Maija Lassila, Brian Mackern, Nadija Mustapic, Ana Peraica, Angelo Plessas, Andreas Treske and Mai Ueda.

5 P.N. Stearns, *American Cool: Constructing a Twentieth-century Emotional Style* (New York: New York Univeristy Press, 1994).

6 Ibid., 1.

7 Ibid., 231.

8 Ibid., 293.

9 Ibid., 310.

10 Ibid., 244.

11 C. Nancarrow and P. Nancarrow, 'Hunting for cool tribes', in: B. Cova, R. Kozinets and A. Shankar (eds.), *Consumer Tribes* (Oxford: Elsevier, 2007), 132.

12 Ibid., 133.

13 Ibid., 134.

14 Ibid., 135.

15 A. Liu, *The Laws of Cool: Knowledge Work and the Culture of Information* (Chicago, IL: University of Chicago Press, 2004).

16 'Cool is information designed to resist information.' Ibid., 179.

17 Ibid., 76.

18 From an interview with Alan Liu by Geert Lovink, 28 February 2006. Web: http://networkcultures. org/wpmu/geert/interview-with-alan-liu (accessed 24 May 2010).

19 R.F. Thompson, 'An Aesthetic of the Cool', in: B. Beckley and D. Shapiro (eds.), *Uncontrollable Beauty: Toward a New Aesthetics* (New York: Allworth, 2002).

20 Ibid., 372.

21 Ibid., 374.

22 It is interesting to note the reference to the concept of 'cool' in Baudrillard's definition of 'pop' in *La Société de consommation* (1970): 'Pop is a "cool" art: it demands not aesthetic ecstasy or affective or symbolic participation ("deep involvement"), but a kind of "abstract involvement", a sort of *instrumental curiosity*. And this retains something of a child-like curiosity, a näive enchantment of discovery.' J. Baudrillard, *La Société de consommation* (Paris: Gallimard, 1970); translation: *The Consumer Society: Myths and Structures* (London: SAGE, 1998), 120.

23 Web: http://www.youtube.com/watch?v=TZ86oP4iTaM (accessed 24 May 2010).

24 I am referring to a concept of beauty that recalls only 'beautiful things' and not to the wider one (that has been evident in aesthetic theories since the ancient past) that includes thoughts, attitudes and habits.

25 I want to thank one of my students, Alessandro Mantico, for this valuable report (I also finally understood what a neighbour of mine cries every afternoon).

26 Web: http://bookchin.net/projects/massornament.html (accessed 24 May 2010).

27 S. Kracauer, *Das Ornament der Masse: Essays* (Frankfurt: Suhrkamp, 1963); translation: *The Mass Ornament: Weimer Essays* (Cambridge, MA: Harvard University Press, 1995).

28 Web: http://www.youtube.com/watch?v=2Uu_qI4GbgM (accessed 24 May 2010).

Chapter V
Remix as Compositional Practice

Innovation and Repetition

1 R.E. Krauss, *The Originality of the Avant-Garde and Other Modernist Myths* (Cambridge, MA: MIT Press, 1986 [1985]).

2 Ibid., 157.

3 Ibid., 157-158.

4 Ibid., 158.

5 Ibid., 160.

6 Ibid.

7 Ibid.

8 A similar position can be found in: G. Di Giacomo and C. Zambianchi (eds.), *Alle origini dell'opera d'arte contemporanea* (Rome: Laterza, 2008).

9 F. Jameson, *Postmodernism, or, The Cultural Logic of Late Capitalism* (1991) (Durham, NC: Duke University Press, 1997), 397.

10 A. Dal Lago and S. Giordano, *Meracnti d'aura. Logiche dell'arte contemporanea* (Bologne: Il Mulino, 2006).

11 The decision to focus on DJ culture adheres to the claim made by Eduardo Navas, who identifies the roots of remix culture within that specific cultural sphere of the 1970s.

12 Web: http://web.archive.org/web/20080209234547/http://ethnomus.ucr.edu/remix_culture/remix_ history.htm (accessed 2 June 2010).

13 R. Middleton, *Studying Popular Music* (Philadelphia, PA: Open University Press, 1990).

14 In this specific field of music, for example, it is already largely historical fact that in the passage from American house music to British acid house the original associations, such as African American and homosexual cultures, were lost. Meanwhile, new forces of subversion, such as the consumption of ecstasy and the uptake of the music by those suffering from new forms of social disadvantage emerged – although these were, however, peculiar to a predominantly white and straight audience, mainly belonging to working-class and English provincial towns.

15 M. Maffesoli, *Le temps des tribus. Le déclin de l'individualisme dans les sociétés de masse* (Paris: Méridiens Klincksieck, 1988); translation: *The Time of the Tribes: The Decline of Individualism in Mass Society* (London: SAGE, 1996), 76.

16 The sources of this brief history of the remix are 'Wikipedia' - http://en.wikipedia.org/wiki/Remix; 'Indopedia' - Web: http://www.indopedia.org/index.php?title=Remix. In both cases my last access is 5 July 2009.

17 E. Navas, *Remix Defined* (2006). Web: http://remixtheory.net/?page_id=3 (accessed 2 June 2010). Navas quotes as his main source: B. Brewster and F. Broughton, *Last Night a DJ Saved my Life: The History of the Disc Jockey* (New York: Grove Press, 1999).

18 Ibid.

19 Ibid. A similar argument can be found in: U. Poschardt, *DJ Culture* (1995) (London: Quartet Books, 1998).

20 Ibid.

21 J. O'Neil, *The Remix Aesthetic: Originality, Mixed and Mashed-up* (2006), 3-4. Web: http://www.mcluhan-remix.com/images/Oneil_Remix_1D_SHORT.pdf (accessed 2 June 2010).

22 O'Neil writes: 'The aesthetics of remix does not require a precise historical knowledge of "originals" in the conventional sense, but a more complex view of history that seeks to continually reinterpret itself.... remix denies the very concept of the original. In remix, the "original" is impossible, because the world (or paradigm) is one of copies of copies, a place where we have lost touch, moreover, lost *faith* in the possibility of an original.' Ibid., 7.

23 Web: http://www.rebirthofanation.com.

24 'No matter what form it takes, the remix is always allegorical, meaning that the object of contemplation depends on recognition of a pre-existing cultural code. The audience is always expected to see within the object a trace of history.' E. Navas, *Remix: The Bond of Repetition and Representation* (2009). Web: http://remixtheory.net/?p=361 (accessed 2 June 2010).

25 L. Lessig, *Remix: Making Art and Commerce Thrive in the Hybrid Economy* (New York: Penguin Press, 2008).

26 Ibid., 56.

27 Ibid., 68.

28 Ibid., 69.

29 Web: http://120years.net (accessed 2 June 2010).

30 Web: http://120years.net/machines/mellotron/index.htm (accessed 2 June 2010)l.

31 Web: http://en.wikipedia.org/wiki/Mellotron (accessed 2 June 2010).

32 On the impact of synthesizers and in particular the Moog on music see: T. Pinch and F. Trocco, *Analog Days: The Invention and Impact of the Moog Synthesizer* (Cambridge, MA: Harvard University Press, 2004).

33 As Florian Cramer observes: 'The whole musical genre of bootleg pop remixes would not exist without the programs *Acid* by Sonic Foundry and *Traktor* by Native Instruments.' F. Cramer, *Words Made Flesh: Code, Culture, Imagination* (Rotterdam: Piet Zwart Institute, 2005), 85.

34 On this point, see: P. Maysles, 'Dubbing The Nation', *Small Axe*, no. 11 (March 2002), Indiana, IN.

35 This passage is quoted in: *Annali d'Italianistica*, no. 22 (2004) of the University of Notre Dame, Department. of Modern and Classical Languages, Italian Section, 307.

36 'Repetition, in a way that needs to be examined, reaches out to return the future to the past, while drawing on the past also to reconstruct the future.' A. Giddens, 'Living in a Post-Traditional Society', in: U. Beck, A. Giddens and S. Lash, *Reflexive Modernization: Politics, Tradition and Aesthetics in the Modern Social Order* (Stanford, CA: Stanford University Press, 1994), 62.

37 This assumption is central to Brett Gaylor's unmissable documentary *RiP: A Remix Manifesto* (2008). Web: http://www.ripremix.com (accessed 2 June 2010).

38 R. Barthes, 'The Death of the Author' (1967), in: Stephen Heath (ed.), *Image, Music, Text* (New York: Hill and Wang, 1977), 146.

39 M. de Certeau. *L'Invention du Quotidien*, vol. 1, Arts de Faire (Paris: Union générale d'éditions, 1980); translation: *The Practice of Everyday Life* (Berkeley, CA: University of California Press, 1984).

40 Web: http://www.netvibes.com (accessed 2 June 2010).

41 Think of Google Wave, a platform that is still in testing as I write. Google Wave is designed to transform e-mail, instant messaging, podcasts, VoIP, streaming content and so forth into a single flow accessible through a single web application. Web: http://wave.google.com/about.html (accessed 2 June 2010).

42 'Caravaggio: una mostra impossibile', Castel Sant'Elmo, Naples (6 April – 1 June 2003). Web: http://www.caravaggio.rai.it/index_en.htm (accessed 2 June 2010).

43 P. Panza, 'Arte, la copia è meglio dell'originale' (an interview with Peter Greenaway), *Corriere della Sera*, 01 June 2009, 27 [translation by the author].

44 Two web applications that eloquently demonstrate how easily one can create personalized forms of multimedia objects, by mixing together web materials, are: *YouTube Mixer* by 2Roqs (http://v3ga.net/ YouTubeMixer) and *Mother Fucking Crossfader* by Jake Elliott (http://twoyoutubevideosandamotherfuckingcrossfader.com) (both accessed 2 June 2010).

45 L. Manovich, *Software Takes Command* (version: 20 November 2008), 28. Web: http://softwarestudies.com/softbook/manovich_softbook_11_20_2008.doc.

46 Ibid., 229.

47 Ibid., 230.

48 Ibid., 231.

49 Ibid., 233.

50 Ibid.

51 Ibid., 236.

52 Ibid.

53 Ibid.

54 Ibid., 238.

55 Ibid., 242.

56 Ibid., 28.

57 Ibid.

58 Ibid., 92.

59 Ibid.

60 G. de Tarde, 'L'inter psychologie', *Bulletin de l'Institut général psychologique* (1903).

61 Manovich, *Software takes command*, op. cit. (note 45), 185.

62 Navas, *Remix: The Bond of Repetition and Representation*, op. cit. (note 24).

63 Ibid.

64 Ibid.

65 Ibid.

66 Ibid.

67 E. Navas, *The Author Function in Remix* (2008). Web: http://remixtheory.net/?p=309 (accessed 2 June 2010). Navas's use of the word 'text' is, as he specifies, to be considered in the wider sense of 'visual arts and media at large'.

68 G. de Tarde, *The Laws of Imitations* (New York: Henry Holt, 1903), 43.

69 It must be remembered that McKenzie Wark attaches to *hack* some of the properties that I have associated with the remix. Indeed, he claims that the *hack* is the creative gesture that turns 'repetition into difference, representation into expression, communication into information'. See: M. Wark, *A Hacker Manifesto* (Cambridge, MA: Harvard University Press, 2004), 130.

70 The term derives from the Latin *originàlem: orìginem* (beginning, origin) + *alem* (belonging).

71 Already in the mid-1980s, Iain Chambers had written that: 'With electronic reproduction offering the spectacle of gestures, images, styles and cultures in a perpetual collage of disintegration and reintegration, the "new" disappears into a permanent present. And with the end of the "new" – a concept connected to linearity, to the serial prospects of "progress", to "modernism" – we move into a perpetual recycling of quotations, styles and fashions; an uninterrupted montage of the "now".' I. Chambers, *Popular Culture: The Metropolitan Experience* (London: Routledge, 1986), 190.

72 N. Bourriaud, *Postproduction. La culture comme scénario: comment l'art reprogramme le monde contemporain* (Dijon: Les presses du Réel, 2001); translation: *Postproduction. Culture as Screenplay: How Art Reprograms the World* (New York: Lukas & Sternberg, 2002).

73 Ibid., 5.
74 Bourriaud writes: 'The activities of DJs, Web surfers, and postproduction artists imply a similar configuration of knowledge, which is characterized by the invention of paths through culture. All three are "semionauts" who produce original pathways through signs. Every work is issued from a script that the artist projects onto culture, considered the framework of a narrative that in turn projects new possible scripts, endlessly. The DJ activates the history of music by copying and pasting together loops of sound, placing recorded products in relation with each other. Artists actively inhabit cultural and social forms. The Internet user may create his or her own site or homepage and constantly reshuffle the information obtained, inventing paths that can be bookmarked and reproduced at will. When we start a search engine in pursuit of a name or a subject, a mass of information issued from a labyrinth of databanks is inscribed on the screen. The "semionaut" imagines the links, the likely relations between disparate sites. A sampler, a machine that reprocesses musical products, also implies constant activity; to listen to records becomes work in itself, which diminishes the dividing line between reception and practice, producing new cartographies of knowledge. This recycling of sounds, images, and forms implies incessant navigation within the meanderings of cultural history, navigation which itself becomes the subject of artistic practice. Isn't art, as Duchamp once said, "a game among all men of all eras"? Postproduction is the contemporary form of this game.' Ibid., 11.
75 Ibid., 13.
76 Web: http://www.youtube.com/watch?v=WhwbxEfy7fg (accessed 2 June 2010).
77 Web: http://www.thelonelyisland.com (accessed 2 June 2010).
78 'The scene in the Barry Levinson film *Diner* (1982), in which Mickey Rourke places his penis inside a box of popcorn at a movie theater to win a bet and a scene in the Claude Pinoteau film *La Boum* (1980), in which a junior high school student performs an identical act for fun.' Source: 'Wikipedia', http://en.wikipedia.org/wiki/Dick_in_a_Box (accessed 2 June 2010).
79 Web: http://www.bustedtees.com/dickinabox#male (accessed 2 June 2010).
80 Web: http://www.youtube.com/watch?v=s9pklHJglXE (accessed 2 June 2010).
81 Web: http://www.purpleduckfilms.com/index.html (accessed 2 June 2010).
82 '*Last Night a DJ Saved My Life* is a song written by Michael Cleveland for R&B/dance group Indeep. It features vocals from Reggie and Rose Marie Ramsey, and its protagonists recall how they were bored to death until a DJ played a hot song and saved their lives by giving new energy to the night. The song was released as a single in 1982 and became the most popular and successful hit released by their record label: Sound of New York.' Source: 'Wikipedia', http://en.wikipedia.org/wiki/Last_Night_a_DJ_Saved_My_Life_(song) (accessed 2 June 2010).

Remix It Yourself

1 T. Bazzichelli, *Networking: The Net as Artwork* (Aarhus: Digital Aesthetics Research Center, Aarhus University, 2008), 27.
2 Lévi-Strauss relates *bricolage* to mythical thinking: it is in fact the method by which primitives organized their myths, their worldview, their language, their society and – ultimately – their thinking and its rules.
3 C. Lévi-Strauss, *La Pensée sauvage* (Paris: Librairie Plon, 1962); translation: *The Savage Mind: The Nature of Human Society Series* (Chicago, IL: University of Chicago Press, 1966), 17-18.
4 'He interrogates all the heterogeneous objects of which his treasury is composed to discover what each of them could signify.' Ibid.
5 G. Deleuze and F. Guattari, *L'Anti-Oedipe* (Paris: Minuit, 1972); translation: *Anti-Oedipus: Capitalism and Schizophrenia* (London: Continuum, 2004), 5-6.
6 Web: http://www.eastgate.com/catalog/PatchworkGirl.html.
7 A. Tursi, *Estetica dei nuovi media. Forme espressive e network society* (Milan: Costa & Nolan, 2007), 124 [translation by the author]. George P. Landow uses similar words in: *Hypertext 2.0* (Baltimore, MD: Johns Hopkins University Press, 1997).
8 Ibid., 126-127.

9   M. Novak, *Transmitting Architecture: The Transphysical City* (1995). Web: http://www.cluster.eu/v2/
    themes/novak (accessed 2 June 2010). An Italian version of this passage is quoted by Tursi in *Estetica*
    dei nuovi media, op. cit. (note 7), 128. See also: M. Novak, 'Transmitting Architecture revisited', *Cluster*,
    no. 7, Transmitting Architecture' (2008), 74-81.

10 L. Manovich, *Software Takes Command* (version: 20 November 2008), 175. Web: http://softwarestudies.
    com/softbook/manovich_softbook_11_20_2008.doc.

11 I have written 'tend to become' but I must underline that there are authoritative voices who consider
    the development of technology a process that has always been independent and self-operative. In this
    sense, it could be enough to recall that Marx believes that a critical history of technology will high-
    light how small the part played by the individual is in determining the inventions of the eighteenth
    century: 'A critical history of technology would show how little any of the inventions of the eight-
    eenth century are the work of a single individual.' K. Marx, *Kapital. Kritik der politischen Ökonomie*, vol.
    I (1867); translation: *Capital: A Critique of Political Economy*, vol. I (New York: Penguin Classics, 1976),
    493, note 4.

12 Manovich, *Software Takes Command*, op. cit. (note 10), 247.

13 Ibid., 248.

14 Web: http://www.oliverlaric.com/5050.htm (accessed 2 June 2010).

15 Web: http://www.oliverlaric.com/touchmybody.htm (accessed 2 June 2010).

16 from the Latin *lator*. In Tursi's original text the word 'latore' is used , which in Italian sounds like a
    mix of the words *autore* and *lettore*, or 'author' and 'reader' respectively.

17 Tursi, *Estetica dei nuovi media*, op. cit. (note 7), 60 [translation by the author].

18 N. Thrift, *Knowing Capitalism* (London: SAGE, 2005), 133.

19 J. Howe, *Crowdsourcing: Why the Power of the Crowd is Driving the Future of Business* (New York: Crown
    Business, 2008). Web: http://www.crowdsourcing.com (accessed 2 June 2010).

20 On this issue, I particularly recommend: G. Lovink and N. Rossiter (eds.), *MyCreativity Reader:*
    A Critique of Creative Industries (Amsterdam: Institute of Network Cultures, 2007).

21 Manovich, *Software Takes Command*, op. cit. (note 10), 276. Similar words are used by David Garcia
    and Geert Lovink in the introduction/manifesto to *Next Five Minutes* (De Waag Society, Amsterdam,
    September 2003) entitled: 'The ABC of Tactical Media'. Web: http://www.nettime.org/Lists-Archives/
    nettime-l-9705/msg00096.html (accessed 2 June 2010). The issue of tactical media has recently been
    deepened by Rita Raley. See: R. Raley, *Tactical Media* (Minneapolis, MN: University of Minnesota Press,
    2009).

Remix Ethics

1   Eyal Weizman uses the expression 'elastic geography' and writes: 'The frontiers of the Occupied
    Territories are not rigid and fixed at all ... These borders are dynamic, constantly shifting, ebbing and
    flowing; they creep along, stealthily surrounding Palestinian villages and roads.' E. Weizman, *Hollow*
    Land (London: Verso, 2007), 6-7.

2   T. Bazzichelli, *Networking: The Net as Artwork* (Aarhus: Digital Aesthetics Research Center, Aarhus
    University, 2008), 27.

3   It is interesting to note that plagiarism didn't become a crime until the advent of typographical
    culture. During the Middle Ages, in fact, everyone had the right to copy any work, indeed it was con-
    sidered meritorious to copy and even to put into circulation the work of someone else. Even after the
    invention of the movable type printing press, nothing prevented a bookseller from printing a previ-
    ously published work, in fact there was an enormous choice of works that could be published, while
    the need for books was at such a level to justify multiple editions of the same text. The situation
    changed drastically when printed books began to reach a certain number, and especially when works
    by contemporary authors began to be printed. The first attempt at exclusivity devised by editors was
    to use royal privileges, but the privilege system proved unsuited to counter 'pirated copies' and was
    ineffective in an international context, as each sovereign granted privileges that were valid only in
    their kingdoms. This situation continued until the adoption of the English Copyright Act of 1709,
    which is the first legislative measure to establish the relationships between publishers and authors.

This was imitated by France in 1793, and then by other states, while it was not until 1886 that the Berne Convention establishes the principle of international reciprocity of rights. Most interestingly, perhaps, is the fact that authors received no fees from publishers until the eighteenth century, and even when they did they were ashamed of receiving payment: Voltaire's anger at a species so miserable it writes to make a living is well known. Source: M. Baldini, *Storia della comunicazione* (Rome: Newton & Compton, 2003), 68-71. Copyright is not the result of authors' commercial interest, however. The interest behind copyright is due to publishers' economic concerns. Similarly, today the vast majority of intellectual property laws are aimed at protecting the economic interests of publishers, record labels, multinational software companies, etcetera. The livelihood of authors and the defence of their creativity are, in essence, always the arguments used to justify the existence of exclusive rights of which – paradox of paradoxes – the authors benefit only in small part.

4 In Lessig's reconstruction, analogue technologies were marked by 'natural' limitations that somehow limited consumers' opportunities to compete with producers. Digital technologies have eliminated these constraints, rendering any cultural content completely manipulable. When the *content industry* became aware of this, it was terrified, 'and thus were born the copyright wars'. L. Lessig, *Remix: Making Art and Commerce Thrive in the Hybrid Economy* (New York: Penguin Press, 2008), 38-39.

5 M. Lazzarato, *La politica dell'evento* (Catanzaro: Rubettino, 2004), 25.

6 In South Africa, recent statistics from the Department of Health (http://www.doh.gov.za) report 1,700 new cases of HIV infection each day, and a total of 6-8 million people infected (of a population of about 40 million).

7 In 1997 Nelson Mandela, the former president of South Africa, enacted the Medical Act, a law authorizing South African industries to produce drugs to treat AIDS without having to purchase them at huge cost from pharmaceutical companies. The estimates of UNAIDS (the Joint United Nations Programme for fighting AIDS) report a situation in which about 25.3 million of the 36.1 million people worldwide infected with HIV live in Africa, most of them in the Sub-Saharan region. However, the African continent, with 70 per cent of infections of the number worldwide, represents only 1 per cent of the global market for drugs, compared with 80 per cent represented by the USA, Western Europe and Japan. In view of this scandal, the expression 'health apartheid' formulated by Médecins Sans Frontières appears profoundly justified. The struggle between the right to health and the defence of companies' profits inspired the novel *The Constant Gardener* (2001) by John Le Carré: a harsh indictment of the economic interests of pharmaceutical companies.

8 J. Rifkin, *The Age Of Access: The New Culture of Hypercapitalism, Where All of Life is a Paid-For Experience* (New York: J.P. Tarcher/Putnam, 2000).

9 L. Lessig, *Free Culture: How Big Media Uses Technology and the Law to Lock Down Culture and Control Creativity* (New York: Penguin Press, 2004).

10 Web: http://creativecommons.org (accessed 2 June 2010).

11 For a critical reading of the presuppositions of Free Culture and an original exposition of the main positions emerging in the debate around Creative Commons, see: M. Pasquinelli, *Animal Spirits: A Bestiary of the Commons* (Rotterdam/Amsterdam: NAi Publishers/Institute of Network Cultures, 2008).

12 K.A. Appiah, *Cosmopolitanism: Ethics in a World of Strangers* (New York: W.W. Norton & Co., 2006). On the issue of artistic and, more particularly, archaeological objects, Appiah considers it laughable for modern states to claim as national heritage the objects of historical and artistic interest found within their territories. According to Appiah these objects should instead be considered the heritage of all humanity, and therefore be made accessible to everybody. If this reasoning is applied to cultural production as a whole, a cosmopolitan view leads to the conclusion that any cultural object should be accessible and usable (for new production) by all.

13 Lessig himself, in his recent work *Remix*, states that before entering a legal plan it is essential to take the crucial matter to be that the 'right to quote – or as I will call it, to remix – is a critical expression of creative freedom that in a broad range of contexts, no free society should restrict'. Lessig, *Remix*, op. cit. (note 4), 56.

14 A very enjoyable parody of the 'relationship rules' to be adopted on Facebook is offered by the video *Facebook Manners And You.* Web: http://www.youtube.com/watch?v=iROYzrm5SBM (accessed 2 June 2010).

15 M. Deseriis and G. Marano, *Net.art. L'arte della connessione* (Milan: Shake, 2003), 84 [translation by the author]. In this book, which offers a brilliant interpretation of the pioneering phase of net.art, it is possible to read a precise reconstruction of the history of 'plagiarisms' to which I refer (See: 78-85).

16 Private conversation between Deseriis, Marano and 010010111010110.org, quoted in: Ibid., 82-84 [translation by the author].

17 Elsewhere I defined the contemporary art system as 'a hologram of a vanished world, the representation of an ancient society in which everything was weighed up in terms of atoms'. See: Vito Campanelli (ed.), *L'arte della Rete l'arte in Rete. Il Neen, la rivoluzione estetica di Miltos Manetas* (Rome: Aracne, 2005), 85.

18 Web: http://www.dangermousesite.com (accessed 2 June 2010).

19 D. Keller, 'The Musician as Thief', in: P.D. Miller (ed.), *Sound Unbound: Sampling Digital Music and Culture* (Cambridge, MA: MIT Press, 2008), 136.

Machinic Subjectivity

1 G. Lynn, 'Blobs (or Why Tectonics is Square and Topology is Groovy)', *ANY*, no. 14, 'Tectonics Unbound: Kernform and Kunstform Revisited!' (May 1996), 58-62.

2 A. Vidler, *Warped Space: Art, Architecture, and Anxiety in Modern Culture* (Cambridge, MA: MIT Press, 2000).

3 The word 'net art' in itself arises by chance in an email infected with a virus, received by the artist Vuk Cosic. At the heart of this corrupt mail, among a number of words in bulk, the words 'net' and 'art' appeared alongside one another. It is not known whether this story is real or the fruit of Cosic's fantasy, but no matter. What I think is emblematic is that the *mitopoiesis* (mythmaking) of net.art blames a machinic intervention for the birth of the new art form.

4 Web: http://marknapier.com/presskit/mn_statement.html (accessed 2 June 2010).

5 Web: http://www.obn.org/generator, or: http://net.art-generator.com (both accessed 2 June 2010). For an artistic autobiography see: C. Sollfrank, *Net.art Generator* (Nürnberg: Verlag für Moderne Kunst, 2005). More recently Sollfrank has further investigated the issue of obsolescence of such concepts as 'original' and 'copyrighted' in: C. Sollfrank (ed.), *Expanded Original*, (Ostfildern-Ruit: Hatje Cantz, 2009).

6 Web: http://www.artwarez.org/femext/index.html (accessed 2 June 2010).

7 F. Cramer, *Words Made Flesh: Code, Culture, Imagination* (Rotterdam: Piet Zwart Institute, 2005), 83-84.

8 According to Focillon: 'Each historical style exists under the aegis of one technique that overrides other techniques and that gives to the style its tonality.' H. Focillon, *Vie des formes* (Paris: Leroux, 1934); translation: *The Life of Forms in Art* (New York: Zone Books, 1989), 51.

9 M. Costa, *Dimenticare l'arte. Nuovi orientamenti nella teoria e nella sperimentazione estetica* (Milan: FrancoAngeli, 2005), 47-51 [translation by the author].

10 Ibid., 43-47 [translation by the author].

11 Ibid., 44-48 [translation by the author].

12 Ibid., 47 [translation by the author].

13 Ibid., 44-45 [translation by the author]. It is easy to discern in Costa echoes of similar key reconstructions of technological milestones, particulary in the similarity between the terms 'neo-technologies' and Lewis Mumford's 'neotechnics', introduced in 1934. See: L. Mumford, *Technics and Civilization* (New York. Harcourt, Brace & Company, 1934).

14 Ibid., 48 [translation by the author].

15 Ibid., 103-104 [translation by the author].

16 Web: http://www.ekac.org/move36.html.

17 This is a reworked extract from: V. Campanelli, 'Move 36, il confine fra umano ed il non umano', *Neural* (2004). Web: http://www.neural.it/nnews/move36.htm (accessed 2 June 2010).

18 Web: http://www.lxxl.pt/artsbot. See also: L. Moura and H.G. Pereira, *Man + Robots: Symbiotic Art* (Villeurbanne: Institut d'Art Contemporain, 2004).

19 Web: http://www.leonelmoura.com/artsbot.html (accessed 2 June 2010).
20 Ibid.
21 Ibid.
22 Ibid.
23 Ibid. In another text Moura and Pereira write: 'The art object is the product of a human non-entity, indifferent to concerns about representation, essence or purpose.' Web: http://www.lxxl.pt/artsbot (accessed 2 June 2010).
24 Ibid.

Bibliography

Günther Anders, *Die Antiquiertheit des Menschen. Band I: Über die Seele im Zeitalter der zweiten industriellen Revolution* (Munich: Beck, 1956)

Günther Anders, *Philosophische Stenogramme* (1965) (Munich: Beck, 2002)

Kwame Anthony Appiah, *Cosmopolitanism: Ethics in a World of Strangers* (New York: W.W. Norton & Co., 2006)

Giulio Carlo Argan and Achille Bonito Oliva, *L'arte moderna, 1770-1970* (1970). *L'arte oltre il Duemila* (1991) (Florence: Sansoni, 2002)

Roy Ascott, 'The Architecture of Cyberception', *Leonardo Electronic Almanac*, vol. 2, no. 8, August 1994

Marc Augé, *Où est passé l'avenir?* (Paris: Éditions du Panama, 2008)

Jacques Aumont, Alain Bergala, Michel Marie and Marc Vernet, *Aesthetics of Film* (Austin, TX: University of Texas Press, 1992)

Mikhail M.Bakhtin, *Estetika slovesnogo tvorchestva* (Moscow: Iskusstvo, 1979); translation in French: *Esthétique de la création verbale* (Paris: Gallimard, 1984)

Mikhail M.Bakhtin, *Esthétique et théorie du roman* (Paris: Gallimard, 1978)

Massimo Baldini, *Storia della comunicazione* (Rome: Newton & Compton, 2003)

James Mark Baldwin, *Social and Ethical Interpretations in Mental Development: A Study in Social Psychology* (London: Macmillan, 1897)

Iain M. Banks, 'Descendant', in: Banks, I.M., *The State of the Art* (London: Orbit, 1991)

Roland Barthes, 'The Death of the Author' (1967), in: Heath, S. (ed.), *Image, Music, Text* (New York: Hill and Wang, 1977)

Charles Baudelaire, *Paris Spleen* (1865) (New York: New Directions, 1970)

Jean Baudrillard, *Le Système des objets* (Paris: Gallimard, 1968); translation: *The System of Objects* (London: Verso, 2005)

Jean Baudrillard, *La Société de consommation* (Paris: Gallimard, 1970); translation: *The Consumer Society: Myths and Structures* (London: SAGE, 1998)

Jean Baudrillard, *Art and Artefact* (Thousand Oaks, CA: SAGE, 1997)

Jean Baudrillard, *Illusion, désillusion esthétiques* (Paris: Sens & Tonka, 1997)

Jean Baudrillard, 'Le Complot de l'art', *Libération*, 20 May 1996. Web: http://usm.maine.edu/~bcj/issues/two/baudrillard_2.html (accessed 6 April 2010)

Jean Baudrillard, *Le crime parfait* (Paris: Galilée, 1995); translation: *The Perfect Crime* (London: Verso, 1996)

Jean Baudrillard, *L'illusion de la fin, ou, la grève des événements* (Paris: Galilée, 1992); translation: *The Illusion of the End* (Stanford, CA: Stanford University Press, 1994)

Jean Baudrillard, *L'Échange symbolique et la mort* (Paris: Gallimard, 1976); translation: *Symbolic Exchange and Death* (London: SAGE, 1993)

Zygmunt Bauman, *Consuming Life* (Cambridge: Polity, 2007)

Zygmunt Bauman, *Legislators and interpreters - On Modernity, Post-Modernity, Intellectuals* (New York: Cornell University Press, 1987)

Tilman Bäumgartel, 'Media Piracy and Independent Cinema in Southest Asia', in: Lovink, G. and Niederer, S. (eds.), *Video Vortex Reader: Responses to YouTube* (Amsterdam: Institute of Network Cultures, 2008)

Tilman Bäumgartel, 'The Culture of Piracy in the Philippines', in: Shin Dong Kim and David, J. (eds.), *Cinema in / on Asia* (Gwanju: Asian Culture Forum, 2006)

Tatiana Bazzichelli, *Networking: The Net as Artwork* (Aarhus: Digital Aesthetics Research Center, Aarhus University, 2008)

Konrad Becker and Felix Stalder, (eds.), *Deep Search: The Politics of Search beyond Google* (Innsbruck: Studien, 2009)

Walter Benjamin, 'Paris, die Haupstadt des XIX. Jahrhunderts', in: *Schriften* (2 vols.) (Frankfurt: Suhrkamp, 1955); translation: 'Paris the Capital of the Ninenteenth Century', in: *Selected Writings: 1935-1938* (Cambridge, MA: Harvard University Press, 2002)

Walter Benjamin, *Das Kunstwerk im Zeitalter seiner technischen Reproduzierbarkeit* (1936); translation: 'The Work of Art in the Age of Mechanical Reproduction', in: *Illuminations* (New York: Schocken, 1969)

Yochai Benkler, *The Wealth of Networks: How Social Production Transforms Markets and Freedom* (New Haven: Yale University Press, 2006)

John Berger, *Ways of Seeing* (London: Penguin Books, 1972)

Marshall Berman, *All That Is Solid Melts into Air: The Experience of Modernity* (New York: Simon and Shuster, 1982)

Tim Berners-Lee and Mark Fischetti, *Weaving the Web: The Original Design and Ultimate Destiny of the World Wide Web By Its Inventor* (San Francisco: HarperCollins, 1999)

Giuseppe Bianco, 'La mano virtuale della cyber-democrazia. Utopia e ideologia delle NTIC', in: Lévy, P., *Cyberdemocrazia. Saggio di filosofia politica* (Milan: Mimesis, 2008)

Cristina Bignardi, *L'espressione delle emozioni all'origine della teoria warburghiana sul simbolo estetico* (1998). Web: http://www.parol.it/articles/bignardi.htm (accessed 12 March 2010)

Susan Blackmore, *The Meme Machine* (Oxford: Oxford University Press, 1999)

Jay David Bolter and Richard Grusin, *Remediation: Understanding New Media* (Cambridge, MA: MIT Press, 1999)

Daniel J. Boorstin, *The Image: A Guide to Pseudo-Events in America* (New York: Harper & Row, 1961)

Pierre Bourdieu, *Raisons pratiques. Sur la théorie de l'action* (Paris: Le Seuil. 1994); translation: *Practical Reason: On the Theory of Action* (Stanford, CA: Stanford University Press, 1998)

Nicolas Bourriaud, *Postproduction. La culture comme scénario: comment l'art reprogramme le monde contemporain* (Dijon: Les presses du Réel, 2001); translation: *Postproduction. Culture as Screenplay: How Art Reprograms the World* (New York: Lukas & Sternberg, 2002)

Philippe Breton, *L'utopie de la communication. Le mythe du village planétaire* (Paris: La Découverte, 1992)

Philippe Breton, *Le culte de l'Internet. Une menace pour le lien social?* (Paris: La Découverte, 2000)

Bill Brewster and Frank Broughton, *Last Night a DJ Saved My Life: The History of the Disc Jockey* (New York: Grove Press, 1999)

Richard Brodie, *Virus of the Mind: The New Science of the Meme* (Seattle: Integral Press, 1996)

Mathias Bruhn, *Aby Warburg (1866-1929): The Survival of an Idea* (2001). Web: http://www.educ.fc.ul.pt/hyper/resources/mbruhn/ (accessed 12 March 2010)

Ron Burnett, *Cultures of Vision: Images, Media, and the Imaginary* (Bloomington, IN: Indiana University Press, 1995)

Matei Calinescu, *Faces of Modernity: Avant-Garde, Decadence, Kitsch* (Bloomington, IN: Indiana University Press, 1977)

Guido Calogero, *Filosofia del dialogo* (Milan: Edizioni di Comunità, 1962)

Vito Campanelli, 'Move 36, il confine fra umano ed il non umano', *Neural*, 2004. Web: http://www.neural.it/nnews/move36.htm (accessed 2 June 2010)

Vito Campanelli, 'Internet Landscape: Shapes and Places of the Web in the Work of Marco Cadioli', in: Vito Campanelli (ed.), *Internet Landscapes (2003-2007)* (Naples: MAO, 2009)

Vito Campanelli, *L'arte della Rete l'arte in Rete. Il Neen, la rivoluzione estetica di Miltos Manetas* (Rome: Aracne, 2005)

Manuel Castells, *The Rise of the Network Society. The Information Age: Economy, Society and Culture* vol. 1 (1996) (Oxford: Blackwell, 2009)

Iain Chambers, *Culture After Humanism: History, Culture, Subjectivity* (London: Routledge, 2001)

Iain Chambers, *Migracy, Culture, Identity* (London: Routledge, 1994)

Iain Chambers, *Border Dialogues: Journeys in Postmodernity* (London: Routledge, 1990)

Iain Chambers, *Popular Culture: The Metropolitan Experience* (London: Routledge, 1986)

Galeazzo Ciano, *Diario 1937-1943* (Milan: Rizzoli, 1946)

Mario Costa, *Dimenticare l'arte. Nuovi orientamenti nella teoria e nella sperimentazione estetica* (Milan: FrancoAngeli, 2005)

Mario Costa, 'Appunti per l'estetica a venire', in: Vassalo, S. and A. Di Brino (eds.), *Arte tra azione e contemplazione. L'interattività nelle ricerche artistiche* (Pisa: ETS, 2004)

Mario Costa, *Internet e globalizzazione estetica* (Naples: Cuzzolin, 2002)

Mario Costa, 'For a New Kind of Aesthetics', *Leonardo*, vol. 34, no. 3, June 2001, 275-276

Mario Costa, *Il sublime tecnologico. Piccolo trattato di estetica della tecnologia* (1990) (Rome: Castelvecchi, 1998)

Donna Cox, 'Metaphoric Mappings: The Art of Visualization', in: Paul Fishwick (ed.), *Aesthetic Computing* (Cambridge, MA: MIT Press, 2006)

Florian Cramer, *Words Made Flesh: Code, Culture, Imagination* (Rotterdam: Piet Zwart Institute, 2005)

Valentina Culatti, 'Memetic Simulation no. 2, memetic shoot 'em up', *Neural*, 2008. Web: http://www.neural.it/art/2008/04/memetic_simulation_no_2_shooti.phtml (accessed 12 March 2010)

Alessandro Dal Lago and Serena Giordano, *Meracnti d'aura. Logiche dell'arte contemporanea* (Bologne: Il Mulino, 2006)

Arthur C. Danto, *Beyond the Brillo Box: The Visual Arts in Post-Historical Perspective* (New York: Farrar, Stratus and Giroux, 1992)

Arthur C. Danto, 'L'esperluète et le point d'exclamation', *Les Cahiers du Musée national d'art moderne*, no. 37, "Visions", October 1991

Arthur C. Danto, *The Transfiguration of the Commonplace: A Philosophy of Art* (Cambridge, MA: Harvard University Press, 1981)

Richard Dawkins, *Unweaving the Rainbow: Science, Delusion and the Appetite for Wonder* (London: Penguin Books, 1998)

Richard Dawkins, *The Selfish Gene* (Oxford: Oxford University Press, 1976)

Michel de Certeau, *L'Invention du Quotidien*, vol. 1, Arts de Faire (Paris: Union générale d'éditions, 1980; translation: *The Practice of Everyday Life* (Berkeley, CA: University of California Press, 1984)

Francesco De Sanctis, 'L'idea e l'estetica dello Hegel' (1858), in: Francesco De Sanctis, *Opere* (Turin: Einaudi, 1965)

Gabriel de Tarde, *Les lois de l'imitation*, (Paris: Félix Alcan, 1890); translation: *The Laws of Imitation* (New York: Henry Holt, 1903)

Gabriel de Tarde, 'L'inter psychologie', *Bulletin de l'Institut général psychologique*, 1903

264

Guy Debord, *La société du spectacle* (Paris: Buchet-Chastel, 1967); translation: *The Society of the Spectacle* (New York: Zone Books, 1995)

Guy Debord, *Commentaires sur la société du spectacle* (Paris: Gerard Lebovici, 1988); translation: *Comments on the Society of the Spectacle* (London: Verso, 1998)

Gilles Deleuze and Félix Guattari, *L'Anti-Oedipe* (Paris: Minuit, 1972); translation: *Anti-Oedipus: Capitalism and Schizophrenia* (London: Continuum, 2004)

Gilles Deleuze and Félix Guattari, *Mille Plateaux* (Paris: Minuit, 1980); translation: *A Thousand Plateaus: Capitalism and Schizophrenia* (London: Continuum, 2004)

Gilles Deleuze, *Le Pli. Leibniz et le Baroque* (Paris: Minuit, 1988); translation: *The Fold: Leibniz and the Baroque* (London: Continuum, 2006)

Gilles Deleuze, *Francis Bacon. Logique de la sensation* (Paris: La différence, 1981); translation: *Francis Bacon: The Logic of Sensation* (London: Continuum, 2005)

Daniel C. Dennett, *Darwin's Dangerous Idea: Evolution and the Meanings of Life* (New York: Simon & Schuster, 1995)

Daniel C. Dennett, *Consciousness Explained* (Boston: Little Brown, 1991)

Daniel C. Dennett, 'Memes and the Exploitation of Imagination', *Journal of Aesthetics and Art Criticism*, vol. 48, no. 2, 1990. Web: http://cogprints.org/258/ (accessed 12 March 2010)

Fortunato Depero, 'Il futurismo e l'arte pubblicitaria', *Numero unico futurista Campari 1931*, 1931

Jacques Derrida, *De l'hospitalité* (Paris: Calmann-Lévy, 1997); translation: *Of Hospitality* (Stanford, CA: Stanford University Press, 2000)

Jacques Derrida, *Le monolinguisme de l'autre, ou, la prothèse d'origine* (Paris: Galilée, 1996); translation: *Monolingualism of the Other, or, The Prosthesis of Origin* (Stanford, CA: Stanford University Press, 1998)

Marco Deseriis and Giuseppe Marano, *Net.art. L'arte della connessione* (Milan: Shake, 2003)

John Dewey, *Art as Experience* (1934) (New York: Perigee, 2005)

John Dewey, *Experience and Nature* (1925) (Whitefish, MT: Kessinger, 2003)

Giuseppe Di Giacomo and Claudio Zambianchi, (eds.), *Alle origini dell'opera d'arte contemporanea* (Rome: Laterza, 2008)

Martin Dodge and Rob Kitchin, *Atlas of Cyberspace* (London: Pearson Education, 2001)

Gillo Dorfles, *Horror Pleni. La (in)civiltà del rumore* (Rome: Castelvecchi, 2008)

Gillo Dorfles, *L'intervallo perduto* (Turin: Einaudi, 1980)

Roger F. Fidler, *Mediamorphosis: Understanding New Media* (Thousand Oaks, CA: Pine Forge Press, 1997)

Vilém Flusser, *Für eine Philosophie der Fotografie* (Göttingen: European Photography, 1983); translation: *Towards a Philosophy of Photography* (London: Reaktion Books, 2000)

Vilém Flusser, *Dinge und Undinge.Phänomenologische Skizzen* (Munich: Hanser, 1993); translation: *The Shape of Things: A Philosophy of Design* (London: Reaktion Books, 1999)

Henri Focillon, *Vie des formes* (Paris: Leroux, 1934); translation: *The Life of Forms in Art* (New York: Zone Books, 1989)

Ernesto L. Francalanci, *Estetica degli oggetti* (Bologne: Il Mulino, 2006)

Matthew Fuller, *Behind the Blip: Essays on the Culture of Software* (New York: Autonomedia, 2003)

Bob Gallagher and Alexander Wilson, 'Michel Foucault. An Interview: Sex, Power and the Politics of Identity', *The Advocate*, no. 400, 7 August 1984

Clara Gallini, *Cyberspiders. Un'etnologa nella rete* (Rome: Manifestolibri, 2004)

Alexander R. Galloway, *Protocol: How Control Exists After Decentralization* (Cambridge, MA: MIT Press, 2004)

David Garcia and Geert Lovink, *The ABC of Tactical Media* (2003). Web: http://www.nettime.org/Lists-Archives/nettime-l-9705/msg00096.html (accessed 2 June 2010)

William Gibson, *Neuromancer* (New York: Ace Books, 1984)

Anthony Giddens, 'Living in a Post-Traditional Society', in: U. Beck, A. Giddens and S. Lash, *Reflexive Modernization: Politics, Tradition and Aesthetics in the Modern Social Order* (Stanford, CA: Stanford University Press, 1994)

E.H. Gombrich, *Aby Warburg: An Intellectual Biography* (London: The Warburg Institute, University of London, 1970)

E.H. Gombrich, *Art and Illusion: A Study in the Psychology of Pictorial Representation* (London: Phaidon, 1960)

Danny Goodman, *Spam Wars: Our Last Best Chance to Defeat Spammers, Scammers, and Hackers* (New York: SelectBooks, 2004)

Algirdas Julien Greimas, *De l'imperfection* (Périgueux: Pierre Fanlac, 1987)

Lisa Gye, Anna Munster and Ingrid Richardson, (eds.), 'Distributed Aesthetics', *FibreCulture*, no. 7, 2005. Web: http://journal.fibreculture.org/issue7/issue7_abstracts.html (accessed 12 March 2010)

Mark B.N. Hansen, *New Philosophy for New Media* (Cambridge, MA: MIT Press, 2004)

Michael Hardt and Antonio Negri, *Empire* (Cambridge, MA: Harvard University Press, 2000)

Pikka Himanen, *The Hacker Ethic and the Spirit of the Information Age* (New York: Random House/Vintage, 2001)

Jeff Howe, *Crowdsourcing: Why the Power of the Crowd is Driving the Future of Business* (New York: Crown Business, 2008)

Andreas Huyssen, *After the Great Divide: Modernism, Mass Culture, Postmodernism* (Bloomington, IN: Indiana University Press, 1986)

Francesco Ianneo, *Meme. Genetica e virologia di idee, credenze e mode* (Rome: Castelvecchi, 1999)

Margaret Iverson, *Alois Riegl: Art History and Theory* (Cambridge, MA: MIT Press, 1993)

Fredric Jameson, *Postmodernism, or, The Cultural Logic of Late Capitalism* (1991) (Durham, NC: Duke University Press, 1997)

Daphne Keller, 'The Musician as Thief', in: Paul D. Miller (ed.), *Sound Unbound: Sampling Digital Music and Culture* (Cambridge, MA: MIT Press, 2008)

Michael Kelly (ed.), *Encyclopedia of Aesthetics* (Oxford: Oxford University Press, 1998)

Friedrich A. Kittler, *Grammophone, Film, Typewriter* (Stanford, CA: Stanford University Press, 1999)

Friedrich A. Kittler, *Grammophon, Film, Typewriter* (Berlin: Brinkmann & Bose, 1986); translation: 'Grammophone, Film, Typewriter', in: Friedrich A. Kittler (ed.), *Literature, Media, Information Systems: Essays* (New York: Routledge, 1997)

Eric Kluitenberg, *Delusive Spaces: Essays on Culture, Media and Technology* (Rotterdam/Amsterdam: NAi Publishers/Institute of Network Cultures, 2008)

Leonard Koren, *Wabi-Sabi, For Artists, Designers, Poets & Philosophers* (Point Reyes, CA: Imperfect, 2008)

Siegfried Kracauer, *Das Ornament der Masse: Essays* (Frankfurt: Suhrkamp, 1963); translation: *The Mass Ornament: Weimer Essays* (Cambridge, MA: Harvard University Press, 1995)

Rosalind Krauss, *The Originality of the Avant-Garde and Other Modernist Myths* (1985) (Cambridge, MA: MIT Press, 1986)

George P. Landow, *Hypertext 2.0* (Baltimore, MD: Johns Hopkins University Press, 1997)

Maurizio Lazzarato, *La politica dell'evento* (Catanzaro: Rubettino, 2004)

Gustave Le Bon, *Psychologie des foules* (Paris: Félix Alcan, 1895); translation: *The Crowd: A Study of the Popular Mind* (New York: Dover, 2002)

Gustave Le Bon, *Les lois psychologiques de l'évolution des peuples* (Paris: Félix Alcan, 1895); translation: *The Psychology of Peoples* (New York: Macmillan, 1899)

James Leach, *Creative Land: Place and Procreation on the Rai Coast of Papua New Guinea* (New York: Berghahn Books, 2003)

Lawrence Lessig, *Remix: Making Art and Commerce Thrive in the Hybrid Economy* (New York: Penguin Press, 2008)

Lawrence Lessig, *Free Culture: How Big Media Uses Technology and the Law to Lock Down Culture and Control Creativity* (New York: Penguin Press, 2004)

Emmanuel Levinas, *Autrement qu'être ou au-delà de l'essence* (The Hague: Martinus Nijhoff, 1978); translation: *Otherwise than Being or Beyond Essence* (Pittsburgh, PA: Duquesne University Press, 2000)

Emmanuel Levinas, *Totalité et infini. Essai sur l'extériorité* (The Hague: Martinus Nijhoff, 1961); translation: *Totality and Infinity: An Essay on Exteriority* (Pittsburgh, PA: Duquesne University Press, 1969)

Claude Lévi-Strauss, *La Pensée sauvage* (Paris: Librairie Plon, 1962); translation: *The Savage Mind: The Nature of Human Society Series* (Chicago, IL: University of Chicago Press, 1966)

Pierre Lévy, *Cyberdémocratie. Essai de philosophie politique* (Paris: Odile Jacob, 1992)

George A. Lindbeck, *The Nature of Doctrine: Religion and Theology in a Postliberal Age* (Philadelphia: Westminister Press, 1984)

Alan Liu, *The Laws of Cool: Knowledge Work and the Culture of Information* (Chicago, IL: University of Chicago Press, 2004).

Geert Lovink, 'The Data Dandy', in: Adilkno, *The Media Archive* (New York: Autonomedia, 1988)

Geert Lovink, *Zero Comments: Blogging and Critical Internet Culture* (New York: Routledge, 2007)

Geert Lovink, 'The Art of Watching Databases', in: M. Gerritzen and I. van Tol (eds.), *New Cultural Networks* (Amsterdam: Stichting All Media, 2008)

Geert Lovink, 'Society of Query: The Googlization of our Lives', in: K. Becker and F. Stalder (eds.), *Deep Search: The Politics of Search beyond Google* (Innsbruck: Studien, 2009)

Geert Lovink and Ned Rossiter, (eds.), *MyCreativity Reader: A Critique of Creative Industries* (Amsterdam: Institute of Network Cultures, 2007)

Alessandro Ludovico, 'Decasia, a film made of recycled celluloid', *Neural*, 2003. Web: http://www.neural.it/nnews/decasiae.htm (accessed 24 May 2010)

Alessandro Ludovico, 'Inside the Spam Cartel', *Neural*, 2005. Web: http://www.neural.it/nnews/inside-thespamcartel.htm (accessed 6 April 2010)

Alessandro Ludovico, *Spam, the Economy of Desire* (2005). Web: http://www.neural.it/art/2005/12/spam_the_economy_of_desire.phtml (accessed 6 April 2010)

Greg Lynn, 'Blobs (or Why Tectonics is Square and Topology is Groovy)', *ANY*, no. 14, 'Tectonics Unbound: Kernform and Kunstform Revisited!', May 1996

Jean-François Lyotard, *La condition postmoderne. Rapport sur le savoir* (Paris: Minuit, 1979); translation: *The Postmodern Condition: A Report on Knowledge* (Manchester: Manchester University Press, 1984)

Michel Maffesoli, *Le temps des tribus. Le déclin de l'individualisme dans les sociétés de masse* (Paris: Méridiens Klincksieck, 1988); translation: *The Time of the Tribes: The Decline of Individualism in Mass Society* (London: SAGE, 1996)

Lev Manovich, *Software Takes Command* (version: 20 November, 2008). Web: http://softwarestudies.com/softbook/manovich_softbook_11_20_2008.doc

Lev Manovich, 'Database as a Symbolic Form', in: V. Vesna (ed.): *Database Aesthetics: Art in the Age of Information Overflow* (Minneapolis, MN: University of Minnesota Press, 2007)

Lev Manovich, *Information as an Aesthetic Event* (2007). Web: http://www.manovich.net/DOCS/TATE_lecture.doc (accessed 12 March 2010)

Lev Manovich, *The Language of New Media* (Cambridge, MA: MIT Press, 2001)

Lev Manovich, *Macromedia and Micro-media* (2000). Web: http://www.manovich.net/DOCS/macro_micro.doc (accessed 24 May 2010)

Lev Manovich, *Database as a Symbolic Form* (1998). Web: http://www.manovich.net/docs/database.rtf (accessed 8 August 2009)

Laura U. Marks, *The Skin of the Film: Intercultural Cinema, Embodiment and the Senses* (Durham, NC: Duke University Press, 1999)

Karl Marx, *Kapital. Kritik der politischen Ökonomie*, vol. I (1867); translation: *Capital: A Critique of Political Economy*, vol. I (New York: Penguin Classics, 1976)

Philip Maysles, 'Dubbing The Nation', *Small Axe*, no. 11, March 2002, Indiana, IN

Marco Mazzeo, *Tatto e linguaggio. Il corpo delle parole* (Rome: Editori Riuniti, 2003)

Marshall McLuhan, *Understanding Media: The Extensions of Man* (New York: McGraw Hill, 1964)

Richard Middleton, *Studying Popular Music* (Philadelphia, PA: Open University Press, 1990)

Paul D. Miller, 'In Through the Out Door: Samping and the Creative Act', in: P.D. Miller (ed.), *Sound Unbound: Sampling Digital Music and Culture* (Cambridge, MA: MIT Press, 2008)

Walter Molino and Stefano Porro, *Disinformation Technology* (Milan: Apogeo, 2003)

Patricia Moran, *Poetics of Correspondence* (2009). Web: http://www.vjtheory.net/web_texts/text_moran.htm (accessed 17 May 2010)

Leonoel Moura and Henrique Garcia Pereira, *Man + Robots: Symbiotic Art* (Villeurbanne: Institut d'Art Contemporain, 2004)

Lewis Mumford, *Technics and Civilization* (New York. Harcourt, Brace & Company, 1934)

Anna Munster and Geert Lovink, 'Theses on Distributed Aesthetics: Or, What a Network is Not', *FibreCulture*, no. 7, 'Distributed Aesthetics', 2005. Web: http://journal.fibreculture.org/issue7/issue7_munster_lovink.html

Anna Munster, *Data Undermining: The Work of Networked Art in an Age of Imperceptibility* (2009), Web: http://munster.networkedbook.org/data-undermining-the-work-of-networked-art-in-an-age-of-imperceptibility

Frieder Nake and Susanne Grabowski, 'The Interface as Sign and as Aesthetic Event', in: P. Fishwick (ed.), *Aesthetic Computing* (Cambridge, MA: MIT Press, 2006)

Clive Nancarrow and Pamela Nancarrow, 'Hunting for Cool Tribes', in: Bernard Cova, Robert Kozinets and Avi Shankar (eds.), *Consumer Tribes* (Oxford: Elsevier, 2007)

Eduardo Navas, *Remix: The Bond of Repetition and Representation* (2009). Web: http://remixtheory.net/?p=361 (accessed 2 June 2010)

Eduardo Navas, *The Author Function in Remix* (2008). Web: http://remixtheory.net/?p=309 (accessed 2 June 2010)

Eduardo Navas, *The Latency of the Moving Image in New Media* (2007). Web: http://remixtheory.net/?p=190 (accessed 24 May 2010)

Eduardo Navas, *Remix Defined* (2006). Web: http://remixtheory.net/?page_id=3 (accessed 2 June 2010)

Joseph Nechvatal, *Towards an Immersive Intelligence: Essays on the Work of Art in the Age of Computer Technology and Virtual Reality 1993-2006* (New York: Edgewise, 2009)

Jakob Nielsen, *Designing Web Usability: The Practice of Simplicity* (Indianapolis, IN: New Riders, 1999)

Marcos Novak, 'Transmitting Architecture revisited', *Cluster*, no. 7, 'Transmitting Architecture', 2008

Marcos Novak, *Transmitting Architecture: The Transphysical City* (1995). Web: http://www.cluster.eu/v2/themes/novak (accessed 2 June 2010)

Jamie O'Neil, *The Remix Aesthetic: Originality, Mixed and Mashed-up* (2006). Web: http://www.mcluhan-remix.com/images/Oneil_Remix_1D_SHORT.pdf (accessed 2 June 2010)

Pierluigi Panza, 'Arte, la copia è meglio dell'originale' (an interview with Peter Greeneway), *Corriere della Sera*, 1 June 2009

Jussi Parikka and Tony D. Sampson (eds.), *The Spam Book: On Viruses, Porn and Other Anomalies From the Dark Side of Digital Culture* (Cresskill, NJ: Hampton Press, 2009)

Matteo Pasquinelli, *Animal Spirits: A Bestiary of the Commons* (Rotterdam/Amsterdam: NAi Publishers/Institute of Network Cultures, 2008)

Mario Perniola, *Contro la comunicazione* (Turin: Einaudi, 2004)

Mario Perniola, *Il sex appeal dell'inorganico* (Turin: Einaudi, 1994); translation: *The Sex-appeal of the Inorganic* (London: Continuum, 2004)

Trevor Pinch and Frank Trocco, *Analog Days: The Invention and Impact of the Moog Synthesizer* (Cambridge, MA: Harvard University Press, 2004)

Andrea Pinotti, 'Un'immagine alla mano. Note per una genealogia dello spettatore tattile', in: A. Somaini (ed.), *Il luogo dello spettatore. Forme dello sguardo nella cultura delle immagini* (Milan: Vita e Pensiero, 2005)

Andrea Pinotti, *Il corpo dello stile. Storia dell'arte come storia dell'estetica a partire da Semper, Riegl, Wölfflin* (Milan: Mimesis, 2001)

Ulf Poschardt, *DJ Culture* (1995) (London: Quartet Books, 1998)

Jeffrey Posluns, *Inside the Spam Cartel: Trade Secrets from the Dark Side* (Rockland, MA: Syngress, 2004)

Neil Postman, *Technopoly: The Surrender of Culture to Technology* (1992) (New York: Vintage Books, 1993)

Rita Raley, *Tactical Media* (Minneapolis, MN: University of Minnesota Press, 2009)

Géza Révész, *Die Formenwelt des Tastsinnes* (The Hague: Martinus Nijhoff, 1938)

Aloïs Riegl, *Die spätrömische Kunstindustrie nach den Funden in Österreich-Ungarn* (Vienna: Österreichisches Archäologisches Institut, 1901): translation: *Late Roman Art Industry* (Rome: G. Bretschneider, 1985)

Jeremy Rifkin, *The Age Of Access: The New Culture of Hypercapitalism, Where All of Life is a Paid-For Experience* (New York: J.P. Tarcher/Putnam, 2000)

Rainer Maria Rilke, 'Gong' (1925), in: S. Mitchell (ed. and trans.), *Selected Poetry of Rainer Maria Rilke* (New York: Random House/Vintage, 1989)

Luigi Russolo, *L'arte dei rumori* (Milan: Direzione del Mvimento Fturista, 1913); translation: *The Art of Noises* (New York: Pendragon, 2005)

Richard W. Semon, *Die Mneme als erhaltendes Princip im Wechsel des organischen Geschehens* (Leipzig: Engelmann, 1904)

Raymond Murray Schafer, *The Tuning of the World: The Soundscape* (New York: Knopf, 1977)

Emanuele Severino, *Tecnica e architettura* (Milan: Raffaello Cortina, 2003)

Lucien Sfez, *Critique de la communication* (Paris: Seuil, 1988)

John F. Simon Jr, 'Unfolding Object', in: VV.AA., *Stretched Paint #1/ Web as Canvas* (Madrid: Anaya Multimedia, 2002)

Cornelia Sollfrank (ed.), *Expanded Original* (Ostfildern-Ruit: Hatje Cantz, 2009)

Cornelia Sollfrank, *Net.art Generator* (Nürnberg: Verlag für Moderne Kunst, 2005)

Peter N. Stearns, *American Cool: Constructing a Twentieth-century Emotional Style* (New York: New York Univeristy Press, 1994)

Bruce Sterling, *Shaping Things* (Cambridge, MA: MIT Press, 2005)

Daisetz Teitarō Suzuki, *Zen and Japanese Culture* (1936) (London: Taylor & Francis, 1970)

Władysław Tatarkiewicz, *Dzieje sześciu pojęć*, (Warsaw: PWN, 1976); translation: *A History of Six Ideas: An Essay in Aesthetics* (The Hague: Martinus Nijhoff, 1980)

Robert Farris Thompson, 'An Aesthetic of the Cool', in: B. Beckley and D. Shapiro (eds.), *Uncontrollable Beauty: Toward a New Aesthetics* (New York: Allworth, 2002)

Nigel Thrift, *Knowing Capitalism* (London: SAGE, 2005)

Tzvetan Todorov, *Avanguardie artistiche e dittature totalitarie* (Florence: Le Monnier Università, 2007)

Tzvetan Todorov, *Mikhail Bakhtin: The Dialogical Principle* (Manchester: Manchester University Press, 1984)

Antonio Tursi, *Estetica dei nuovi media. Forme espressive e network society* (Milan: Costa & Nolan, 2007)

Anthony Vidler, *Warped Space: Art, Architecture, and Anxiety in Modern Culture* (Cambridge, MA: MIT Press, 2000)

Paul Virilio and Sylvére Lotringer, *Pure War* (New York: Semiotext(e), 1983)

Paul Virilio, *L'Art à perte de vue* (Paris: Galilée, 2005); translation: *Art as Far as the Eye Can See* (Oxford: Berg, 2007)

Jean-Baptiste Waldner, *Nanocomputers and Swarm Intelligence* (New York: John Wiley & Sons, 2008)

McKenzie Wark, *A Hacker Manifesto* (Cambridge, MA: Harvard University Press, 2004)

Eyal Weizman, *Hollow Land* (London: Verso, 2007)

Heinrich Wölfflin, *Renaissance and Baroque* (New York: Cornell University Press, 1967)

Heinrich Wölfflin, *Kunstgeschichliche Grundbegriffe. Das Problem der Stilentwicklung in der neueren Kunst* (Munich: Bruckmann, 1915); translation: *Principles of Art History: The problem of the Development of Style in Later Art* (New York: Dover, 1950)

Matt Woolman, *Digital Information Graphics* (London: Thames & Hudson, 2002)

Slavoj Žižek, *Ein Plädoyer für die Intoleranz* (Wien: Passagen, 1998)

Also available in this series:

Ned Rossiter
Organized Networks
Media Theory, Creative Labour, New Institutions

The celebration of network cultures as open, decentralized, and horizontal all too easily forgets the political dimensions of labour and life in informational times. *Organized Networks* sets out to destroy these myths by tracking the antagonisms that lurk within Internet governance debates, the exploitation of labour in the creative industries, and the aesthetics of global finance capital. Cutting across the fields of media theory, political philosophy, and cultural critique, Ned Rossiter diagnoses some of the key problematics facing network cultures today. Why have radical social-technical networks so often collapsed after the party? What are the key resources common to critical network cultures? And how might these create conditions for the invention of new platforms of organization and sustainability? These questions are central to the survival of networks in a post-dotcom era. Derived from research and experiences participating in network cultures, Rossiter unleashes a range of strategic concepts in order to explain and facilitate the current transformation of networks into autonomous political and cultural 'networks of networks'.
Australian media theorist Ned Rossiter works as a Senior Lecturer in Media Studies (Digital Media), Centre for Media Research, University of Ulster, Northern Ireland and an Adjunct Research Fellow, Centre for Cultural Research, University of Western Sydney, Australia.
ISBN 978-90-5662-526-9
252 pages

Eric Kluitenberg
Delusive Spaces
Essays on Culture, Media and Technology

The once open terrain of new media is closing fast. Market concentration, legal consolidation and tightening governmental control have effectively ended the myth of the free and open networks. In *Delusive Spaces*, Eric Kluitenberg takes a critical position that retains a utopian potential for emerging media cultures. The book investigates the archaeology of media and machine, mapping the different methods and metaphors used to speak about technology. Returning to the present, Kluitenberg discusses the cultural use of new media in an age of post-governmental politics. *Delusive Spaces* concludes with the impossibility of representation. Going beyond the obvious delusions of the 'new' and the 'free', Kluitenberg theorizes artistic practices and European cultural policies, demonstrating a provocative engagement with the utopian dimension of technology.
Eric Kluitenberg is a Dutch media theorist, writer and organizer. Since the late 1980s, he has been involved in numerous international projects in the fields of electronic art, media culture and information politics. Kluitenberg heads the media programme of De Balie, Centre for Culture and Politics in Amsterdam. He is the editor of the *Book of Imaginary Media* (NAi Publishers, 2006) and the theme issue 'Hybrid Space' of *OPEN*, journal on art and the public domain (2007).
ISBN 978-90-5662-617-5
392 pages

Matteo Pasquinelli
Animal Spirits
A Bestiary of the Commons

After a decade of digital fetishism, the spectres of the financial and energy crisis have also affected new media culture and brought into question the autonomy of networks. Yet activism and the art world still celebrate Creative Commons and the 'creative cities' as the new ideals for the Internet generation. Unmasking the animal spirits of the commons, Matteo Pasquinelli identifies the key social conflicts and business models at work behind the rhetoric of Free Culture. The corporate parasite infiltrating file-sharing networks, the hydra of gentrification in 'creative cities' such as Berlin and the bicephalous nature of the Internet with its pornographic underworld are three untold dimensions of contemporary 'politics of the common'. Against the latent puritanism of authors like Baudrillard and Žižek, constantly quoted by both artists and activists, *Animal Spirits* draws a conceptual 'book of beasts'. In a world system shaped by a turbulent stock market, Pasquinelli unleashes a politically incorrect grammar for the coming generation of the new commons.

Matteo Pasquinelli is an Amsterdam-based writer and researcher at the Queen Mary University of London and has an activist background in Italy. He edited the collection *Media Activism: Strategies and Practices of Independent Communication* (2002) and co-edited *C'Lick Me: A Netporn Studies Reader* (2007). Since 2000, he has been editor of the mailing list Rekombinant (*www.rekombinant.org*).

ISBN 978-90-5662-663-1

240 pages